CN01081381

# Philosophy Inc.

Santiago Iñiguez

# Philosophy Inc.

## Applying Wisdom to Everyday Management

palgrave
macmillan

Santiago Iñiguez
IE University
Madrid, Spain

ISBN 978-3-031-20482-1      ISBN 978-3-031-20483-8   (eBook)
https://doi.org/10.1007/978-3-031-20483-8

This Palgrave Macmillan imprint is published by the registered company Springer Nature Switzerland AG.
The registered company address is: Gewerbestrasse 11, 6330 Cham, Switzerland

*For Diego del Alcázar Benjumea*

# Acknowledgments

"*Gaudeamus igitur, iuvenes dum sumus*" (Let us rejoice, for we are still young), the opening lines of the quintessential academic hymn, have been sung at university graduation ceremonies the world over for centuries by young men and women about to join the adult world and begin their careers. As well as encouraging us to live each day to the full, its message is also that education keeps us young: Continued learning over the years helps us retain a sharp and lively mind.

I consider myself fortunate to have a career in education; my years spent in intellectual contemplation, research, teaching, as well as academic management have far exceeded my dreams and expectations when I too graduated. Looking back over my career, I am filled with gratitude, aware that so many of our achievements and successes are the result of teamwork, of the support and collaboration of so many people. Luck or serendipity has also played their part, sometimes overshadowing any personal merit as I remember my successes and setbacks.

My first line of thanks goes to Diego del Alcázar Silvela, Founder of IE University, friend, mentor and personal and professional touchstone, with whom I have had the immense fortune of working over the last three decades. Diego has been my fundamental source of learning and advice as a visionary and entrepreneur, the origin of countless ideas and projects, a lover of the Humanities, a profound connoisseur of people and the educational environment.

I would also like to express my gratitude to Diego del Alcázar Benjumea, CEO of IE University, who has taken over from his father with admirable gravitas, intelligence and professionalism. It is a source of boundless satisfaction for me to see IE University grow under his strategic direction as a leading educational institution, operating in the sphere of the best universities in the world, consolidating its research and teaching. My appreciation also goes to Maria Benjumea and Isabela del Alcázar for their admirable dedication and support for our university.

Chance has been especially kind to surround me with extraordinary colleagues and collaborators, to whom I owe a debt of gratitude for having been able to ride on the shoulders of giants. Salvador Carmona, Rector of IE University, whose leadership has been the pillar of our academic consolidation. Also Juan José Güemes, Economic Vice President, the person who allows us to sleep peacefully. Macarena Rosado, our Legal Advisor; and Gonzalo Garland, Vice President of the IE Foundation. My collaborators at the head of the different educational units: Manuel Muñiz, Provost and Dean of IE School of Global and Public Affairs; Lee Newman, Dean of IE Business School; Martha Thorne, Dean of IE School of Architecture and Design; Soledad Atienza, Dean of IE School of Law; Ikhlaq Sidhu, Dean of IE School of Science and Technology; and Teresa Martín-Retortillo, Director of IE XL. Similarly, thanks go to Antonio de Castro, Adriana Angel, Ines Drieselmann, Sabine Yazbeck, Martín Rodríguez Jugo, Ignacio Sanjuanbenito and Geoffroy Gerard.

The support of IE University's communications and digital marketing team has been fundamental in disseminating myriad contributions through different media, some of which are included in this book. My gratitude, in particular, to Javier Ayuso, Juncal Sánchez Mendieta, Yolanda Regodón, Kerry Parke, Igor Galo, Pablo Sun Li, Rosa Aranda, Cristina Manzano, Carlos Saldaña, Emanuel Díaz and Iratxe Piñeiro.

There is a core group of people directly involved in all my editorial projects and publications, to whom I must profess my recognition and special thanks. Nick Lyne, my English editor, who enhances my ideas and writing, with whom I have worked for the last decade. Felix Valdivieso, friend, advisor and spur to my literary forays. Liz Barlow, my editor at Palgrave Macmillan, who has encouraged and advised me in the publication of my last three books. Cynthia Fernandez, who coordinates all my publishing projects and encourages me to explore new themes and formats. Virginia Collera, Editor of LinkedIn Spain, for all her support in the most influential social network in the professional field. Andrés Borisenko, who assists me in the different social networks in which I participate. And Igone Jayo, my right hand and Personal Assistant, without whom my work would be gibberish.

Finally, I lack the words to convey my immeasurable gratitude to Juan Ramón Zamorano, who has patiently listened to readings and re-readings of this manuscript; friend and companion, advisor and support.

There are many other people who deserve space here, especially all the members of IE University, but also of the networks, institutions and organizations of which I am a member, with whom I have exchanged many of the ideas contained in this book, and to whom I would like to express my deep appreciation. To all of them I personally address the final words of the aforementioned academic hymn: "*Vivat Academia, vivant professores. Vivat membrum quodlibet, vivant membra quaelibet, semper sint in flore.*" (Long live the University, long live the professors. Long live each and every one of its members, may they always shine.)

# Guide to This Book

For some people, the word philosophy brings back unhappy memories; perhaps, they were forced to study classical thinkers while still too young to understand the meaning or relevance of their ideas, unable to join up the dots, something they may have been able to do with maturity and experience. This book is aimed especially at them, in the spirit of making philosophy a tool to help us make better decisions as managers and entrepreneurs and also to better understand how we can be happier. The aim is not to make philosophy superficial, but to make it accessible to the general public, to nonacademics and nonexperts.

That said, a hopefully unnecessary caveat: Philosophy does not provide categorical, one-size-fits-all solutions to the problems we face as managers. But it can help us to articulate our thoughts better, make sense of our intuitions and find better arguments to justify our decisions. In any case, your experience as a manager will have shown you that the relevant issues, the cardinal dilemmas you have to solve in your company, require reflection, weighing up the pros and cons, gathering all the substantial information. You cannot, or should not, simply appeal to arguments of authority—"the boss said so"—or to factual arguments that are debatable: data that can be interpreted in any number of ways, experiences that are countered by anecdotes. By now, you will have understood that momentous questions often have no single correct answer.

Turning to philosophy can help you to think better, to argue more confidently, to give meaning and consistency to your decisions. This book is intended to help you along that path.

"Philosophy Inc." consists of six distinct parts, which open with introductions to explain their content and scope. Each part, and each section, can be read independently or in sequence. Some of the sections have conclusions or takeaways to assist in the application of the ideas discussed in concrete situations.

Some of the sections that make up this book have been previously published on LinkedIn, as part of the interaction I maintain as an influencer with my followers, and also in other media such as "The Conversation" or "IE Insights," but many other sections have been prepared specifically for this book.

I hope that the reflections that make up this book will be as useful to you as they have been for me. As I state in several places, "Management is Philosophy in action," and if you better understand the philosophy, values and principles that guide your performance, I believe you will become a better manager.

RN, Brazil                                                                    Sibaúma
August 27, 2022

# Contents

# 1

# Part I: Wisdom—Why Should We Practice Philosophy?

The purpose of philosophy is to provide insights that help us to better understand the world, answers to the question of who we are, or reasoning to justify how we should act. Its scope is multidisciplinary, and virtually every important question has a philosophical background. The early philosophers attempted to explain the world, nature, institutions and our behavior. Their method was argumentative, often in dialogue with others, providing reasons or evidence in their defense. Over time, philosophy has become specialized and confined mainly to academia. There are any number of fine thinkers and gurus out there, but the spirit of the classical philosophers, who applied their prescience to the burning questions of life, seems gone forever.

Notwithstanding, the life of any of us, the most important milestones, our key decisions, can still be explained using philosophical values or principles, in the same way that the activity of a company or any other organization can be analyzed based on a school of thought. Therefore, the first reason to philosophize is to take the reins of interpretation of your own existence, or of the company you run, before someone else does it for you.

Moreover, philosophy provides depth and meaning to our projects and our activities. This first section offers an introduction to the philosophical analysis of some central questions, both for personal reflection and professional practice. Reasons are given as to why philosophizing is not an activity reserved solely for intellectual giants, but instead for all those who want to reflect on the meaning of their life and behavior. It also offers an example of the pragmatic dimension of philosophy, represented by Baltasar Gracián, a Spanish philosopher whose central work has served as a guide for many politicians and businessmen. Some implications of meritocracy, the central system of

S. Iñiguez, *Philosophy Inc.*, https://doi.org/10.1007/978-3-031-20483-8_1

recognition and distribution of resources in most liberal democracies—and business—are discussed, as well as recent criticisms of meritocracy's elitist drift. Finally, I share some of John Locke's advice on the education of children.

## 1.1    What Does Philosophy Have to Tell Us About Business?

*"Life unexamined is not worth living,"*[1] said Socrates, considered by many the father of Western Philosophy. He argued that what distinguishes us from other species is our capacity for self-reflection and for asking ourselves profound questions about who we are, what we should do, or what we can know.

These and related basic questions about the World and how we interact with it are the stuff that philosophy is made of.

Indeed, the task of philosophers was originally concerned with the major issues that all human beings deal with at key moments in their lives, those questions that may give significance to our existence, aspirations and achievements.

Asking ourselves such questions is a meaningful exercise in itself, regardless of any answers we may come up with, and one that we may sometimes only reach over the course of our lives, or maybe—in the opinion of some—never.[2] It is often said that the best coaches are those who raise questions that make us reflect, rather than those who offer quick fixes or ready-made advice. Similarly, Socrates was better known for the questions he posed to his students, which were radical and systematic, rather than the answers he provided, which are not always entirely persuasive. As with other human endeavors, Socrates and many other philosophers have not always succeeded in providing conclusive arguments as to the meaning of life.

The fact that philosophers have raised similar basic questions throughout history is evidence of the closeness of human beings and the similarity of our concerns across generations and centuries, regardless of social, cultural, or geographical diversity.

Needless to say, the responses to those questions were not all the same, and instead varied, based on the different beliefs, values and methods of diverse thinkers. However, philosophical enquiry was originally not just conceived as a mental or speculative exercise, intended as an intellectual endeavor. Ideally, the findings and conclusions of philosophical discourse were aimed at influencing and guiding our behavior in life.

In fact, the classical philosophers strived to live in accordance with their beliefs, for better or worse. "*If I don't reveal my views in a formal account, I do so by my conduct. Don't you think that actions are more reliable evidence than words?*",[3] said Socrates, arguably the epitome of aligning one's beliefs with how one lives. He even respected an unjust death sentence to show his obedience to authority, declining exile and offers to escape or to challenge his accusers. The final hours of his life before drinking hemlock, narrated with moving affection by his disciple Plato,[4] were spent in a discussion with his friends on the immortality of the soul, human life and death and the duty to obey the law.

Later philosophers also tried to live their lives according to their beliefs. Montaigne was as adventurous and experiential as his writings, Rousseau suffered exile for his work, and Nietzsche's final madness had probably something to do with his passionate and turbulent stream of ideas: "*strife is the perpetual food of the soul.*"[5]

In short, as recounted in hagiographies by the likes of Diogenes Laertius and Plutarch,[6] the ancient philosophers lived exemplary lives, acting according to their beliefs, earning themselves immortality.

Nowadays, consistency between one's beliefs and personal behavior, coherence between what one thinks and does, is often called authenticity or integrity. It is a virtue highly respected by society, not only expected of philosophers and thinkers but in general of all professionals.

For example, integrity is an essential virtue for doing business, the success of which is based on trust. Moreover, when a person has integrity, we can predict to a certain degree how they're going to behave. The opposite of integrity is hypocrisy and inconsistency. Entrepreneurs tend to shy away from dilettanti or erratic people whose values or principles are uncertain: Predictability is one of the essential attributes for doing business.

It is also interesting how integrity is taken into account by recruiters in job interviews. For example, there are tests that make it possible to assess with a relatively high degree of probability whether interviewees are inconsistent in answering about their values or principles.

That said, integrity does not imply a closed mind or intransigence. Rather, it is understood to be the result of a reflective exercise, the search for answers to the big questions we ask ourselves, not because we have absorbed the received wisdom. In other words, the search for answers is an iterative exercise that continues throughout our lives, in dialogue with others, and our principles and values are transformed and become clearer with experience and knowledge. That is why flexibility and openness are characteristics of integrity. As our knowledge is limited and progresses with the development of science and collective knowledge, a person of integrity is one who knows how to adapt his or her values and principles.

In fact, open-mindedness, flexibility in weighing different ideas and systematic questioning of major issues are fundamental features of philosophical thinking. This inquiring and questioning attitude is what distinguishes those who cultivate philosophy, as opposed to those who work in the fields of religion or theology, where its proponents assume a series of unquestioned truths or dogma.

As I commented above, the proposals of most of the great philosophers are not just conceptual, but a model for living. That is why philosophy is particularly interesting and relevant for managers. The fundamental thesis of this book is that *management is philosophy in action*. Therefore, all conceptions of management, theories about the mission of companies or the specific vision for a particular business are the concrete application of a particular philosophy. Denying one has a particular philosophical conception is in itself a philosophy.

Nevertheless, some thinkers insist on the impossibility of finding answers to the great questions of philosophy, or even the sense in asking such questions. These detractors can be classified into two main groups.

The first are the defenders of Skepticism.[7] Their fundamental approach is methodological. What they question is whether there are procedures or intellectual resources able to answer any major philosophical issue. In their opinion, propositions about what is true or false, about what is good or bad, are indemonstrable. According to this approach it would be impossible to justify whether it is immoral or not to pay a bribe, since we lack a reliable method of finding this out. As Aristotle—who was not a skeptic—once said, *"the fire burns in Hellas and Persia, but the ideas of right and wrong vary across the board."*[8] However, it is often said that skepticism refutes itself, because the first proposition whose veracity could be questioned is precisely its central argument: that nothing is demonstrable or reasonable.

The second group of detractors are the Existentialists. Søren Kierkegaard, the first exponent of this world view, questioned the relationship between reality and reason, the basic approach of philosophy that there is a reason for everything that exists. For example, the Danish philosopher believed that suffering as such does not exist; instead, there are simply people who believe they experience it, but lack the arguments to explain its meaning, failing in the process to understand that the essential state of existence is anguish. Anguish is what drives us and determines the meaning that can be given to human life. It is interesting how Kierkegaard's thought anticipates in some way the foundations of psychoanalysis.[9]

Another of the best known existentialists, who gave his name to the movement, was Jean Paul Sartre, the twentieth-century French philosopher who argued that "*hell is other people.*"[10] In another revealing passage, Sartre explained that "*human existence is an absurd passion, fulfilled only to the extent that, in the eyes of others, I become definitively this or that, this or that.*"[11]

Existentialism has appeal for those who see life as an unfolding tragedy, which is why it is not a philosophy likely to be found in the entrepreneurial among us, those with the will to transform society, to generate value or to grow a company. Therefore, with respect to its defenders, we will leave it parked here. Moreover, although many entrepreneurs have existential doubts at some point in their lives, maybe on rainy days or when they launch IPOs, they tend to remain optimistic, seeking opportunities for growth, fostering relationships with other people as a source of business. In short, an existentialist entrepreneur is an oxymoron.

Existentialism ruled out, I return to the idea of coherence and aligning our ideas with personal conduct, the ideal of integrity. This is a particularly commendable virtue in CEOs, and many of the biographies of business leaders emphasize how their values and principles led them to create and develop their companies.

Originally, philosophers addressed a wide range of issues, along with the big questions with which this chapter opened. Over the centuries, however, as philosophy was confined as a profession to the boundaries of university departments, philosophical inquiry became more focused, specialized and theoretical. The point of inflection toward this professionalization is probably marked by Immanuel Kant, a university professor who never left his native city of Königsberg once in his entire life.[12] Kant kept such an orderly schedule that his countrymen checked the time of day against the thinker's routines. Compare this with Plato's audacious life, who after the death of his master travelled around Italy, Sicily, Egypt and Cyrene, an epic voyage for a Greek 25 centuries ago.[13] Thinkers who engaged in philosophy relied on rational discussion and exchange of ideas to try to answer the big questions.

A number of conclusions can be drawn from this introductory chapter:

- The fundamental role of philosophy is to provide questions that give meaning to our lives, both looking forward and backward. The development of the sciences or the specialization of philosophy does not detract from or question its function as a guide for making major life decisions. Philosophy belongs to the humanities, which have a necessary and complementary role to the disciplines known as STEM (Science, Technology, Economics, Mathematics).

- Integrity, understood as consistency between our ideas and behavior, is highly prized in our societies, and long promoted by philosophers. It is also an ideal sought by successful managers, and a personal characteristic valued by companies, for example, in recruitment and promotion.
- Personal integrity is not synonymous with intransigence, conservatism or closed-mindedness. The truly integrous person is flexible and open to adapting his or her values and principles as circumstances change or as thinking evolves.
- Understanding the history of philosophy and ideas allows us to engage with the debate that has developed throughout history between people of different backgrounds, habits and ways of thinking. It connects us with other generations and other cultures, where we find the mirror of our own concerns and questions.

Socrates said that he went to the Oracle of Delphi, the sacred place where prophecies were heard, to ask who was the wisest man in Greece. The Oracle's answer was that it was him, which surprised him and led him to contrast it by talking to the wisest men he knew. These enquiries led him to realize that even the most prominent were not only ignorant of basic questions about their professions, or had no answer as to the purposes for which they performed them or their results, but even disdained to ask such questions. After the surprise, Socrates concluded that the meaning of the Oracle is that he was wiser because he knew his own ignorance. Hence, the profundity of one of the Greek sage's best-known proverbs: "*I only know that I know nothing*" is the starting point of any experience of knowledge.[14] Humility and modesty to understand that there are still many things to learn is the requirement to continue learning and become wiser.

## 1.2   Why Managers Should Develop the Habit of Examining Their Actions

Seen in philosophical terms, management is about praxis. Among the defining characteristics of a good manager is the ability to take decisions swiftly, handle meetings efficiently and generally to improve the organization's productivity. Time is the most valuable resource in management and must be administered efficiently: A good chairman of the board ensures that meetings cover all the topics on the agenda in good time.

Similarly, innovative companies focus on "time to market," in other words, getting new services or products to customers. Most business leaders would agree that making the best use of time so that competitors must copy products or services is the best guarantee of innovation. Flexibility and speed are two pillars of successful companies.

In which case, in a business world where opinions must be formed and decisions taken on the move, how can we find time to cultivate an interest in philosophy, taking time to ponder our next move? While philosophy ponders the fundamental questions and offers a model for life, it also pushes us to understand ideals such as liberty, justice and equality, liberal democracy, the law and economics.

The challenge business leaders face today is finding the time to reflect on their values, and how to apply these to setting goals. Whether it's during a long plane journey, a weekend in the country, joining a retreat or developing mindfulness techniques, we need to find a balance: Action and thought are two sides of the same coin, as Iris Murdoch points out in *The Sovereignty of Good*: "*The task of attention goes on all the time and at apparently empty and everyday moments we are 'looking', making those little efforts of imagination.*"[15]

As I hope this book shows, philosophy is a fundamental part of human life, and thus has a role to play in the practice of management. Whether we are aware of it or not, business decisions reflect our world view, because they are based on assumptions about the meaning of business.

Going further, I would argue that denying a link between management and our principles is an expression of a philosophy, perhaps as extreme as nihilism, cynicism, or relativism, outlooks that are essentially contradictory.[16]

Fortunately, business educators and executives now recognize the importance management theories based on core values and principles, for which they have turned to the humanities.

A pioneer in this regard was Ayn Rand, the American writer who attempted to rationalize individualism through the philosophy of Objectivism. Addressing West Point graduates in 1974, she made a speech called *Philosophy: who needs it?*, telling her audience: "*Without abstract ideas, you would not be able to deal with concrete, particular, real-life problems. You would be in the position of a newborn infant, to whom every object is a unique, unprecedented phenomenon. The difference between his mental state and yours lies in the number of conceptual integrations your mind has performed. You have no choice about the necessity to integrate your observations, your experiences, your knowledge into abstract ideas, i.e., into principles.*"[17]

Going further, she highlighted how a philosophic system is an integrated view of existence. "*As a human being, you have no choice about the fact that you need a philosophy. Your only choice is whether you define your philosophy by a conscious, rational, disciplined process of thought and scrupulously logical deliberation—or let your subconscious accumulate a junk heap of unwarranted conclusions.*"[18]

In other words, because everything we do reflects certain values and principles, we should take the time to identify and understand them.

As we shall see, one of the growing demands on entrepreneurs and managers is to justify their decisions to shareholders. Philosophy provides the arguments we need to do that by linking the decisions taken by the management of a company with a certain vision of the world, with shared values and principles, giving them meaning and facilitating their acceptance.

In addition to this strategic objective, philosophy will also give personal meaning to the individual, professional and personal trajectory of managers. It will increase their confidence and allow them to achieve greater levels of well-being and happiness.

## 1.3 Philosophy and Common Sense: Lessons from a Seventeenth-Century Cleric

The motto of this book is that *Management is philosophy in action*. This simple theory has certainly given business educators food for thought over the years. Yet, it is still no easy task to find a balanced and palatable guide to how thought and action should interact in the corporate arena.

The history of philosophical literature written by politicians provides good examples of manuals of a practical nature, written with the purpose of serving as reference books, collections of advice or thoughts applicable to daily chores, especially for the exercise of leadership. In some cases, they are compendiums of tactical, operative maxims, often lacking any moral component—although this absence of ethics is also a philosophy, even if frowned on by most people. In other cases, values, principles and constructive intent are apparent. Some of the most popular books of this genre are the *Meditations*, by the Emperor Marcus Aurelius, the *Politician's Breviary* by Cardinal Mazarin, and the *Reflections*, or *Sentences and Moral Maxims* by François de La Rouchefoucauld.[19]

Along these lines, allow me to introduce Baltasar Gracián, the seventeenth-century Spanish cleric and thinker who, though he may not have achieved the same widespread fame as his literary counterparts, nevertheless played an influential role in the European Enlightenment.

Such a highly qualified commentator as Nietzsche hailed him as the author of one of the world's greatest works of practical philosophy. His main contribution to strategy, *The Art of Worldly Wisdom: a Pocket Oracle*[20] comprises 300 elegantly crafted maxims that are as astonishingly appropriate to the running of a twenty-first-century global business corporation as they were to Spanish society more 300 years ago.

If an editor were to throw in references to e-mails, laptops and cell phones, you would hardly notice that you were reading words written several centuries ago.

Gracián's recommendations for achieving a powerful blend of ethical behavior and earthly success are both readable and instructive, not to mention practical.

The canny observations and humanistic approach of this chaplain, confessor, preacher and academic administrator are a far cry from the naked cynicism of other classics of the genre, and far more applicable to the kind of corporate environment we now aspire to.

The virtue of his writing lies in providing just the right blend of thought and action in management. For example, Gracián's contributions could provide the answer to the debate sparked by the late professor Sumantra Ghoshal, of London Business School, who in a posthumously published article lamented what he saw as business educators' over-emphasis on the "*homo economicus* theory" as the cornerstone of management science.[21] In brief, this states that economic agents are rational wealth-maximizers who behave strategically, trying to anticipate the possible reactions of other economic agents to their decisions. Social well-being does not enter the equation.

This model is a traditional one, found in such classics as Machiavelli's *The Prince*, another manual filled with practical advice for leaders[22] which has topped bestseller lists for centuries and still forms part of the strategic management syllabus at some business schools. But for many people, it is a "nightmare" model, based on the idea that human nature is intrinsically aggressive, and that people will always put their own interests first. We should remember, however, that the nightmare model is based on supposedly indisputable facts, and that we are not discussing whether or not these facts are good or bad.

In short, it is an attempt to describe the way things are rather than condone them, nevertheless, it can be criticized on at least that basis, namely that it may not actually be an accurate depiction of reality.

This criticism seems to be Ghoshal's main line of attack, in that the *homo economicus* theory leaves no room for other patterns of behavior, such as altruism. What's more, Ghoshal disagreed with Management's inclusion, as an academic discipline, among the social sciences: "*Our theories and ideas have done much to strengthen the management practices that we are all now so loudly condemning.*"[23] He argued that the social sciences have an inferiority complex, what he called "physics envy," because its assumptions, models and conclusions are not governed by causal paradigms. Instead, the social sciences' prevailing model is functional, an attempt to explain how individuals behave. What's more, as he points out, there's a reductionist aspect to fitting our behavior to functional paradigms. [No scientific theory]… *"explains the phenomenon of the organized complexity… [of companies] possibly because companies are not empirically observable natural phenomena like volcanoes or animals, or follow any predeterminable pattern."*[24] The risk of reducing the study of management to the level of scientism has been to downgrade humans to little more than economic maximizers.

Enter the noble dream, as advocated by numerous supporters of sustainable business. According to this model, politicians and managers must take ethical responsibility for their actions, the underlying idea being that it is the essential duty of managers to create wealth, while helping improve the environment, eradicate poverty, and enhance society in general.

In fact, politicians, managers and business educators are neither angels nor demons, but instead tend to embrace both of these two extremes. And although today's authors may proffer a wide range of recommendations on how to deal with this paradox, the classics, those building blocks of modern thought, remain sadly silent.

Baltasar Gracián provides a much-needed exception. His contribution to the nightmare versus noble dream argument provides us with a realistic approach to the problem. The great appeal of his work is that his observations of human nature are viable from all perspectives.

The reader is, for example, instructed that *"knowledge and honorable intentions ensure that success will bear fruit"* and that *"character and intelligence are the axes your talent revolves around. It isn't enough to be intelligent; you must also have the right character."*[25]

Integrity scores highly with Gracián, not only as a virtue, but in purely pragmatic terms.

If you *"only act with honorable people,"* then the chances of a successful outcome are multiplied, given that *"their honor is the best guarantee of their behavior, for they always act according to their character."*[26]

It may sound as if Gracián was setting his readers up to be sitting ducks for the first corporate shark they encounter, but rest assured that he also took care to equip his readers for the darker side of the business world. *"Do not be too much of a dove,"* he warns, *"but remember that you must 'use', but not 'abuse', cunning."*[27]

Timeless business advice abounds in this small, but perfectly formed volume. Gracián even pays tribute to networking: "*One of the gifts of the hero is the ability to dwell with heroes. This ability is a wonder of nature, both because it is so mysterious and because it is so beneficial.*"[28]

He was also a great advocate of current "must-dos" such as innovation. As he so eloquently puts it, "*Renew your brilliance. Excellence grows old and so does fame,*" which sounds so much more pleasant than "innovate or die."[29]

Comments like, "*have original and out-of-the-way views*" and "*float a trial balloon to see how well something is received*" would not be out of place among the practices of any of today's leading companies.[30]

Globalization is also addressed: "*Avoid the defects of your country. No country, not even the most refined, has ever escaped some innate defect or other, and these weaknesses are seized on by neighboring countries as defense or consolation.*"[31]

He had already grasped that dispelling stereotyped perceptions is crucial when it comes to developing an internationally respected profile and is an essential skill when leading cross-cultural teams.

True visionaries are hard to find, but when one does come to light it is particularly encouraging to discover that both heart and business brain are in the right place, and that they are able to be optimistic without being naïve. Gracián's pocket oracle says: "*Wisdom has one advantage. She is immortal. If this is not her century, many others will be.*"[32]

For me, Baltasar Gracián remains a visionary, a yardstick of how philosophy can be part of managerial thinking, and that it can be of immense practical use. However, now is the time to visit the dark side, to better understand Machiavelli's thinking, and what he wanted to convey to those who were considering leading a state or an organization.

## 1.4    Does Meritocracy Apply to Business?

Do you think that the best possible government, or that the best company, should be run by the smartest in society? It's certainly what Plato thought, and he outlined his ideas about governance in *The Republic*, arguing that those with the best education are also the most just, and therefore the most fit to run things.[33] Having a deeper and more cultivated knowledge of reality, intelligent people grasp ideas more quickly and are better equipped to identify problems and offer more effective solutions. On the contrary, for Plato, ignorance and a lack of culture lead to barbarism and disorder.

Plato's social structure was a pyramid. The wise men occupied the top, at the next level were the soldiers, and at the bottom the workers. Furthermore, women had no rights and slaves were an essential part of the economy.

Ignoring the autocratic nature of society according to Plato, would you agree that our rulers should also be the most intelligent among us? Imagine if pre-election debates included intelligence tests, general knowledge tests, and other exercises that would reveal the intellectual, and even managerial, capabilities of the candidates. Would you use this information to decide who to vote for?

The truth is that, regardless of whether such information is available, experience shows that many of us do not vote based on rational criteria, and are instead motivated by other factors that have nothing to do with the candidates' intelligence.[34]

Most of us would accept that that intelligence implies better reasoning ability, and therefore results in more expert and potentially successful decisions. And most of the highly regarded politicians down the ages have usually been possessed of attributes that are associated with intelligence such as good communication skills, vision, prudence or gravitas. In this regard, some studies show that most US presidents have above-average IQs, with John Quincy Adams and Thomas Jefferson leading the way.[35] Logically, the race for the presidency tests all the attributes generally associated with wisdom.

The idea of a government of the wise seems meritocratic, the recognition of people who exercise their abilities, generally intellectual, and achieve results that make them worthy of the top prize. Meritocracy has been the alternative for organizing democratic societies, as well as for distinguishing and rewarding the contribution of citizens, at least since the French Revolution of 1789, replacing aristocratic regimes where the distribution of goods was determined by birth. In his 2021 book *The Aristocracy of Talent*, journalist and writer Adrian Wooldridge argues that meritocracy is still the best of the available alternatives, despite being the target of much criticism.[36]

His definition of meritocracy goes beyond the autocratic approach formulated by Plato and includes the most relevant contributions that liberal philosophy has been incorporating since the Enlightenment. "*A meritocratic society combines four qualities which are each in themselves admirable. First, it prides itself on the extent to which people can get ahead in life on the basis of their natural talents. Second, it tries to secure equality of opportunity by providing education for all. Third, it forbids discrimination on the basis of race and sex and other irrelevant characteristics. Fourth, it awards jobs through open competition rather than patronage and nepotism.*"[37]

This liberal ideal of meritocracy has recently been questioned from two different sides.

Firstly, from a radical liberal position, which, in view of the increase in social inequality, and in particular racial discrimination—conceived as structural, embedded in social institutions—maintains that meritocracy perpetuates the privileges of the wealthier classes. One of the best-known figures in this movement is Michael Sandel, whose 2020 best-seller *The Tyranny of Merit* argues that access to the best US universities has been distorted, giving admission priority to candidates related to "legacy," for example, the children of graduates or donors. In addition, he believes that there is an unavoidable relationship between access to resources or having grown up in a prosperous environment and having a better education or one's talent nurtured. In his opinion, it would be more equitable to select students through a lottery than through the current system.[38]

Writing from a communitarian perspective, Daniel Markovits' *The Meritocracy Trap* also criticizes how access to prestigious universities and the labor market favors the scions of the wealthy. His arguments, and some of his proposals, are similar to those of Sandel. In his opinion, access to the most prestigious universities should be broadened to allow the entry of young people from a wide range of backgrounds, as well as strengthening the labor market for mid-skilled workers.[39]

Curiously, the initiative to promote the labor segments most affected by globalization and the outplacement of mid-skilled jobs is also shared by the other group of the detractors of meritocracy, conservative populists. The arguments put forward by their representatives may be fallacious, but are now part of public discourse. The targets of their attacks are mainly intellectual elites, historical political parties and the advocates of progress, globalization and sustainability. These populists lambast meritocracy as the system that has favored the rise of technocrats, entrepreneurs and consequently globalization, and thus the displacement of jobs to developing countries.

Wooldridge uses his dialectical skills to deploy a wide range of arguments, dismantling both sides' attacks on meritocracy.[40] Aware that meritocracy needs to be renewed, and above all that it must respond to critiques based on communitarianism, he puts forward proposals that I summarize below, at the risk of simplifying the sophisticated arguments he uses.

Firstly, the need for universal, quality education from preschool (kindergarten) level. As he explains, the early stages of personality development, from infancy, are crucial for acquiring skills, fostering behavioral habits, inculcating virtues and awakening interest in knowledge. It has been proven that countries that pay special attention to the early stages of education achieve better aggregate results in all the following stages of their citizens' education. Education is the best instrument for equality, and it is more effective if it is implemented early on.

Secondly, the use of IQ-related tests to select the beneficiaries of scholarships and study grants, regardless of their social background, so as to include the largest number of people. In return, the recipients of these benefits would commit themselves to work for the state for a period of their professional career, contributing to the improvement of the public sector. Here we see the connection between Wooldridge and Plato.

However, it is worth noting that ever since the first attempts to analyze and measure intelligence, there has been speculation about what determines a higher IQ, whether it is primarily the result of genetics, environment or education. The "nature vs. nurture" debate is still very much alive, but what is decisive is that all the factors mentioned above contribute, to varying degrees, to the development of intelligence.[41] On the other hand, cognitive psychology has shown that there are different forms of intelligence, that sometimes emotional intelligence is more decisive than analytical intelligence for personal success, and that in any case, even defining intelligence is a controversial exercise.[42]

- Wooldridge also calls for a moral regeneration of leaders in all types of social institutions, from politics to business to academia. His recommendation is enigmatic, because advocates of meritocracy, such as Stephen Pinker, often believe in the idea of moral progress as well.[43] I understand that he is referring to promoting the principles of professional deontology and good citizenship, as well as the ideals of the culture of sustainability, which is especially prevalent among millennials.

- Similarly, Wooldridge proposes strengthening vocational training, so as to offer more opportunities to segments of workers who have been left behind in the digital economy. Perhaps this proposal could be complemented by the need for continuous training and learning, which is very much in line with a meritocratic approach and the need for renewed personal effort throughout one's career.

Wooldridge's conclusion is that the best way to defend meritocracy and combat its critics is to strengthen meritocratic institutions in society. Goethe's maxim seems particularly applicable here: "*If you want to feel the satisfaction of your own merit, you must concede merit to the world.*"[44]

## 1.5    Do We Deserve Our Talent? Not According to John Rawls

Anybody who has read the Gospels will be familiar with two of the best-known parables: the Workers in the Vineyard,[45] and the Talents, both from the Book of Matthew.[46] The first can seem at odds with the message of Jesus, while the latter is usually understood and accepted.

In the Parable of the Workers in the Vineyard, a winemaker recruits several laborers over the course of the day to pick grapes from his property. He goes out early in the morning to the village and hires a team, offering them a denarius for their day's work; at noon he goes out again, and so on three more times until late in the afternoon, hiring different groups each time. When the time comes to settle the wages at the end of the day, the owner pays everyone the same: a denarius. When those hired earliest protest at having worked longer, the owner replies that he has acted justly, and that he is free to pay whatever he wants to his workers, as long as he keeps his word.

The parable has generally been interpreted by theologians as an illustration that even those who repent at the last moment can also attain eternal life. It also illustrates the ideal that, as long as compensation is reasonable, discrimination can help create a more egalitarian community, regardless of individual effort. After all, those recruited later had initially worried that no one would hire them.

By the same token, we accept that a progressive tax scale means higher contributions from those who earn more, even if they have worked harder or longer.

In short, the parable attaches little importance to the concept of merit, that our actions make us worthy of reward or punishment. In the opinion of the owner of the vineyard, the workers he hired first do not deserve a greater reward than the latecomers, even if they have worked longer, their effort greater, or the result of their work is more valuable. One could imagine a community that is governed without regard to merit, where salaries for all are equal, regardless of the content or type of work, or the time spent working. A different question is how many of the most deserving—those who work harder or more productively than average—would choose to remain in such a community.

Similarly, if the owner of the vineyard had announced at the beginning of the day that the wage would be the same regardless of the number of hours worked, perhaps some would have waited until the last shift; as a rule, we are not predisposed to effort without reward.

In the Parable of the Talents, a businessman who has to leave on a trip divides his money equally among three of his workers: to the first he gives five talents, the Roman currency of the day; two to the second, and to the third, just one. He returns from his trip and asks his employees what they did with the money. The first two have doubled theirs by investing it. The owner praises them as *"good and faithful servants."*[47] The third, however, has buried his talent for fear of losing it. The employer accuses him of being lazy and takes away his coin. The parable concludes with an enigmatic phrase: *"For he that hath, to him shall be given: and he that hath not, from him shall be taken even that which he hath."*[48]

This parable reflects the liberal sentiment, the ideal of meritocracy, whereby we are rewarded according to our effort, our abilities, dedication and ingenuity, while those who have failed to take advantage of their talents are punished. The basis of compensation here is merit, understood as decisions or actions deserving of reward or punishment. The episode might also be called the parable of the entrepreneur, because it emphasizes risk-taking, free enterprise and the search for growth, as opposed to saving, routine and inertia. Curiously, the Catholic Church uses the expression "good and faithful servant," taken from this parable, to refer to those who have been beatified. What would have happened, however, if one of those who invested his talents had lost them as a result of a bad decision or some external factor? Perhaps the servant who had buried his talent would not have been reprimanded so harshly.

In short, the idea of merit, mechanisms of individual compensation or personal recognition, is woven into many of our social institutions and practices. From the earliest years in the family or at school, effort and the value of actions are rewarded, excellence is praised and perfection is extolled. We laud triumphant athletes, praise brilliant writers and study successful entrepreneurs.

That said, sometimes, in the family or education, interpersonal differences are counterbalanced that can benefit even the most disadvantaged, giving them more attention, lowering demands or boosting stimuli, for example the syndrome of the youngest child.

From the perspective of merit, the two parables can be interpreted as alternative answers to a fundamental philosophical question for society: how to distribute resources, the criteria for establishing taxes, or for recognizing and rewarding the contribution of individuals to the collective. The Parable of the Workers in the Vineyard is an expression of communitarianism, the logical conclusion of which is communism, whereas the Parable of the Talents represents the liberal ideal, which carried to the maximum, results in libertarianism. In the continuum between these two poles, represented by freedom and equality, values that are often in conflict, there is room for moderate options, and possibly a balanced approach to create a durable, cohesive, and possibly more just society. How can the tension between these dual values be moderated?

Perhaps an exercise using the latest available technologies could help us find a solution. Imagine you have been elected with a group of people in a metaverse to discuss and approve the principles for distributing goods and establishing obligations in a society. The aim of the metaverse is to detach the participants from their present circumstances, so that they are not conditioned by their present environment—families, jobs, interests—and can think generically, taking into account the whole of humanity. It is a perspective similar to that which Immanuel Kant, the German Enlightenment philosopher, proposed with his categorical imperative: to act in such a way that your behavior in a particular situation becomes a universal standard, so that anyone in the same situation would have a reference.[49] And in our particular metaverse, participants would adopt that universal view.

Continuing with our experiment, avatars are distributed randomly so as to distance the participants from their current identities, allowing them to assume alternative worldviews; for example, different gender, sexual orientation, or races.

This experimental metaverse is very similar to what John Rawls, one of the most influential contemporary philosophers, outlined in his 1971 book *A Theory of Justice* as a procedure for establishing the basic principles that should govern a democratic society.[50] Rawls proposed an "original position," in which participants do not know what kind of life they are going to live, how talented they will be, as well as the limitations, illnesses, wealth, luck or misfortunes they are going to experience in the future. They are behind what he calls the "veil of ignorance" of personal circumstances, which would make them prudent in defining the distribution of goods and responsibilities, and support win-win decisions, because there is a high probability that their experience will be comparatively worse than that of others: sickness, poverty, misfortune.

Under these circumstances, Rawls argued that the participants would devise a system that is as fair as possible, because nobody knows how life is going to turn out, but they would at least want to be happy. Three principles would result from this process, and would govern social institutions:

(1) The maximization of the freedom of individuals, limited only to preserve precisely that freedom. For example, prohibitions could be established for political parties that deny basic liberties or propose the elimination of the political system by force.

(2) Equality for all, allowing only those discriminations that benefit the most disadvantaged in society, what Rawls calls the "difference principle." For example, the establishment of progressive taxation to redistribute wealth.

(3) Equality of opportunity and the elimination of inequality of opportunity generated by factors related to birth or wealth. For example, Rawls would be against the admission of applicants to US universities through legacy, which is to say the children of alumni or donors.[51]

Rawls' proposal, described as "qualified egalitarianism,"[52] generated one of the most intense philosophical debates of recent decades. It has the merit of establishing itself as an entire theory of justice, as an autonomous system with the vocation of completeness. Moreover, it has had a relevant influence beyond the academic sphere, with repercussions in the legislative and judicial spheres beyond the United States.[53]

Nevertheless, there have been many critics of *A Theory of Justice*.[54] Perhaps the most effective are those that question why anybody should accept the arrangements of those who were in the "original position" if they did not participate in those decisions. Furthermore, it would even be possible to dispute those decisions even if one had participated in them: The subsequent reality, our experiences, could lead us to challenge the whole procedure. Something similar happens with contracts that are presumed to be for life. Think, for example, of the frequency of divorces, even if the marriage is assumed to be forever. Similarly, agreements made in ignorance of all the facts could be refuted by decisive circumstances that change our world view. Do we have the right to selfishness in maturity if we have been generous when young?

In Thomas Nagel's opinion, the reduction of a global social agreement to so few and concise principles turns the Rawlsian proposal into a *"thin theory of justice."*[55] Its basic principles are so generic that they require further development in order to be applied to concrete decisions, and this is where the problems of detail generate contradictions and inconsistencies. On the other hand, there are many other substantive issues related to social justice that could not be decided by such principles. Certainly, most of the constitutions of democratic countries have a much more extensive articulation, which is still insufficient to resolve many social dilemmas and require further interpretation.

Rawls' *Theory of Justice* attempts to correct the personal or environmental conditions that determine our future, among them luck, wealth or the benefits derived from where one is born, but also talent or natural intelligence. In his opinion, letting those who are more talented accumulate assets without any redistribution would mean duplicating the effect of a "natural accident" such as being more intelligent, more extroverted, or more handsome, factors that contribute to personal success. It therefore adjusts the spaces of freedom and equality of opportunity in favor of greater real equality, especially for the most disadvantaged.

Rawls' contribution is still the source of many communitarian ideas, which prioritize the greater good and the redistributive function of the state and institutions over the primacy of individualism and personal merit. One of its exponents is Michael Sandel, who defends replacing the current admission system to Ivy League universities, arguing that the supposed merit enjoyed by successful candidates is in fact the result of privilege.[56]

Rawls would probably have been more sympathetic to the Parable of the Vineyard Workers, and arguably have questioned the moral of the Parable of the Talents. As with his "original position," the rest of us lack the arguments to take sides, and we adapt our conception of what is just and deserved over the course of our lives.

## 1.6   The Matthew Effect: Michael Sandel on Merit

Most institutions are based on meritocracy, a system that supposedly adjudicates reward based on talent, effort and achievement. Typically, admission to universities, access to grants or scholarships, selection for jobs, assessment of work, professional promotion and most public distinctions, among many other practices, are meritocratic.

One of the earliest explanations of the concept of merit can be found in the mentioned Parable of the Talents[57] where a farmer divides his wealth among three workers and returns after some time asking the three to account for their money. While the first two have doubled their investment, while the third has buried his talent for fear of losing it. The owner criticizes the latter for his laziness and praises the first two for their diligence.

Calling this "the Matthew Effect," US sociologist Robert Merton explains how success typically leads to further success, the generation of wealth leads to the concentration of goods, in the same way that the exercise of power leads to the accumulation of greater power, as well as something similar with prestige or fame. In short, the rich get richer and the poor get poorer.[58]

In his latest book, *The Tyranny of Merit*, Michael Sandel offers a timely critique of meritocracy, arguing forcefully that it generates inequality and social unrest.[59] A Harvard professor, Sandel is often associated with the philosophy of communitarianism, the belief that our identity comes from belonging to the whole, as opposed to liberalism, which emphasizes individualism.

Sandel analyzes US society over recent decades and the underlying philosophy that, in his opinion, has characterized politics and economics regardless of which party has been in power.

In his view, the rise of populism is fundamentally due to two factors. Firstly, the adoption of the technocratic model, and secondly, the enshrinement of the meritocratic system that defines who we call winners and losers.

Sandel focuses on two spheres of social activity to illustrate his argument: higher education and the work environment. In both, the concept of merit plays a decisive role. For example, admission and evaluation systems in universities, or selection for jobs, as well as professional promotion and recognition in the business world. Sandel also highlights how, in his opinion, access to the most prestigious American universities has reinforced elitism and inequality over time. For instance, a high percentage of those admitted to Ivy League universities are the children of alumni or donors to the university, or are given sports scholarships. This has reinforced elitism and hindered access to education.

To counter this, Sandel formulates the following proposal. Let us assume that Harvard University receives approximately 40,000 admission applications, but can only admit 2000 students, of whom more than half come from families associated with the university. At the same time, studies show that some 20,000 applicants have the right profile. To avoid elitism and the Matthew Effect, the ideal would be to draw lots to determine which of those 20,000 would be admitted. Luck, limited by some coefficients that would guarantee, for example, gender diversity and other categories, would guarantee a fairer result.

I won't go into whether Sandel's suggestion would be a better approach than letting the admissions department decide. I suspect that many people would dismiss the proposal by saying that there are enough inequalities due to luck in our lives.

My main criticism of Sandel is that he is merely proposing another exclusive model of university access, albeit using different selection mechanisms. Instead, why not widen the windows of opportunity for education, instead of reducing it to a single, once-in-a-lifetime card?

This is where continuing education throughout our careers, makes sense, and where universities can play a role. The populism Sandel discusses has in large part been driven by an electorate of older people who lack the skills needed in today's labor market. The best solution would be to offer more educational options for these professionals to regain employability or explore entrepreneurship, not to fight globalization to regain jobs that have been offshored to emerging countries, as Sandel proposes, incidentally, in line with Donald Trump.[60]

At the same time, the pandemic has shown the potential of online education thanks to platforms such as edx, Coursera and Openclassrooms, among others.[61] Contrary to what was thought only two years ago, quality online training can significantly expand universal access to education. For example, the Justice course taught by Michael Sandel himself at Harvard University, one of the most demanded by students, is available on edx for everyone.[62] A very effective way to combat elitism.

Given that the concept of meritocracy is intrinsic to the functioning of many institutions, educators would be better focused on instilling self-confidence in their students, underlined by a sense of commitment to society and the virtue of modesty. That could be achieved by business schools emphasizing the responsibilities that come with attending school and entering a profession.

Universities try to instill the confidence in their students that will allow them to analyze, establish goals and assume risks. The challenge for educators and for students is how to balance the self-assurance needed to lead people and to take decisions with the modesty required to avoid over-confidence and losing touch with reality. Openness and modesty are two recommendable attitudes to start any learning experience with. In fact, they are key for those entering an MBA program, since much of learning comes from fellow participants. I tend to kick off the inaugural speech I give to MBA students at my school with the same words Socrates used when addressing new students: "*The only true wisdom is knowing that you know nothing.*"[63] This sometimes ruffles a few feathers, since MBA students normally have a very high opinion of themselves, believing that they are where they are on merit.

Similarly, business schools with students from a wide range of cultures, with different world views encourages tolerance and openness to new ideas and confronts students with a reality of multiple references, thus making it harder to see themselves as belonging to a single, elite group.

Finally, I think it pays to revisit the concept of merit, something Sandel hints at in his work. One promising avenue is to understand that success in life does not depend on what was traditionally considered talent, but to extend it to many other forms of intelligence that, according to evidence and experience, provide more opportunities to succeed.

## 1.7 Inculcating Knowledge in the Young: John Locke's Golden Rules of Children's Education

"*The little, or almost insensible impressions on our tender infancies, have very important and lasting consequences.*"[64] Widely shared by psychologists and pediatricians today, this insight was written more than 300 years ago by British philosopher John Locke in his treatise *Some Thoughts Concerning*

*Education*, his response to a request by an aristocratic friend for advice on how to bring up his children. Published in 1693, the book soon became a reference work within the English-speaking world.

When a good friend of mine, a young father, recently asked if I could recommend a book on bringing up children, I thought of Locke. There are any number of more recent studies, but I opted for a classic work, one linked to the Humanist philosophical strain.

While some may question the value of humanism in education or personal and professional development, I find it very useful to revisit my grounding in the classics. Growing numbers of parents, for varying reasons, are content for their children to be occupied for hours on end with smartphones or video games, despite the associated risks of addiction from uncontrolled use of these kinds of technology from an early age. Some are now debating the practicalities of robots designed to attend to children when both parents are at work and nannies are not an option, while critics say we are in danger of creating a dehumanized world where AI will perform the duties once carried out by parents, teachers and coaches.

I believe technology offers myriad resources to personalize and boost learning, for adults and children, and I also continue to trust in the contribution the Humanities and the Classics can make to education.

Locke formulates two key principles regarding children's education. The first is that the task is primarily the responsibility of parents, even if it is sometimes necessary to delegate to other members of the family, teachers and even the state. This belief is particularly relevant today, when in most cases, people are able to plan their families and the decision to start a family is increasingly the result of mutual consent between partners.

At the same time, based on its responsibility to guarantee the right to an education, the state and other public administrations are obliged to help parents in their endeavors. Given the importance of the early years in creating our personality, setting our values and developing our skills, the state, particularly in advanced countries, needs to provide free, high-quality nursery care. For example, infants find it much easier to learn new languages and are much more open to new information, as well as developing the basic characteristics that will shape their personality.

Locke's second principle is that education is the best investment one can make in one's children, above any material assets. He refers expressly to the cost of good tutors. Fiction and real life have provided us with any number of examples of parents who strive to create empires for their children. A staunch proponent of private property, Locke doesn't downplay the importance of inheritances, but he was aware of the value of education over material goods:

*"...the difference to be found in the manners and abilities of men is owing more to their education than to anything else."*[65]

In the final analysis, says Locke, we are the sum of what we accrue through education. Locke rejects the idea that we are what we are for innate reasons, what today we would call genetics, or the sole outcome of our environment or material assets. When we are born, he explains, we are a tabula rasa, ready to be written on. This idea is at the heart of empiricism, which argues that the only source of human knowledge is experience and that each proposition we make should be subjected to the information our senses and experience provide us with. Locke was one of the principal exponents of Empiricism, along with Berkeley and Hume.[66] Empiricism would have a huge influence over the development over analytical philosophy and positivism, which are still important aspects of thinking in the English-speaking world.

Locke further argues that educating our children is not just about spending time with them: He criticizes parents who spoil their offspring, saying this deforms their character and results in willful and unreliable adults. Using an analogy from the Classics, Locke draws a parallel between education and the journey between Scylla and Charybdis, as told in *The Odyssey*.[67] In Ulysses' time, only experienced sailors knew how to chart this course through the Strait of Messina, with the whirlpools on one side created by Charybdis, which swallowed boats, and the rocks of Scylla on the other. Parents must find the balance between love and discipline. Locke says many parents make the mistake of trying to be their children's friends, but it is only in adulthood, when we are able to reason and to understand the value of friendship that parents can establish this type of relationship with their children.

Locke attacks the use of physical punishment on children, although this was widespread at the time, and would continue to be until just a few decades ago. He says corporal punishment should only be used in extreme cases of obstinacy.

Rather than the carrot and the stick, says Locke, it is better to praise children publicly when they do well, while criticism, often simply through a look, should be made in private. I have found this approach to work well with adults over the course of my career.

Locke was a pioneer in other aspects of education: The first chapters of his book anticipate the current theories of wellness. Employing Juvenal's maxim *mens sana in corpore sano* (a healthy mind in a healthy body),[68] he recommended regular sport, time in the open air and a balanced diet, and was especially keen on swimming, citing the Roman maxim applied to the badly brought up: *nec literas nec natare* (he neither reads nor swims). He was also a keen proponent of cold showers and light clothing as a way to toughen up the young. His later influence is clear: The idea of combining physical exercise with intellectual development is at the core of all modern teaching methods.

His ideas regarding nutrition reflect his study of medicine while at Oxford: He understood the benefits of eating certain foods, as well as of healthy habits, all of which are outlined in *Some Thoughts Concerning Education*. He recommended a moderate diet, chewing one's food, avoiding too much meat, as well as abstinence, noting *"The Romans usually fasted till supper."*[69]

Locke also highlighted the importance of learning a trade or profession, one compatible with the study of the Humanities and the Liberal Arts. This is significant, given that his recommendations were being made to the nobility, who at that time didn't work. In this sense, Locke can be seen as a forerunner of the educational model adopted later by many universities, combining generalist disciplines with a specialization intended to be applied to the world of work following graduation.

In general, Locke followed the classic tradition of focusing children's education on developing virtues and habits. Once again, virtues are not innate qualities, but acquired. To learn virtues, Locke provides examples: *"Children do most by example,"* he explains, particularly their parents'. *"We are all sort of chameleons."*[70]

Children's literature did not exist as a genre in Locke's day, but he recommends Aesop's Fables for young people, a choice I would agree with, along with other books written later that have played an important role in our education, such as the tales of Hans Christian Andersen.[71]

In short, *Some Thoughts Concerning Education* is a surprisingly modern book and one I would recommend to any parent. Locke's knowledge, his intuition and his wisdom are particularly noteworthy given that he never had children. A modern, original and still very relevant author.

## Notes

1. Plato, *Apology*, 38 a 5–6, in *The Last Days of Socrates: Euthyphro; Apology; Crito; Phaedo* (ed. H. Tarrant) (London: Penguin, 2003).
2. Skepticism and Cynicism are the two main philosophical streams questioning whether we can actually know. Vid M. Proudfoot and A.R. Lacey, *The Routledge Dictionary of Philosophy*, 4th ed. (London: Routledge, 2020).
3. From Xenophon's *Memorabilia,* quoted by J. Miller, Examined Lives. Form Socrates to Nietzsche (New York: Farrar, Straus and Giroux, 2011), p. 7.
4. Plato, op. cit. ibidem.

5. R.J. Hollingdale, *Nietzsche. The Man and His Philosophy* (Rev. ed.) (Cambridge: Cambridge University Press, 1999), p. 25.
6. Diogenes Laertius, *Lives of the Eminent Philosophers* (Oxford: Oxford University Press, 2020); and Plutarch, *The Makers of Rome: Nine Lives* (ed. I. Scott-Kilver) (London: Penguin, 1965).
7. J. Greco (ed.), *The Oxford Handbook of Skepticism* (Oxford, Oxford University Press, 2011).
8. Aristotle, *The Nicomachean Ethics* (trans. H. Tredennick & J.A.K. Thomson) (London: Penguin, 2004), Ch. 10.
9. N. Warburton, *A Little History of Philosophy* (New Haven, Conn.: Yale University Press, 2011), Ch. 26.
10. J.P. Sartre, *No Exit* (New York: Samuel French Inc., 1958).
11. J.P. Sartre, *Being and Nothingness* (Trans. H: E Barnes) (London: Routledge, 1993), and *Essays in Existentialism* (New York: Citadel, 1976).
12. J. Miller, Examined Lives. From Socrates to Nietzsche, op. cit., p. 268.
13. Ibid., pp. 43–72.
14. Plato, Apology, op. cit., 21d.
15. I. Murdoch, *The Sovereignty of the Good* (London: Routledge, 1979); p. 35.
16. T. Baldwin, "There Might Be Nothing". 56 *Analysis* 4, pp. 231–238; N. Warburton, op. cit., Ch. 3.
17. A. Rand, "Philosophy: Who Needs It?" (New York, NY: Penguin; Signet, 1984); p. 5.
18. Ibidem.
19. Marcus Aurelius, *Meditations* (London: Penguin, 2006); Cardenal Mazarino, *Breviario de los politicos* (Barcelona: Acantilado, 2007); La Rouchefoucauld, *Maxims* (London: Penguin, 1982).
20. B. Gracian, *The Art of Worldly Wisdom: a Pocket Oracle* (New York: Snowball, 2012).
21. S. Ghoshal: "Bad Management Theories Are Destroying Good Management Practices," *Academy of Management Learning & Education IV* (2005), pp. 75–91.
22. N. Machiavelli, The Prince (London: Penguin, 2003).
23. S. Ghoshal, op. cit., p.75.
24. Ibid., p.79.
25. B. Gracián, op.cit., 16, p. 38.
26. Ibid., 26, p. 138.
27. Ibid., 243, p. 265.
28. Ibid., 44, p. 66.
29. Ibid., 81, p. 163.
30. Ibid., 164, p.186.
31. Ibid., 9, p. 31.
32. Ibid., 4, p. 26.
33. Plato, *The Republic* (London: Penguin, 2007), IV, 428e.

34. D. Kahnemann, *Thinking Fast and Slow* (New York: Farrar, Straus and Giroux, 2013).
35. IQ of American presidents https://www.usnews.com/news/blogs/data-mine/2015/05/27/poindexter-in-chief-presidential-iqs-and-success-in-the-oval-office.
36. A. Wooldridge, *The Aristocracy of Talent. How Meritocracy Made the Modern World* (Penguin: London, 2021).
37. Ibid., p.1.
38. M. Sandel, *The Tyranny of Merit. Can We Find the Common Good?* (Farrar, Straus & Giroux, 2020).
39. D. Markovits, *The Meritocracy Trap. How America's Foundational Myth Feeds Inequality, Dismantles the Middle Class, and Devours the Elite* (New York: Penguin, 2019).
40. A. Wooldridge, op. cit., Part V.
41. R. Plomin, *Blueprint: How DNA Makes Us Who We Are* (Boston: MIT Press, 2019). https://www.psychologytoday.com/us/basics/nature-vs-nurture.
42. H. Gardner, *Multiple Intelligences. New Horizons in Theory and Practice* (New York: Basic Books, 2006).
43. S. Pinker, *Enlightenment Now. The Case for reason, Science, Humanism, and Progress* (London: Penguin, 2019).
44. J.W. Goethe, quoted by S. Zweig, *The struggle against the devil: Hölderlin—Kleist—Nietzsche* (Madrid: El Acantilado, 2021) (Spanish Edition), p. 78.
45. Mathew, 20: 1–16.
46. Matthew, 25: 14–30.
47. Ibidem.
48. Ibidem.
49. I. Kant, *Groundwork of the Metaphysic of Morals* (ed. C.M. Korsgaard, M. Gregor, and J. Timmermann) (Cambridge: Cambridge University Press, 2012).
50. J. *Rawls, A Theory of Justice* (Oxford: Oxford University Press, 2005).
51. Rawls' MAXIMIN [abbreviation of "maximum minimorum"] is the rule of choice that asks that, in any distribution, the most disadvantaged situation be considered first (that of the individual who benefits least from the distribution).
52. N. Warburton, op. cit., Ch. 38.
53. Ibidem.
54. C. Kukathas and P. Pettit, *Rawls: A Theory of Justice and Its Critics* (Stanford, CA: Stanford University Press, 1990), and N. Daniels (ed.), *Reading Rawls. Critical Studies on Rawls' 'A Theory of Justice'* (Stanford, CA: Stanford University Press, 1989).
55. T. Nagel, "Rawls on Justice", *82 The Philosophical Review 2* (April 1973), pp. 220–34.
56. M. Sandel, op. cit.

57. Matthew, 25: 14–30.

58. https://www.science.org/doi/10.1126/science.159.3810.56.

59. M. Sandel, op. cit.

60. https://www.reuters.com/article/us-usa-trump-outsource-idUSKBN1CF1IF.

61. S. Iniguez and P. Lorange (eds.), *Executive Education after the Pandemic: A Vision for the Future* (London: Palgrave Macmillan, 2021).

62. https://www.edx.org/es/bio/michael-j-sandel.

63. Plato, *Apology*, op. cit. Ibidem.

64. J. Locke, *Some Thoughts concerning Education* (London: Kypros Press, 2016), Kindle ed.

65. Ibid., 32, loc. 339.

66. N. Warburton, op. cit., Ch. 15.

67. Homer, *The Odyssey* (London: Penguin, 2003), Books 12–14.

68. Juvenal, *The Satires* (Oxford: Oxford University Press, 1991).

69. J. Locke, op. cit., 14, loc. 167.

70. Ibid., 67, loc. 728.

71. Aesop, *The Complete Fables* (trans. O. Temple) (London: Penguin, 1998); H.C. Andersen, *The Emperor's New clothes and Other Stories* (London: Penguin, 1995).

# 2

# Part 2: Leadership—Who Do I Want to Be?

The ideas of Friedrich Nietzsche, the nineteenth-century German philosopher famous for his assertion that "*God is dead*," have influenced management theories in the West over the last century. In *Thus Spoke Zarathustra*, he celebrates the übermensch, or superman, destined to run the world.

> *I teach you the [Übermensch]. Man is something that shall be overcome.... All beings so far have created something beyond themselves ... What is the ape to man? A laughingstock or a painful embarrassment. And man shall be just that for the [Übermensch]: a laughingstock or a painful embarrassment.... The [Übermensch] is the meaning of the earth.... I beseech you, my brothers, remain faithful to the earth, and do not believe those who speak to you of otherworldly hopes!*[1]

Nietzsche's influence in the United States is noticeable from the beginning of the twentieth century, coinciding with the translation into English of his works, along the rise of the first business tycoons and large corporations, creating oligopolies in key sectors of the economy.[2] Nietzsche admired the American thinker Ralph Waldo Emerson, and his work was commented on and criticized by other US writers such as William James.[3]

For Nietzsche, there are essentially two types of morality, that of the master and that of the slave. The former applies to the leaders of society, who establish their own values and rules. Slave morality applies to the masses, who in turn see the behavior of their masters as evil. Little matter: The masters are "*beyond good and evil*" and set their own rules, while the masses accept mediocrity and try to hold back the true leaders. There are echoes of Nietzsche's writing in management literature on leadership in the 1980s: "*To give style to one's character—a great and rare art! He practices it who surveys all that his*

S. Iñiguez, *Philosophy Inc.*, https://doi.org/10.1007/978-3-031-20483-8_2

*nature presents in strength and weakness and then molds it to an artistic plan until everything appears as art and reason, and even the weakness delights the eye …. It will be the strong, imperious natures which experience their subtlest joy in exercising such a control, in such a constraint and perfecting under their own law."[4]*

Moving on, Nietzsche's arguments also seem to justify the excesses of the 1990s.

> *… the secret of realizing the greatest fruitfulness and the greatest enjoyment of existence is to live dangerously! Build your cities on the slopes of the Vesuvius! Send your ships out into uncharted seas! Live in conflict with your equals and with yourselves! Be robbers and ravagers as long as you cannot be rulers or owners, you men of knowledge! The time will soon be past when you could be content to live concealed in the woods like timid deer!*[5]

Fortunately, business schools have largely abandoned the masters of the universe mentality admired by Nietzsche and his followers, and instead tend to focus on purpose and social commitment. Indeed, there has been something of a recovery of business ethics, even as one business scandal after another emerges, sometimes triggering financial crises. A good example of new styles of leadership theory is the idea proposed by Harvard's Jim Collins: the "Level 5 Leader,"[6] who combines traditional leadership qualities such as tenacity with other attributes like humility.

Nevertheless, leadership and charisma, in accordance with Nietzsche's thinking, are still widely associated, something that is addressed in the next section.

## 2.1   Beware of the Charismatic Candidate

Over the course of my career, I have interviewed a great many people, either for posts where they would report directly to me, or for other departments. Furthermore, during my first stint at IE Business School as Associate Director of the MBA and Executive MBA programs, I also interviewed numerous applicants.

While this experience has helped hone my listening skills, I fear any other benefits have probably been neutralized by my innate capacity for distraction, combined with a tendency grown over the years to talk too much, which seems to be a natural part of management. And while I have learned to evaluate the personality and professional background of applicants, I often fail in unraveling the idiosyncrasies of the person I'm talking to, let alone predict the success or otherwise of his or her future performance. So, to gain better perspective, I usually consult colleagues who are better at reading people, more intuitive and generally sociable and well-intentioned.

That said, one of the lessons I have learned over the years is not to place too much importance on that most subjective of qualities, charisma. My hard-earned experience is that charismatic people are not necessarily the best leaders or the most effective managers. Based on this personal knowledge, I venture to make the most salient recommendation of this section: do not be blinded by the charisma of your candidates. Obviously, it would be perverse to dismiss charisma entirely, nevertheless, we should look for additional qualities when choosing the right person.

What is this attribute we call charisma, and so often associated with leadership? Conventionally, it is understood as "the powerful personal quality that some people have to attract and impress other people."[7] A trait that is usually associated with prominent figures in the fields of politics, the stage, the arts, and of course business.

Max Weber, the German sociologist and political scientist, is often regarded as the first thinker to analyze the phenomenon of charisma and attempt to dissect its characteristics. Weber lived at the time of the resurgence of Caesarism in Europe, embodied by characters such as Otto von Bismarck, the father of German unification. "*Charisma is a certain quality of an individual personality by virtue of which he is set apart from ordinary men and treated as endowed with supernatural, superhuman, or at least specifically exceptional powers or qualities. These as such are not accessible to the ordinary person, but are regarded as of divine origin or as exemplary, and on the basis of them the individual concerned is treated as a leader,*" wrote Weber in *The Theory of Social and Economic Organization.*[8]

Weber saw something semidivine in charisma, identifying it as an innate gift, but experience and research show that it can be cultivated and developed, even later in life, along with the skills of managerial leadership. Some people associate charisma with extroversion,[9] but we should also remember that introversion does not exclude leadership. Research by Adam Grant shows that extrovert leaders typically perform better when they have passive teams around them, while introverts work better with proactive employees, which means that the latter perform better when innovation is the goal.[10]

The introverts among us looking to develop their charisma can always turn to Charisma Leadership Tactics (CLT), which provide training in habits and practices to enhance our ability to influence others.[11] There is even evidence to show how circadian rhythms can influence people,[12] that is, the time of day when our organism is at its biological peak; some of us are larks who perform better in the morning, while others are night owls.

In their article *Learning Charisma*, John Antonakis, Marika Fenley and Sue Liechti identify 12 tactics to reinforce our charisma.[13] Nine of them are related to verbal language such as comparisons, the use of metaphors, similes and analogies; referencing through stories and anecdotes; formulating contrasts; using rhetorical questions; structuring our arguments in three points—a magic number; emphasizing moral convictions; reflecting shared feelings in the group—promoting empathy; proposing ambitious goals; and conveying confidence that they are achievable.

Three of their tactics have to do with nonverbal communication: intonation, facial expressions—which is why some people rehearse speeches in front of a mirror—and the use of hand and body gestures. They also offer other effective resources, such as creating a sense of urgency, invoking history, talking about sacrifice—recalling Churchill's "*I promise you blood, sweat and tears*"[14]—and the use of humor.

We may not like to accept it, but appearance is often key to projecting charisma. Gordon L. Patzer's *Looks: Why They Matter More Than You Ever Imagined* explains that Personal Attractiveness (PA) is a decisively favorable factor in many social situations. For example, people with a high PA are more likely to be selected for a job, to be promoted within a company, to succeed in politics or in professions with public exposure, and even to receive more attention, and better grades—from their teachers. As Patzer explains: "*While shared values and common life goals are important, by far the most important factor is what can be gleaned from the picture accompanying the person's online profile (…)* although "*online daters often discover cover that the photo they fell in love with, like the carefully written profile that it accompanies, doesn't tell the whole story.*"[15]

When I raise the question of charisma with my students, many say the term should be limited to the morally acceptable exercise of leadership, and that characters such as Hitler or Stalin, for example, should be excluded. The problem with this selective restriction is that there are any number of charismatic leaders whose behavior is open to question. At the same time, there are young charismatic men and women who have not yet fulfilled their mission, meaning that any identification of their qualities is independent of the evaluation of their achievements. In conceptual terms, we have to accept that charisma is independent of whether it is exercised for noble ends, purely for self-interest, or in pursuit of evil, and has to be weighed against other personal virtues.

With that in mind, we should be careful in attributing qualities such as charisma to those responsible for crimes against humanity. This brings to mind Hannah Arendt's description of Adolf Eichmann, who masterminded the Final Solution and who was kidnapped in Argentina after the second world war by Israeli agents, and taken to Jerusalem where he was tried for crimes against humanity in 1961.[16] Arendt attended the trial, and was struck by Eichmann's attitude, famously describing his seeming composure as the banality of evil. Arendt was attempting to demythologize evil, the idea that only somebody who was sick in the mind would be capable of such terrible acts. Her conclusion was that any number of ordinary people are capable of acts of great cruelty. Eichmann was not a psychopath who was not responsible for his actions, but instead a sentient man carrying out a policy to kill millions of people and who insisted he had never personally killed anybody. Arendt's insight is proof of how sometimes people who seem normal to us can commit horrendous crimes, and that we need to isolate the concept of charisma when assessing people's morality.

As for whether it's a good idea or not for organizations to have charismatic leaders, the research suggests it depends on a range of factors. Weber explained that the relationship between people with charisma and the group is paradoxical. In times of crisis, groups demand clear direction, firm leadership, and are willing to follow the leader unquestioningly.[17] The dictators of Ancient Rome originally took power to deal with a major crisis, for example, a barbarian invasion, and we've seen during the pandemic how the role and powers of leaders were strengthened.[18]

That said, charismatic people do not necessarily make effective managers. John P. Kotter clarified the difference between the two when he explained that management is about balancing complexity, organizing and allocating resources and people, controlling and planning, whereas leading is dealing with change, developing a vision, motivating and inspiring and, above all, aligning a team toward a mission. Although management seems a more rational practice than leadership, akin perhaps to organizational engineering, leadership should not be perceived as a mysterious or mystical quality. "*It has nothing to do with having 'charisma' or some other exotic personality trait. It is not the territory of a select few,*" he explains. Instead, it is a skill that develops over time and comprises a set of characteristics that require deep communication with the parties involved, much deeper than what a manager needs.[19]

Given that charisma tends to blind our critical judgment about a leader's qualities, what can we do to avoid this? Below is some advice, based on my experience.

- Be wary of charismatic leaders who are sharply critical of others, especially their predecessors, colleagues or successors. Fake leaders gain credibility by discrediting of others, rather than on their own merits. Conversely, systematic and sincere praise is an indication of humility and honesty.

- Praise is not the same as flattery, and it is advisable discourage flattery or adulation, not only to expose charismatic people with nothing to offer, but also as an exercise in personal modesty.
- External references from people who know a candidate are valid, especially when it comes to leaders with charisma, because they can provide us with information that proves their management skills. If your enquiry solicits silence, you may have confirmation that your doubts are justified.
- Voluntary turnover or short stays in various positions, blaming others or disparaging former employees can also be an indication of unauthentic charisma. This is the case of seemingly impressive people, but with whom no one wants to work. Perhaps you have come across some similar cases.

Finally, my experience as a teacher on hybrid programs, which combine quality online training with face-to-face modules, has helped me to get to know my students better, both their intellectual facets and their leadership skills. Hybrid formats test the multiple capabilities of managers and can be a good testing ground to check the balance between their multifaceted qualities.

A report from the French Artillery Academy where Napoleon Bonaparte studied read: "*Corsican in character and birth, this young man will go far if circumstances help him.*"[20] Napoleon would not originally be the archetype of charisma: bald, short, he spoke French with an Italian accent, graduated in the middle of his class, and was an introverted child. Sometimes, luck, serendipity, or circumstances, release our hidden charisma.

## 2.2    Why Humility Is a Sign of Strength

Humility is not a virtue that typically characterizes powerful people, whether politicians, business leaders or intellectuals, who tend to associate it with the also-rans of this world. As seen, Friedrich Nietzsche inspired the concept of modern charismatic leadership and the idea of the "superman" and believed that humility is the response of the weak to avoid the wrath of the powerful.[21]

In most religions, pride—as opposed to humility—remains one of the cardinal sins. Lucifer's fall is due to his arrogance in challenging God, and he assumes his punishment with recalcitrance, declaring it is better to live in hell as a master in hell than in heaven as a servant, in the words of poet John Milton.[22]

Similarly, in the book of Genesis, God punishes the builders of the Tower of Babel for their arrogance in aspiring to reach the heavens, condemning them to speak in different languages—the biblical origin of linguistic diversity.[23] A more charitable interpretation of both cases would be that they were overly ambitious rather than arrogant.

In Greek mythology, Icarus's ambition led him and his father Daedalus to build wings made of feathers and wax, and to take flight from the labyrinth of the Minotaur, located on the island of Crete. Disregarding his father's instructions, boastful Icarus flew too close to the sun, the wax melted and he plummeted into the sea near the island of Samos.[24] Perhaps, Icarus' behavior today would have been described as disruptive and innovative, and he might well have been hired by Elon Musk or Richard Branson for their space ventures.

As said, the traditional concept of humility, associating it with prudence, conformism and submission, means it tends to be rejected by leaders. However, humility is not the same as blind obedience. Humility is the recognition of one's limitations, and leads to self-improvement. Rather than limiting our scope, it helps us achieve our goals: Saint Teresa of Jesus, the religious mystic of the Spanish Golden Age, believed that "humility is truth."[25]

For Aristotle, the virtues lie in the middle ground, placing humility between the extremes of insecurity and inferiority at one extreme, and arrogance, vanity or pride at the other.[26] On this spectrum, arrogant people are more annoying than those who are self-conscious, because they are more visible and audible, making their presence hard to bear.

Business schools have sometimes been criticized for encouraging arrogance in MBA students. When I hear this, I reply that not all business schools share the same values, nor do they select or prepare their students in the same way. In any case, the existence of this criticism is reason enough to revisit the learning model and the contents of our teaching, and try to train more committed and modest entrepreneurs. There is an element of service in business, and failure to understand this typically leads to failure.

The fundamental value of humility for entrepreneurs and business people is that it provides a more objective and realistic view of the world. Arrogance provides a shield against other people's ideas, rejecting innovation and obstructing self-criticism, thus success results in pride, and failure in complacency.[27]

One of the sessions I remember most vividly from the International Teacher's Program, a highly successful training course for business school teachers in Europe a few years ago, was a meeting with the great strategist Sumantra Ghoshal, then teaching at London Business School. Ghoshal had analyzed the typical response of large corporations when things are not going well. Poor results are often the result of the same level of sales but declining profit. In many cases, this trend is confirmed and a slippery slope begins that is difficult to reverse, because it depends not only on the company concerned, but also on interaction with competitors and customers. In these cases, Ghoshal explained, senior management tends to become complacent and avoid responsibility, with the blame being shifted to external factors. Even the hackneyed argument about product or market maturity is used. Ghoshal used the term "*satisfactory underperformance*" to describe this process, a nice irony that captures the arrogance of many CEOs and directors.[28]

A truth known to all, although not always assimilated, is that today's success does not guarantee tomorrow's victory. Looking back over my career, I sometimes ask myself if my achievements are enough to maintain my reputation and guarantee my future, to which I normally tell myself that a career is a long-distance race, and is never really over. As the Red Queen in *Alice in Wonderland* pointed out, even to stay in the same place, we have to keep moving.[29] Sometimes I think of the roller coaster analogy to represent the relative arbitrariness of a career: There are ups and downs, not necessarily related to personal effort or work. Luck, moreover, plays an important role.

In short, a measure of humility and modesty is essential for keeping a level head over the years. In the first place, because things rarely turn out as we plan or imagine them, and also because humility will allow us to see other perspectives and other angles, especially if we exercise the opportune habit of listening.

Some of the great teachers I have had the good fortune to meet in my career possessed the gift of listening, a sign of their genuine humility. I remember two episodes that made an impact on me. The first was with Herbert L.A. Hart, former Professor of Jurisprudence and one of my tutors at University College, whom I had the opportunity to drive—on the left—through the Oxfordshire countryside. He was an octogenarian by then, but retained a prodigious mind, an affectionate and detail-oriented man. We had lunch on several occasions, and I remember how he asked questions about Spain, about our culture, about my doctoral work, about my plans for the future. Generally, such wise and experienced people are usually talkative, rarely asking, let alone listening to a young student. Most of the fellows I dealt with at Oxford were prone to cantankerousness. On the other hand, Hart knew Spanish history in depth—he had assisted the Republican army in the Civil War, and kept up to date on Spanish politics and economics. His generosity of heart, caring style and elegant manners provided me with lessons I still value over the years.[30]

The other episode occurred during my first meeting with architect and Pritzker Prize winner Sir Norman Foster. At that time, we were creating IE School of Architecture and Design, and were seeking expert advice for the mission, programs and faculty of the future school. Lord Foster listened to me for almost 40 minutes, without interrupting me or asking questions, attentive and fixing me with his gaze. Eventually, he intervened and then spoke for an equivalent amount of time. I remember his advice, and some of his phrases almost verbatim. One of the lessons I learned from that meeting, which I have tried to practice since, is not to talk for too long—two or three minutes at the most—in the first meeting with a person. To go on for longer than that often means descending to chitchat and can be seen as an expression of vanity and arrogance, whereas listening reflects modesty, and is a sign of intelligence.

How do you react when someone starts to tell you something you already know, about a character, a place, or your own field of work? Do you interrupt to say: "I already know what you are telling me"? I have always considered that keeping quiet and listening in these situations is a sign of humility and refinement, and that is why I usually try to restrain myself, even if I know the story well, or even if I have been the protagonist of the episode being told. With age and experience, this will happen more frequently, and we will find ourselves in déjà vu situations again and again. A good opportunity to exercise modesty.

A professor at IE University recently asked me what advice to pass on to students to give them self-confidence as opposed to arrogance. In short, how to maintain that Aristotelian balance between the two undesirable extremes. Allow me to close with a few recommendations.

- First, preparation. Knowing one's subject confers security, and indicates a mastery of the matter in hand. A lack of foresight, of having worked on a meeting or a presentation, even if we have experience in the matter, is an expression of arrogance and often leads to failure. Improvisation is a gift that also requires work. I am often reminded of Mark Twain's quote: "*To improvise well, I need at least two weeks.*"[31]
- Second, sportsmanship. If you are offended when things don't go as you would have liked, you may not assimilate the lesson. It is preferable to maintain the attitude of the apprentice who continues to learn throughout life, and to consider failures and mistakes as learning opportunities.
- Speak up and participate in meetings, interviews, social gatherings. Humility does not mean mute acceptance of the status quo; rather, quiet self-confidence empowers us to play a leading role.
- Encourage diversity in your dealings with others, and think about how you can include as wide a range of outlooks and input in business. They will allow you to look at problems from different perspectives, to step outside your own perspective, and to cultivate modesty.
- And finally, a tip from Rosabeth Moss Kanter, the organizational behavior expert. Don't try to do everything yourself. Especially if you have managerial responsibilities, you have to learn to delegate and to trust other people.[32]

Reality always puts us in our place, which is usually not center stage.

## 2.3    Where Would Business Be Without Its Supporting Actors?

Two of the awards most eagerly anticipated by movie fans at the Oscars are for best supporting actress and actor. The prize recognizes the decisive contribution of these performers to a film's plot and storyline, and how they provide depth, context by interacting with the other characters. There are few entertaining or successful films with only one main character: Long monologues can be monotonous, and most of the time we only bother paying attention to them the once; a small cast usually means less color, nuance and tone; after all, films reflect our lives, which are social by definition.

In television and film, whether drama or comedy, there have to be connections between characters; supporting actors enhance and underpin the performance of the main characters. Their role in driving the action and providing exposition through dialogue underpins the stars' leading position. Indeed, the better supporting actors frequently help mediocre leads and provide the gravitas needed to save a film; this is typically the case with movies where there are nominations for supporting actors and none for the leads.

I am often reminded of British actor George Sanders' performance in the 1950 movie All About Eve,[33] where he plays a cynical theater critic who drives the career of supposed ingenue Anne Baxter. Providing a female counterpoint in the same film is Thelma Ritter's peerless performance as ageing star Bette Davis' devoted assistant. In fact, Ritter was one of the most nominated actresses in Hollywood history, but never won an Oscar. Perhaps this is the fate of supporting actors: Their role is fundamental, but they never get the recognition they deserve.

Nevertheless, some Oscar winners in the best supporting actor category have also won best actor; notable examples include Meryl Streep, Jessica Lange, Denzel Washington and Jack Nicholson. Indeed, some critics have argued that the litmus test of acting is to be able shine in supporting roles, rising to the challenge of stealing scenes from the star, who will have more screen time.

Before the movies, novelists would create depth and perspective by creating secondary characters. Some of the great nineteenth-century writers, who often published in installments, such as Leo Tolstoy or Charles Dickens,[34] excelled in counterpoint, alternating the stories of the protagonists and the secondary characters, which typically converged toward a common denouement. The secondary characters contributed credibility and realism to the plot, in addition to supporting the lead figure. Without Doctor Watson, Sherlock Holmes is arguably little more than a pedantic autocrat; similarly, Sancho Panza provides an anchor to Don Quijote's flights of fancy.

The analogy of performers or supporting characters in movies and literature can also help explain the role we play in organizations. In the first session of my Strategy course, I usually advise my students, young managers typically aged around 30, that not all of them will go on to become CEOs; regardless of their skills and hard work, luck always plays a fundamental role in reaching that position.

We generally accept that the success of a company does not depend solely, or even primarily, on the CEO, but instead on the mix of workers and managers that make up the company. However, the management literature has given primacy to the analysis of leadership from the CEO's perspective, with far less attention paid to the rest of the team, who in reality create most of the value in an organization. Public opinion, and even economic analysts, also attach special importance to senior managers, and the departure of the CEO of a public company can spark panic in the stock markets.[35]

In reality, large corporations and well-managed companies are based on governance systems, with their checks and balances, along with systems that manage the distribution of power and succession, thus guaranteeing continuity, regardless of the wishes of individuals. Excessive concentration of authority in a single person should be limited by a company's stakeholders, even if we inevitably tend to stamp institutions—from governments to multinationals—with the imprimatur of their leaders.[36]

Business studies literature often talks about work teams as the generators of success in companies, but I prefer to speak of shared leadership, or even of leaders and followers, because in every team, a leader emerges who decides, while the rest implement; even if there is debate and diversity of opinion. The emphasis on the group is a mystification of what in reality are people who contribute in different and often unequal ways. Praising the team as an idea-generating entity can engender "groupthink," which in turn can suffocate critical capacity, innovation and renewal.[37]

As most of us who work for organizations will know by now, we are part of the cast, followers, employees, because even if we reach the highest position, it is usually only for a limited period. What's more, subordination to others is not in itself a negative thing, and the elevation of the role we are given or choose to play in an organization depends on us, on how we take advantage of it and turn it into the best possible supporting role.

I believe that as professionals, we can learn a lot from the poise of the great supporting actors, embracing the secondary roles we are destined to play. When we are younger, it is best to accept that we still have much to learn, expertise to acquire, intelligence to be strengthened and common sense instilled; these are the gifts we will treasure with the passing of the seasons of life. Impatience is a poor mentor, and has nothing to do with the healthy and prudent ambition that can lead us to undertake important missions.

For this reason, I would question the wisdom of some younger people to change companies if they are not promoted within three years; even if they are simply be following the mistaken advice of some experts and coaches. In fact, the research shows that staying with the same company generates better chances of promotion and access to the top than moving continually. The research is supported by the data, and I often advise my students to try to break out of such patterns, to think and act "outside the box" or better still, never to find themselves in a box in the first place.[38]

But it is arguably in the later stages of our careers when we can learn most from the approach of supporting actors, especially for those who have held the highest positions, whatever their profession, after all, it is hard to abandon the throne, to adapt to being treated like a mere mortal after a few years at the top.

Many years ago, some of the more traditional universities would bring an end to a rector's mandate with a public ritual. The institution's teaching staff was assembled, and the outgoing president was stripped of his (it was always a man) black robe and the adornments of office as an expression of his loss of power and returned to teaching duties. Fortunately, this ceremony no longer exists, although its meaning could be related to the temporary nature of leadership, which is not unhealthy for institutions.

Some business students think that having held positions such as CEO, president or general manager, seemingly lesser responsibilities will not be as satisfying or provide the recognition top jobs bring. Which is why it is all the more advisable to prepare and accommodate to the new situation, preferably before formally leaving one's position.

Over the course of my career, I have met CEOs and managers who, for whatever reason, have not come to terms with vacating positions of power. Artists and actors are not the only divas; such behavior is common among many who have exercised active leadership, especially in business. The vacuum left by responsibilities over people and resources is usually filled by dedication to the family, or to other interests. But there is always a tendency to perform functions similar to those that were occupied in the past. For that reason, it might not be a bad idea in the run up to leaving high office to consider the following recommendations:

- Firstly, our later years provide new opportunities to shine more brightly than ever. One example I often cite is Immanuel Kant, one of the most influential philosophers in history, who published his most important work, *The Critique of Pure Reason*, at the age of 63.[39] In the business world, the impact of leaders such as Jack Welch or Richard Branson, or in management thought, figures such as Peter Drucker or Charles Handy, stand out. In the world of cinema, where longevity traditionally comes at a cost, veteran Welsh actor Anthony Hopkins won his first Oscar last year at the age of 83.
- Humility is a fundamental virtue if we are to continue learning, at any stage of life, especially when occupying the highest positions. It is deeply satisfying to know that we can study new things, and besides, such an approach is beneficial for the brain, for our physical and mental health. Frequent restarts help keep us feeling younger, a healthier frame of mind and enable us to better accept disappointments.
- Furthermore, embracing the ups and downs of life makes us more attractive people, projecting self-confidence and strength. In contrast, refusing to accept the inevitable demeans us, making us appear insecure and weak.

In short, moving from the limelight to being a member of the cast doesn't have to be the twilight of our careers. As Robert Kelley wrote in his seminal 1988 HBR article, *In Praise of Followers*, "*the reality is that most of us are more often followers than leaders.*"[40] To support others is far from being an also-ran: just ask the eight men and women who will be hoping take home an Oscar this year.

Sometimes, supporting actors receive their due recognition over time, emerging as true influencers. One of the best examples is Simone de Beauvoir, long overshadowed by her partner Jean-Paul Sartre, and now considered the founder of feminist philosophy. As I explained in my book on female philosophers *In An Ideal Business*, many historians now recognize that Beauvoir has not been given the recognition she deserves. US academic William McBride has argued that *The Second Sex* is in many ways "*both more original than Sartre's writing and more evocative of the spirit of its age.*"[41]

The second reason Beauvoir's work has been ignored is because she focused on women: It is only in recent years, thanks to the work of other feminist writers, along with protest movements such as #MeToo,[42] that her ideas have found broader recognition, and not just among feminists.

De Beauvoir's central role in philosophy is now increasingly appreciated. Sadly, exceptional talent is sometimes recognized late in life or posthumously.

## 2.4    Why Are Geniuses Often Unreasonable? The Case of J.S. Bach

We're all fascinated by geniuses, those beings gifted with special creative or intellectual abilities, unique individuals way above the average. It's often said that companies that want to innovate need mavericks, the latter day equivalent.

The current meaning of the word genius dates back to an essay by Joseph Addison, *On Genius*, published in 1711 in *The Spectator*,[43] which distinguishes between two types: the natural, that is, those born with it, and the learned, those who have acquired it through education and experience. Addison lists Shakespeare, Homer and Pindar among the natural geniuses, while Aristotle, Virgil and Milton among the learned. The basis for Addison's categories were biographical portraits, and thus open to question.

One of the greatest composers, and included in every list of musical geniuses, is Johann Sebastian Bach, who died in 1750 at the age of 65. Is he to be found among the natural or the learned geniuses? He probably would have said the latter, having written about his prodigious capacity for composition: "*I was obliged to be industrious.*" As Kantor at the church of Saint Thomas in Leipzig, his contract required him to compose a cantata each week, which was performed each Sunday at mass. This impressive output created a repertory of cantatas for every Sunday of the year, which could be performed over successive years.

Bach's case is just one of many where works of genius were created through obligation, a contract to produce something within a short timeframe and there are many such examples in the history of music, the arts and even science. Contrary to the Romantic myth of the genius's need for freedom and the absence of any pressure to produce, experience shows that being subject to a deadline and even limited resources, can sharpen our invention and creativity. A musical life may have a vocational element to it, but in the case of Bach, who had 20 children, it was also the means by which he earned his living.

One way to try to understand genius is to look at the family. In Bach's time, children learned their trade or profession at home, which explains dynasties such as the Couperin family in France, the Scarlatti in Naples and the Bachs in Thuringia.[44] Johann Sebastian Bach grew up surrounded by musicians and learned to read and play music at an early age from one of his uncles and his elder brother after he was orphaned. In turn, three of his children became recognized musicians.

It's clear that the family provided the ideal environment for children and young people to learn their trade or profession, and it may be that further study of the musical clans of the seventeenth and eighteenth centuries could provide us with important lessons regarding the management of family-run businesses today. For example, the way family members teach each other, mutual support and assistance, regardless of merit—which today might be seen as nepotism—or selecting and promoting people from the group, as well as the sense of belonging to a time-honored tradition: Bach's son Carl Philip Emmanuel researched the family's history, tracing its origins back four generations.[45]

It would seem reasonable to conclude that while Johann Sebastian was certainly possessed of singular intellectual and creative abilities, there were two factors that contributed decisively to his work. In the first place, his apprenticeship, both within the family and with other musicians. What's more, he learned by transcribing scores written by other musicians, such as Vivaldi and Corelli, whose ideas he would have assimilated.[46]

Bach's creativity was decisively influenced by the pressure of work and the need to meet very demanding deadlines. In short, Bach's genius was forced, driven by circumstances rather than some inner motivation.

How did Bach go about creating his music? Once again, there are many interesting lessons relating to innovation that are applicable to other areas.

As Robert J. Marshall, an expert on the composer, has written, Bach had no time for contemplation: "*Bach and his contemporaries, subject to the hectic pace of production, had to invent or discover their ideas quickly and could not rely on the unpredictable arrival of "inspiration."*[47] Other researchers have argued that this lack of time prevented Bach from experimenting with new musical forms. In any event, he left us a priceless musical legacy of 1,238 pieces, an unparalleled musical output.

Composition in Bach's time was a three-stage process: *inventio, ellaboratio* and *executio*. The first involved the conception of the basic idea; the second saw embellishment and development, experimenting with alternatives; and the third was about interpreting and correcting and generally improving the final result. In general, innovation was associated with inventio. Nevertheless, the three phases are complementary and iterative, related and being interposed in such a way that creativity is present throughout the three.

Given his musical knowledge and experience, Bach was able to cover these three phases with exceptional skill. He was not only able to develop new musical pieces with a multifocal vision that allowed him to store ideas for later works, he was also a consummate soloist, an organ, clavichord and cello virtuoso, and also understood the limitations and technical potential of performing his works. What's more, he had been a choirboy in his youth, which gave him tremendous insight into choral possibilities.

This ability to combine creating music with its performance is something I always highlight when discussing education. Theory and practice are not separate worlds, and history provides us with examples of geniuses who combined both with ease, as is the case with Bach.

Another matter altogether is sociability and respect for authority. Geniuses are frequently portrayed as conflictive, antisocial and rebellious, resistant to hierarchy, custom and the status quo.

Bach's is an interesting case in this regard. On the one hand, he was a deeply religious man, a faithful follower of the Lutheran tradition inherited from his family. At the same time, he had problems with most of his employers of the course of his career: In just five years, he changed jobs three times and frequently complained that he was not paid enough. He showed respect for authority, but had no problem in standing up for himself if he felt he was being exploited.

Few would characterize Bach as lazy or lacking in diligence. He is one of the most prolific composers in history, original and with an unparalleled ability to compose. That said, one court adviser noted that Bach was sometimes prone to disappear without warning: "He has little inclination to work" after the composer left his post to visit a celebrated organist from whom he wanted to learn. "He was not even prepared to explain what happened," added the courtier. Other contemporaries have also commented on Bach's refusal to give explanations when he felt he was in the right. On one occasion, he was sentenced to house arrest for 40 days as a result of a dispute with an employer.

Below, a few takeaways, although I would say the best way to understand and appreciate Bach is by listening to his music.

- Innovation doesn't occur in a vacuum: Genius requires a complex blend of circumstances, among them the family, learning during childhood, and of course education.
- Discipline and necessity, whether external or internal, can drive us to new creative heights and greater and more innovative output. There are any number of geniuses whose talent came about through duty or obligation.
- Managing geniuses, as with all talent, involves special challenges. Given their often highly developed sense of equality and in many cases awareness of their ability, working with geniuses requires recognition, praise and reward. When it comes to creating new ways of developing talent and training, geniuses tend to have an insatiable appetite for knowledge.

It has taken a genius from the modern age, Thomas Edison, a man who certainly worked to tight deadlines and external pressures, to famously sum up his condition and that of Bach: "*Genius is one percent inspiration and ninety-nine percent perspiration.*"[48] And sometimes, that sweat can only be worked up if somebody else is cracking the whip.

## 2.5   True Leaders Only Win the Argument When They're Right

Occasionally, when discussing a business case on my Strategy course, a student will ask me what the right decision would be in a given situation. The question incorrectly assumes that there is a right decision for every business scenario.

When I reply that the best solution depends on a range of factors, such as shareholder values, stakeholder interaction, along with opportunity, not everyone is satisfied. Some students will know that the teacher's guides for Strategy case studies point to plausible solutions, and in many cases we already know the outcome, but there is often an expectation that certain answers will eliminate uncertainty.

In response, I explain that it makes more sense to talk about the "most reasonable" answer to a strategic problem, and in general to any complex business issue, rather than the "right" one. Moreover, as strategists explain, a decisive success rate, say 80%, depends on how a decision is implemented, not on the strategy per se.[49] And luck can also play a huge role.

Traditionally, teachers have been expected to provide the authoritative answer for their students. But the advent of the internet has changed the rules of the game. For example, my students will often be more up-to-date about a company than I am; one or two may even have worked for it and be able to offer the unique insights of an insider. The role of the teacher has shifted to that of an orchestrator of learning. At times, we still play the role of the voice of wisdom, the benchmark for what is right. At other times, I find it's a good idea to simply oversee a debate so as to extract the best ideas from the class, as Socrates did during his conversations with his students.

This process is often played out in companies. Personally, I don't subscribe to the well-known saying that "the boss is always right," and I'm sure many other people don't either. That said, a good number of managers do seem to believe that what they say in meetings or presentations should have priority and that they are somehow systematically correct. This tendency is often rooted in a fear of getting it wrong, which typically unsettles managers. Many feel that if they do not show the best possible judgment in all situations, their leadership is in jeopardy.

However, as with teachers, there is no reason to expect that the boss sees all the angles and has the answer in every situation. What's more, I would say that one of the most-appreciated virtues of a leader is the ability to listen to the ideas of others before making a decision.

The "sustained certainty" some managers like to think they possess, and that some fainthearted subordinates are willing to go along with, is a poor system of governance and decision-making. It destroys all the benefits of teamwork, generates groupthink and stifles innovation.

In *Eristic Dialectics: The Art of Winning an Argument*, the nineteenth-century German philosopher Arthur Schopenhauer explores the concept of *fas and nefas*, that is, fairness and unfairness.[50] Schopenhauer distinguished between *recht haben*, or being right, and *recht behalten*, which we could translate as getting the better in an argument. In the first, one is defending an objectively true proposition, while in the latter, one is imposing an opinion, irrespective of whether the proposition is true or acceptable.

This acerbic treatise offers 38 stratagems that can be used to come out top in a discussion. In addition to presenting the classic arguments used in rhetoric over the centuries, Schopenhauer provides a complete list of legitimate dialectical resources, such as the *petitio principii* (*petition* of principle, in which the fundamental assumption behind an argument is questioned), together with others that are clearly spurious, such as the argument *ad hominem* (attacking the character of one's opponent, rather than their ideas), or even being rude so as to unbalance them.

While Schopenhauer's advice seems to have been taken by many politicians, we know that management meetings in companies are governed by different rules, although I have occasionally attended gatherings at which such dialectical devices have been employed. Years ago, for example, when I was a member of a board discussing business school accreditation, I always marveled at how one of my colleagues systematically reproduced the arguments I had previously made in a more refined and convincing way, without mentioning me. I'm sure you are familiar with this practice, which is not uncommon among some so-called colleagues.

What interests us here, however, is not winning the argument per se, but understanding the relationship between leadership and reasoning. In other words, in which situations is one right, simply on the basis of being the boss?

(1) *Sometimes, imposing one's will is the right thing to do*

One of Karl E. Weick's favorite stories to illustrate the challenges of leadership and strategy was, apparently, true and is mentioned elsewhere in this book.[51] A Swiss police unit lost its way in the mountains in the middle of a snowstorm. They thought they were going to perish, but one of the platoon members pulled a map out of his backpack, and the lieutenant used it to find a village. Once safe, the captain verified that the map was of the Pyrenees, not the Alps. The lesson from this episode is that the map helped maintain calm, provide confidence and move in one direction. Under the circumstances, and perhaps with some luck, any map will do.

Similarly, we can conclude that in a crisis, the leader's judgment should prevail, even if it is not ideal or appears ill-advised. For example, during the pandemic of the past two years, many companies have experienced critical situations in which their managers have made dogmatic decisions, sometimes with no real idea of the outcome. These are the situations when true leadership is tested, and we need to instill confidence in the organization, for somebody to take the helm and set a course; situations when the priority is not being right, but acting quickly and in unison, thereby limiting damage and highlighting communication.

(2)  *When holding judgment is the right thing to do*

Managers often confess to me that they feel at ease in meetings with small groups, rather than large sessions where they do not control the agenda or have sway over the others in attendance. This is normal, because chairing meetings is concomitant with the idea of control, of avoiding disorder and unwanted surprises, which is more likely to happen in large groups.

However, leading an organization also involves coordinating big meetings where unforeseen events will arise and where the participants, while being respectful, will expect to be able to express their views freely.

In many companies, especially innovative ones, meetings are held where a large group of senior management members meet to discuss strategy, analyze the environment, brainstorm, or address specific problems. For example, after Steve Jobs had consolidated his leadership at Apple, he would hold lengthy meetings, often more than two hours long, attended by more than 50 executives, to discuss a wide range of issues.[52]

Some people think that these kind of events are a waste of time, believing that meetings should be as short as possible, have a closed agenda, focus on specific decisions and avoid digression. In contrast, the advantage of these large-format meetings is that they facilitate integration, promote innovation, help identify talent and can contribute to strengthening the leadership of the CEO and managers, if they are managed as a space for formulating ideas.

These are certainly situations when managers should avoid imposing their will, and instead encourage the flow of information and alternative views. Just as in a strategy class a teacher might ask a student directly what they think about a particular topic, it is healthy for managers to organize meetings that allow their colleagues to take the floor, offer their opinion on specific topics, or that provide an opportunity for an expert to provide insight, while inviting everybody to speculate about the future.

With this in mind, herewith a few takeaways to help find that ideal balance between being right and being efficient by seeking the judgment of one's colleagues.

- First, remember that the ability to listen and to question is a significant leadership virtue. When I ask my students in the first session of my course on Strategy what qualities the ideal CEO should have, the one they emphasize most is being able to listen, perhaps because they have already experienced its absence in their careers.
- The important thing for a leader is not "getting the better," but being objectively right. Time will always reveal which decisions were the right ones. However, at times of crisis, it is the leader's reasoning that should prevail.
- Given that a large part of the work of managers takes place in meetings, as Henry Mintzberg pointed out, the best guarantee of being right and avoiding discredit is to prepare the agenda properly. Improvisation can backfire.[53]

Intuition, which comes from experience, is an excellent basis for making judgments. However, as Heraclitus explained, "nothing endures but change"[54]; therefore, it's sometimes advisable to put intuition on hold when younger colleagues come up with novel, innovative or counter-intuitive arguments.

Finally, we should bear in mind that leadership is a long-term exercise, and that throughout our careers there will not only be successes, but failures— which are more natural and frequent than we tend to recognize. To err is human, and if we learn from it, so much the better.

## 2.6 Let's Be Honest, Success Is Usually the Exception

Have you ever played the lottery? If you have, chances are you've never have won anything: statistics and luck. If you buy a ticket once a year for the Christmas lottery, at best, you might win a smaller prize. But lottery tickets are like a tax on hope: secretly we all dream of winning the jackpot, and when we don't, we feel cheated or unlucky.

The same can apply regarding the expectations we harbor about our professional lives.

Logically, I am referring to cases in which there are no objective reasons to justify such expectations, such as poor professional performance, slackness or detachment from our work. Unless we suffer from a marked cognitive dissonance, that is, we lack objectivity in evaluating personal behavior, we usually know when we are at least partially responsible for a downturn in our circumstances.

A friend of mine recently referred to these situations as "guilty failure," explaining that if we stay up late the day before teaching a class, and the session doesn't go well, we are largely responsible.

Conversely, there are situations where we fail for no fault of our own: We might be passed over for a job, excluded from promotion, lose out to a competitor, or a business idea hits the rocks.

In these situations, we're talking about failure simply as the opposite of success, rather than a "guilty failure."

When one of my students tells me of similar frustrations, I often share a personal anecdote. Years ago, after finishing my MBA, I wanted to apply for a PhD in management at Harvard Business School (HBS) with the intention of extending the area of research developed in my previous PhD in applying moral philosophy to business ethics. I prepared my application, substantially improved my GMAT scores, and contacted an acquaintance, then an associate professor at HBS, who very kindly arranged an interview with the then director of the doctoral program. All my ducks seemed lined up. On the day of my interview, I arrived at Soldier's Field in time to meet my acquaintance, and on our walk across campus we passed the director of the doctoral program with whom I had an appointment. After introducing myself, he replied curtly, "I was expecting you an hour ago in my office; I'm sorry but I don't have time for you right now." It turned out that my acquaintance had mistakenly arranged to meet me an hour late. Needless to say, I was not admitted to the HBS doctoral program.

Speculating on what might have happened had I arrived on time is to enter the realm of the counterfactual and a waste of time. Had I been accepted to HBS, my career path and personal life would have been very different, and perhaps I would not be as happy as I am now. I certainly wouldn't have become Dean of IE Business School, nor would I have become the first President of IE University, a fascinating experience that I would not trade today for any other academic career.

When they hear this story, my students are to some degree consoled, aware that everybody else in the world is also subject to the whims of chance and that we are often not responsible when things don't go as we planned.

Joe Moran uses a similar example in *If You Should Fail*, where he explains that most of us fail to achieve our goals.[55] This systematic failure should not depress us; it's is the norm of human activity. It is normal in life to fail or fall short in fulfilling our ambitions. Moran refers to examples from theater and musicals, as well as literature, to show how in most cases productions do not achieve their intended goals, either because of budget constraints or because the works were not that good in the first place. "*None of us are Proust,*" he says, pointing out that it is the exception to succeed, as the exceptional French writer did.[56] In fact, many writers and artists only achieve recognition after death: The paradigmatic example is Impressionist painter Vincent Van Gogh, who died a pauper, but whose works today sell for record prices.[57]

The important thing is to take the drama out of what is sometimes called professional failure: not achieving what we set out to achieve. The truth is that our dreams are often mirages, and their fundamental usefulness is as a road-map, to guide us to reach other more satisfactory achievements. Moreover, we always evaluate our achievements from a temporary perspective, the alternatives to our plans are unknown and, as we mature, we typically change the criteria for assessing our performance.

Referring to literary creativity, which could be transferable to personal development, Moran explains:

> *The fruits of creativity are asynchronous and asymmetrical—a suspended dialogue with the absent and the yet to be born. All we can do is keep the faith that our lone acts of creation occur, like the movements of flocking starlings or shoaling fish, in tandem with others, and that they will one day feed into the accumulated beauty and wisdom of the world. Every creative act joins in this eternal symphony of human life. Failure is the price we pay for our place in the orchestra.*[58]

Moran's approach is similar to the management literature that emerged a few years ago around harnessing failure for personal development, for example the Harvard Business Review compilation in 2011.[59] The motto of this movement could be formulated as "failure is the stepping stone of success" or "failure is the other side of success." The approach tries to be positive, aiming to motivate managers to retry an initiative, to pick themselves up after a setback, to never throw in the towel. "Entrepreneurs are serial failures," is another of the quotes profusely repeated to illustrate how few great ideas are successfully implemented.[60]

Which is why it's worth remembering a few pointers to help overcome the gloom that can descend when we feel we have failed.

Firstly, put so-called triumphs and failures in perspective. Personal development and professional careers are long-distance races, a marathon rather than a sprint. Sometimes early success spoils talent, as has happened so often with young actors or singers, who derail as they mature. Similarly, some young entrepreneurs obsessed with monetizing their inventions and start-ups lose sight of the bigger prize. When we look back on our life from the vantage point of a couple of decades, the contrasts provided by those supposed successes and failures is what gives depth, volume and distinction to our experiences.

Secondly, it is good idea to ignore the guilt complex in the face of setbacks, especially when we are not personally responsible. Remember the analogy of the lottery ticket: It's not our fault we didn't win and the absence of guilt if you don't win. It's often the same in life, where many random factors play a role in the final outcome.

Leaving aside our "guilty failures," there is no reason to feel culpable in the face of misfortunes or setbacks, unless we are prone to the religious sentiment prescribed St. Thomas Aquinas, who argued that disease is the result of sin.[61] Science has shown us that this is not so, but some minds have proved resistant to the evidence.

For his part, the father of psychoanalysis, Sigmund Freud, related our feelings of guilt to episodes experienced during childhood, especially in relation to our parents.[62] So, if you like, blame mum and dad when things go wrong…

But seriously, the important thing is to assume and internalize that we should bear no responsibility for unintentional failure.

A third recommendation is to assume that we live different lives, what I usually call "blended lives," which although they run along the same timeline, can be multiple, and in the case of geniuses or thinkers, often contradictory. We change plans, careers, goals, even personal relationships. This reality can allow us to relativize failures.

Fourthly, we should work on developing the mental muscle that allows us to take setbacks as being part of the game. The best thing to do is shake off despair quickly. Think about what things change your mood, what brings you back to feeling calm. It might be hanging out with friends or family, or reading a book or watching a feel-good movie or television series. We can learn here from the great athletes, who are able to overcome failure or defeat and turn in a winning performance.

Finally, we should never forget that the important thing in life, as philosophy and literature has taught us down the centuries, for example in Homer's Odyssey, that it is not so much the goal, but the journey that counts.

There's an ancient proverb says that *"unlucky at gambling: lucky in love."*[63] I don't know if that's any consolation. Personally, I find the well-known line from Rudyard Kipling's poem *If* more useful: triumph and disaster are both imposters.[64]

## 2.7    Why It's Natural to Sometimes Feel Like an Imposter

As senior managers, at some time it's probable we've suffered from the imposter syndrome: the nagging doubt that we're not qualified to do our job; the feeling of being a fraud and the fear that sooner or later our colleagues will find out. The phenomenon is also very common among academics, who are often assumed to have an encyclopedic knowledge, but similarly, it manifests itself among professionals in changing, innovative and competitive sectors.

This distressing condition is brilliantly explored in Nani Moretti's 2011 comedy *We Have a Pope*.[65] The story begins at a papal conclave, and as is tradition, the College of Cardinals prepares for the announcement from the balcony of St. Peter's Basilica as the new pontiff is being clothed in the finery of God's supreme authority on Earth. But at the last moment, with the *Camarlengo* already before the assembled public, the new pope, overwhelmed by his appointment and his new responsibilities, lets out a cry of despair and is last seen fleeing down the corridors of the Vatican.

I won't reveal how this gentle comedy unfolds, but it certainly made me wonder how I would manage were I to find myself in such a position. Even with popular support, a lifetime appointment brings with it innumerable demands and the challenge of always being up to the task. Sometimes, it simply becomes a trial, as highlighted by the decision of the previous pope, Benedict XVI to abdicate.

On a different scale, many professionals experience similar challenges, and feel insecure about taking on responsibilities for which they feel unprepared.

If all this sounds familiar, let me repeat, do not worry: This is a widespread phenomenon and most professionals have experienced it, and the good news is that they usually overcome it.

A relative of the impostor syndrome is the Peter Principle, formulated by the Canadian academic Laurence J. Peter in the 1960s,[66] which states that people in organizations are promoted to their "maximum level of incompetence." Over time, most of the top positions are filled by incompetents, with the real work done by those below them, who have not yet risen to their level of incompetence.

There's also the Dunning-Kruger effect,[67] a cognitive bias whereby the incompetent overestimate their ability, while the highly competent tend to underestimate theirs. I'm sure that sounds familiar.

But let's be clear about one thing: Humility should not be confused with an inferiority complex. Humility consists in recognizing one's own limitations and that there is still much to learn; revising one's personal beliefs in the light of new arguments; accepting that one can be mistaken. Humility is the starting point of any learning process: the recognition that education is a lifelong task, that knowledge is an endless pursuit.

Indeed, the most intelligent people are usually humble. In the Apology of Socrates, Plato's account of his mentor's trial, Socrates appeals to the recognition of ignorance as the characteristic attitude of philosophers, the starting point of the path that leads to wisdom: *"I only know that I know nothing,"*[68] Socrates affirms in his discourse, which is much more persuasive than that of the accusers who finally condemned him to death.

Humility entails a serene and confident attitude which, far from implying inaction and passivity, is fundamentally proactive: It implies a determined search for ideas and solutions to problems and situations.

In contrast, the inferiority complex is a feeling of insecurity and inadequacy, generally unfounded, and is the basis of the impostor syndrome. How can it be overcome?

- *First of all, it may comfort you to know that the feeling of failure or not measuring up is a fairly common feeling*, much more so than it seems: one study reveals that 70% of managers feel they're out of their depth.

They might not openly acknowledge it, but many CEOs confess this feeling to their coaches. In fact, one of the most common practices when coaching senior executives is to listen and instill self-confidence in them, encourage them to adopt the right perspective to approach challenges, and help them identify potential remedies to address their concerns.

Furthermore, time and experience undoubtedly help us assess and prioritize problems. However, whenever we take on new roles, especially if they are very different from previous tasks, or are performed in different environments or with strangers, the fear of failure can resurface. Under these circumstances it is a good idea to repeat to ourselves the well-known adage: "we have nothing to fear but fear itself."

That said, a certain amount of fear in challenging situations is desirable. It leads us to take new professional challenges seriously and to avoid the over-confidence typified by the Dunning-Kruger effect. The absence of fear leads to recklessness, while assessing it properly inspires the best cases of courage.

- Secondly, avoid trying to be somebody you're not. Over time and through reflection we get to know ourselves better and learn to live with our limitations, which are part of us. This doesn't amount to conformism, because the healthy aspiration for continuous improvement will allow us to iron out and even overcome some defects along the way.

Curiously enough, our friends and acquaintances, including work colleagues, bosses and subordinates, also know us well enough, along with our strengths and weaknesses, perhaps from a better perspective than our own. Therefore, it should be comforting to know that when they entrust us with a responsibility or appoint us to a certain position, they do so after assessing our competence, and probably with greater objectivity. Bearing this in mind should help us to reject the impostor syndrome.

- Thirdly, the attitude of seeing oneself as a lifelong learner, *as* recommended by Andy Molinsky in his book *Reach*,[69] is enormously positive and stress-reducing. Adopting the mindset of a novice, of someone who is undergoing continuous instruction and learning, and who can afford to proceed by trial and error, is enormously helpful.

In microeconomics, the phenomenon of "experience curves" is used to explain how, over time, manufacturing and service costs decrease.[70] This same phenomenon is undoubtedly applicable to the performance of management positions and other responsibilities.

Cultivate personal relationships with others, along with a sense of humor. Being a good person is one of the best ways to reduce the importance of the judgments of others and to avoid the impostor syndrome. The more quickly and deeply we get to know our colleagues, the sooner we will overcome these complexes.

In conclusion, seen from a neurological perspective, the impostor syndrome is simply a cognitive bias that prevents us from improving personally and professionally; a major obstacle to stepping out of our comfort zone, improving performance, or moving to more attractive sectors or countries where we can prosper. Far from reflecting modesty or humility, by succumbing to the imposter syndrome we are letting ourselves down and undermining our potential to do good. Socrates was right: *"know thyself."*[71]

## 2.8   What's in a Name: Do You Want to Be Remembered or Forgotten?

The highlight of university graduation ceremonies is the moment when students are given their diplomas. Having overseen these celebrations for many years, I can testify to the energy, the sense of occasion, perhaps the relief that students feel when they receive the tangible proof of their hard work over the preceding years. Since my university hosts students from more than 136 countries, one of the challenges for the master of ceremonies is reading out the names of our graduates. Correctly pronouncing German, Arabic, Chinese, Spanish, Turkish or Nigerian names, among many others, requires a certain gift for languages, and perhaps most importantly, diligent preparation. One or two errors can be excused, but if the reader systematically stumbles when reading out names, the situation rapidly becomes embarrassing.

Is your name easy to pronounce and remember? For many people, mine isn't. Santiago, with Latin roots, is relatively easy to assimilate, and if someone asks me about its pronunciation I tell them "like the capital of Chile." My first surname, however, is harder. "Iñiguez de Onzoño," with its two "eñes," that unique Spanish letter, can be a bit of a mouthful. Iñiguez is a patronymic, denoting son of Iñigo, and Onzoño indicates the origin of my family: Onzoño is an area on the border between Álava and Vizcaya, in the Spanish Basque Country. When I was younger, I was proud of my name, but with time, and an international career, I have come to understand the difficulties of long, unpronounceable surnames. At conferences, I have learned to accept people's efforts without correcting them. At other times, I cut it down and just keep the first half without the eñe: Iniguez. Other difficulties I sometimes encounter are due to length of surnames on boarding passes, immigration forms, and more recently, vaccination certificates.

The quirkiness or oddity of names extends to other branches of my family. For example, my maternal great-grandfather, who was a professor of medieval history, christened his children with the names of Visigoth kings. My grandfather was named Segismundo, and two of his brothers Leovigildo and Teodorico. As usual, economy in the colloquial language prevailed and in daily dealings they were addressed as Segis, Leo and Teo. A widespread practice, regardless of cultures and languages.

Sometimes I wonder if the oddity of my name scares away possible readers and potential followers on social networks. Several studies in cognitive psychology suggest my concerns might not be unfounded.

In 1948, two Harvard professors carried out a study to find out if there was any correlation between students' names and their academic performance. The result of their research is that, indeed, students with simpler names—the Mikes—obtained, on average, better grades than their counterparts with longer names.[72]

The finding is intuitive and you may have experienced it firsthand if you have a name that can be hard to pronounce. For example, it's hardly surprising that your fellow guests at a cocktail party are going to remember a short, simple name, perhaps making it easier to mingle and network. If you have a more difficult name, it might be wise to develop our distinctive ability to relate, something that involves self-improvement and effort. You can also look for tricks to make yourself remembered. For example, in informal meetings, I introduce myself only as Santiago, to convey a clear and memorable name.

The natural affinity with names that are familiar or normal to us is what is known in psychology as "cognitive ease." Daniel Kahnemann, the Nobel laureate in economics, in his book *Thinking Fast and Slow*, cites three different names: David Stenbill, Monica Bigoutski and Shana Tirana. If asked about familiarity with any of those three names, he would likely choose the first: "Stenbill." "*Words that you have seen before become easier to see again-you can identify them better than other words when they are shown very briefly or masked by noise, and you will be quicker (by a few hundredths of a second) to read them than to read other words. In short, you experience greater cognitive ease in perceiving a word you have seen earlier, and it is this sense of ease that gives you the impression of familiarity.*"[73]

This search for names that are familiar or attractive is what justified a widespread practice in Hollywood, where it was common to change the name of future stars to give them uniqueness, a distinctive identity trait that the public would remember. Margarita Cansino or Roy Fitzgerald may not have enjoyed success if their agents had not renamed them Rita Hayworth or Rock Hudson.[74]

Lane Greene, in his entertaining book *You Are What You Speak*, quotes former British prime minister Winston Churchill, who used to say "*short words are best, and the old words when short are best of all.*" The "old, short" words in English tend, of course, to be of Anglo-Saxon stock.[75] One of the consequences of globalization is the primacy of English as the world's lingua franca, and with it the preeminence of Anglo-Saxon names, especially short ones.

This is evident, for example, in the adoption of Western names by Chinese people who want to integrate more easily into professional and social life in the West. Even though many Chinese names are monosyllabic or bisyllabic, and more than 20% of the population has the surname Wang, Li or Zhang,[76] Westerners rarely make the effort to adapt to their linguistic environment.

One thing we should be wary of is populist and exclusionary nationalist reactions to hearing the surnames of others. Greene also recounts an episode that followed Barack Obama's nomination of Sonia Sotomayor, a Hispanic American born in New York's Bronx. "*When it came to light that she had once praised the virtues of being a "wise Latina" in a speech, conservatives were apoplectic, many flatly calling her a racist. Mark Krikorian, a professional worrier about illegal immigration, found even the prosody of her name galling, writing in the blog of the conservative National Review magazine: 'Deferring to people's own pronunciation of their names should obviously be our first inclination, but there ought to be limits. Putting the emphasis on the final syllable of Sotomayor is unnatural in English … and insisting on an unnatural pronunciation is something we shouldn't be giving in to.'"*[77]

The same phenomenon of cognitive ease appeals to our instincts of familiarity and belonging to a community, which it is desirable to counteract with more knowledge of other cultures, a cosmopolitan awareness and devotion to diversity.

Which prompts the question, would you like to change your name?

If so, you'd be entering the bounds of the philosophical, the metaphysical, after all, a change of name implies a change of identity, and therefore the emergence of a different person. This is the understanding of some people who wish to change their sex, for example. The issue of having diverse identities has been addressed by many philosophers, from John Locke to Derek Parfitt.[78] Locke explained that what makes us the same person is a stream of consciousness that links our present and past experiences and gives meaning to our lives, which would not change, even if we adopted a different identity.

If you have a name that is difficult to remember, you may find it harder to get noticed, and you will have to make an extra effort to be in people's memories. However, if they learn your name, they may retain it forever. Think Thyssen-Bornemisza, Rockefeller or Vanderbilt.

On the other hand, if you have an unusual name, you will have the advantage of appearing at the top of internet searches or in the social networks where you participate. In any case, your friends will always remember you.

In any event, make sure that nobody refers to you as "unmentionable." That simply reflects the fact that there are people who don't hold you in the highest regard.

# Notes

1. F. Nietzsche, *Thus Spoke Zarathustra* (trans. W. Kaufmann) (New York, NY: Modern Library, 1995), pp. 12–13.
2. J. Ratner-Rosenhagen, *American Nietzsche: A History of an Icon and His Ideas* (Chicago: University of Chicago Press, 2012).
3. J. Ratner-Rosenhagen, op. cit., p. 97: *"Religious readers noted increasingly that Nietzsche's novel approach to the study of religion and ethics sounded familiar. It sounded, as one commentator put it, "strikingly anticipatory of William James."*
4. R. J. Hollingdale, *Nietzsche: The Man and His Philosophy* (Cambridge: Cambridge University Press, 1999), p. 143.
5. F. Nietzsche, *Thus Spoke Zarathustra* (trans. R. J. Hollingdale) (London: Penguin, 1974), p. 18.
6. https://www.jimcollins.com/concepts/level-five-leadership.html.
7. Definition provided by the Oxford Dictionary of English. https://www.oxfordlearnersdictionaries.com/us/definition/english/charism.
8. M. Weber, *The Theory of Social and Economic Organization* (trans. A. M. Henderson and T. Parsons) (New York: The Free Press, 1924), pp. 328.
9. https://hbr.org/2012/11/learning-charisma.
10. A. Grant, "Friends at Work? Not So Much", *The New York Times*, September 4, 2015. http://www.nytimes.com/2015/09/06/opinion/Sunday/adam-grant-friends-at-work-not-so-much.html.
11. https://hbr.org/2012/06/learning-charisma-2.
12. https://hbr.org/2021/12/what-time-of-day-are-you-most-charismatic.
13. https://hbr.org/2012/06/learning-charisma-2.
14. https://winstonchurchill.org/resources/speeches/1940-the-finest-hour/blood-toil-tears-sweat/.
15. G L. Patzer, *Looks: Why they Matter More Than You Ever Imagined* (New York: Amacom, 2008), Kindle ed., loc. 275.
16. H. Arendt, *Eichmann in Jerusalem: A Report on the Banality of Evil* (London: Penguin, 2006).
17. M. Weber, op. cit.
18. F. Drogula, *Commanders & Command in the Roman Republic and the Early Empire* (Chapel Hill: University of North Carolina Press, 2015).
19. J. P. Kotter, "What Leaders Really Do," *Harvard Business Review* on Leadership (Boston: Harvard Business Review Press, 1990), p. 38.
20. Stendhal, *Napoleon* (Madrid: Aguilar, 1989); p. 34.
21. F. Nietzsche, *Thus Spoke Zarathustra,* op.cit.
22. J. Milton, *Paradise Lost* (London: Penguin, 2016), 221.
23. Genesis, 10: 8–9.
24. R. Graves, *The Greek Myths* (London: Penguin, 2012).

25. Santa Teresa de Jesús, *Obras Completas* (Madrid: BAC, 1967): "la humildad es andar en verdad".

26. Aristotle, *The Nicomachean Ethics* (trans. H. Tredennick & J.A.K. Thomson) (London: Penguin, 2004), Ch. 10.

27. https://www.ft.com/content/921df7b1-b100-49c8-b6c0-578b6182dd04.

28. https://www.businesstoday.in/opinion/columns/story/when-satisfactory-is-unsatisfactory-121545-2018-12-18.

29. L. Carroll, *Alice's Adventures in Wonderland and Through the Looking Glass* (London: Penguin, 2010).

30. N. Lacey, *A Life of H. L. A. Hart: The Nightmare and the Noble Dream* (Oxford: Oxford University Press, 2004).

31. R. Power, *Mark Twain: A Life* (New York: Free Press, 2006).

32. R. Moss Kanter, "The New Managerial Work", Harvard Business Review (No-Dec, 1989). https://hbr.org/1989/11/the-new-managerial-work.

33. *All about Eve* (20th Century Fox, 1950).

34. G. Law, Graham, "Serials and the Nineteenth-Century Publishing Industry", in L. Brake, M. Demoor (eds.), Dictionary of Nineteenth-Century Journalism (London: Academia Press, 2009), p. 567.

35. https://hbr.org/2022/08/restoring-shareholder-confidence-when-your-stock-is-down.

36. *Harvard Business Review on Corporate Governance* (Boston, Harvard Business Publishing, 2000). And https://hbr.org/2015/03/corporate-governance-2-0.

37. Is Teamwork Overvalued?, in S. Iñiguez de Onzoño, *Cosmopolitan Managers, Executive Development that Works* (London: Palgrave Macmillan, 2016), p. 187.

38. M. Hamori, "Job-Hopping to the Top and Other Career Fallacies," *Harvard Business Review*, July–August 2010.

39. I. Kant, *Critique of Pure Reason* (London: Penguin, 2008).

40. https://hbr.org/1988/11/in-praise-of-followers.

41. W. McBride, *Sartre e Beauvoir all'asse del ventesimo secolo*; in P. Invitto, *La fenomenologia e l'oltre-fenomenologia: Prendendo spunto dal pensiero francese* (Milan: Mimesis Edizioni, 2003); p. 95.

42. Updates from the #Me Too Moment are published by *New York Times* gender editor, Jessica Bennet at: https://www.nytimes.com/series/metoo-moment.

43. J. E. Gardiner, *Bach: Music in the Castle of Heaven* (London: Penguin, 2015).

44. Ibid., p. 51.

45. Ibid., p. 65.

46. Ibid., p. 183.

47. R. L. Marshall, "Toward a Twenty-First-Century Bach Biography", 84 *Musical Quarterly* 3 (Fall 2000), p. 500.

48. This attribution to edition is questioned: https://www.forbes.com/sites/maseenaziegler/2014/09/01/how-we-all-got-it-wrong-women-were-behind-these-7-famously-inspiring-quotes/?sh=536757b41016.

49. R. M. Grant, *Contemporary Strategy Analysis* (New York: John Wiley & Sons, 2021).

50. A. Schopenhauer (ed. A.C. Grayling), *The Art of Always Being Right: Thirty Eight Ways to Win When You Are Defeated* (London: Gibson Square Books, 2004.

51. L. Freedman, *Strategy: A History* (New York: Oxford University Press, 2015), p. 565.

52. https://hbr.org/2020/11/how-apple-is-organized-for-innovation.

53. H. Mitnzberg, *Managing* (Oakland, CA: Berrett-Koehler, 2011).

54. Heraclitus, *The Fragments of The Work of Heraclitus of Ephesus on Nature* (Whitefish, MT: Kessinger Publishing, 2007).

55. J. Moran, *If You Should Fail: Why Success Eludes Us and Why It Doesn't Matter* (London: Penguin, 2021).

56. Ibid., Ch. 5.

57. Although Van Gogh was not poor. https://www.vangoghmuseum.nl/en/art-and-stories/vincent-van-gogh-faq/was-van-gogh-poor; https://www.artbusiness.com/postprice.html.

58. J. Moran, op. cit., p. 125.

59. https://hbr.org/archive-toc/BR1104.

60. https://hbr.org/2011/04/column-entrepreneurs-and-the-cult-of-failure.

61. R. Cross, "Aquinas on Physical Impairment: Human Nature and Original Sin", 110 *Harvard Theological Review* 3, pp. 317–38.

62. S. Freud, *The Interpretation of Dreams* (New York: Basic Books, 2010).

63. https://americaexplained.wordpress.com/2011/03/18/lucky-in-cards/.

64. https://www.poetryfoundation.org/poems/46473/if%2D%2D-

65. *Habemus Papam* (Sacher-Fandango-RAI, 2011).

66. L.J. Peter, *The Peter Principle: Why Things Always Go Wrong* (New York: Harper Collins, 2013).

67. https://www.nytimes.com/2020/05/07/learning/the-dunning-kruger-effect-why-incompetence-begets-confidence.html.

68. Plato, Apology, op. cit., 21d.

69. Andy Molinksy, *Reach: A New Strategy to Help You Step Outside Your Comfort Zone, Rise to the Challenge and Build Confidence* (New York: Penguin, 2017).

70. https://hbr.org/1985/03/building-strategy-on-the-experience-curve.

71. Plato, *Apology*, 38 a 5–6, in *The Last Days of Socrates: Euthyphro; Apology; Crito; Phaedo* (ed. H. Tarrant) (London: Penguin, 2003).

72. https://www.newyorker.com/tech/annals-of-technology/why-your-name-matters.

73. Daniel Kahneman, *Thinking Fast and Slow* (New York: Farrar Straus and Giroux, 2011), p. 61.

74. M. Griffin, *All That Heaven Allows: A Biography of Rock Hudson* (New York: HarperLuxe, 2018).

75. R.L. Greene, *You Are What You Speak* (New York: Random House, 2011), Kindle edition, loc. 3241.
76. https://mandarinhouse.com/100-common-chinese-family-names.
77. R.L. Greene, op. cit., loc. 3828.
78. N. Warburton, *A Little History of Philosophy* (New Haven, Conn.: Yale University Press, 2011), Ch. 14; D. Parfitt, *Reasons and Persons* (Oxford: Oxford University Press, 1986).

# 3

## Part 3: Insight—What Can I know?

One of the main attributes of good managers is being able to understand the environment they operate in, which means nothing more pretentious, nor less operational, than knowing how to interpret changing circumstances, and guessing the behavior of their stakeholders. This ability allows them to make a diagnosis of the situation and make the best possible decisions. That is why the ability to observe, to notice what is important and see details—the trees and the forest—is especially relevant for those who manage organizations and lead people.

The rationality paradigm that we use in the analysis, formulation and implementation of business strategies and managerial decision-making is often formulated in these terms, even though many of the underlying assumptions are open to question.

One of the main reasons is that people often act not entirely rationally, making decisions that are subject to cognitive biases. Psychologists such as Daniel Kahnemann or economists such as Naguib Thaleb[1] have shown that all of us, even the best trained in statistical notions, or with sophisticated knowledge, base our decisions on intuition, previous experiences or prejudices. In this section, I will discuss some of the cognitive biases influencing those decisions, bearing in mind that, despite the difficulties that cloud our reason or exaggerate our reasoning, we have to make judgments and convince others that they are the right ones.

Caution is often a good guide for understanding the context, for managing companies and leading people; but innovators, disruptors and entrepreneurs are characterized by their willingness to take risks and their impatience: They are always in a hurry. In this part, we will look at some of the proposals made by some philosophers to resolve these tensions.

S. Iñiguez, *Philosophy Inc.*, https://doi.org/10.1007/978-3-031-20483-8_3

# 3.1 Why the Days of Magical Realism Are Far from Over

In 1518, an unusual event took place in Strasbourg, then part of the Holy Roman Empire, now France. Frau Troffea, a local woman, took to the streets and began dancing frantically. She was soon joined by others, and eventually, hundreds more joined in. Many, including Frau Troffea, succumbed to exhaustion and died. The phenomenon, historically documented, is known as the Dance Epidemic of 1518. Scholars have come up with various theories, ranging from fungi in rye bread to divine intervention, but have failed to produce a conclusive explanation.[2] The most likely is that it was an outbreak of mass hysteria, an early example of the magical realism depicted in the novels of Gabriel García Márquez, Isabel Allende and other renowned Latin American writers.[3]

Similar social phenomena have occurred over the centuries around the world, and their modern counterparts now largely take place on social networks.

Most of us found ourselves in lockdowns as part of our government's efforts to prevent the spread of the worst pandemic in many decades. As a result, life felt like magical realism, where the virtual, the fantastic and the illusory collided with hard evidence and experience. When future generations read the story of what we went through, they'll probably find our behavior as hard to understand as the antics of Frau Troffea and her followers.

Paradoxically, while our generation has virtually infinite and universal access to information and data of all kinds, knowing what to believe seems harder than ever.

This shouldn't surprise us: We still act collectively, instinctively, as our forebears did when faced with crisis. As a species, we are inherently social, and so in today's world, we connect online in the search for answers, ready to believe just about any theory.

However, in our search for responses and solutions, we may consider what cognitive psychologists call "limited rationality."[4] When we process information or messages, the validity and reliability of our judgments are conditioned by our cognitive limitations and prejudices, as well as the quality of the information and the time constraints for processing it.

In short, we're probably deluding ourselves when we think and make decisions just on a supposed rational basis. The libertarian economist Bryan Caplan has used the concept of rational irrationality to describe contemporary behavior, for example, when voting, which, as recent elections have shown, can be highly unpredictable.[5]

Surely, the best counterweight to improve our critical skills and ability to rationalize is study and reading. Education, thanks to the impressive growth of hybrid formats and liquid learning can also be an opportunity to socialize and share our ideas, subjecting them to the scrutiny of our peers.

At the same time, humor is still one of the best remedies in difficult times: It helps ease our confinement and keeps our spirits up; it unblocks anger, releases tension—especially at work—and often puts things into context. Sigmund Freud argued that jokes are vehicles for releasing repression or untying the knots that society ties us up in.[6]

In contrast, pessimistic and negative messages simply lower our morale: In my opinion, their authors would do well to keep their doom and gloom to themselves. The same for the fake news that circulates at times of uncertainty: How many remedies for the coronavirus have you received from questionable sources in recent days?

In the face of the difficulties we experienced over the past pandemic, or in view of other similar that we may live in the future, herewith some suggestions:

- Try to feel comfortable in our liquid world, where the rational and the irrational are entangled, and where we relate to others not only physically, but virtually as well. The concept of liquid modernity was created by Polish philosopher Zygmunt Bauman, who argued that the way we understand time is no longer linear and is instead pointillist.[7] Bauman was highly critical of what he saw as the impatience of modern society—characterizing this as people preferring juice to peeling an orange. He also questioned the view that education is a product and not a process or path.

I think that during the recent pandemic I interacted more, online, with my colleagues and friends than ever before. In the future, work and interpersonal relationships will continue blending the digital and face-to-face.

Although we understood and subscribed to it, until now some of us had not experienced personally what Charles Darwin, the father of evolution, has been attributed to explain: It is not the strongest or the biggest that survived, but those with the best ability to adapt.[8] As explained before, our lives resemble magical realism literature more than we thought.

- Actively cultivate a sense of humor, several times a day and even in the situations that seem most serious to you. Humor is the younger sister of happiness and, as philosophers have long explained, human beings, especially in times of crisis and epidemics, eagerly seek every scrap of joy they can find. The final part of this book is about happiness, the goal of most people, according to Aristotle.[9]

At the end of García Márquez's timeless novel *Love in the Time of Cholera*, the couple at the center of the story asks the captain to fly a flag warning of an epidemic on board, so they can spend the rest of their lives sailing the Amazon river.[10] For those of us who survived the pandemic in 2020, we disembarked and returned to something approaching normal life, albeit changed. Some of us left loved ones behind, but they will remain in our memories, in our dreams and perhaps even tangibly, as in the novels of magical realism. It will have been an experience that taught us to be more human.

But let's now turn to our need to understand the World.

## 3.2    What David Hume Can Tell Us About Cause and Effect in Business

Filmmaking is one of those businesses where what seems to be a recipe for success can turn out to be a recipe for financial disaster. You might think that the combination of a good script, a distinguished director and high-profile actors would be a dead cert, but sometimes even those magic ingredients don't necessarily guarantee rave reviews or a box office smash. Any number of productions perform poorly, while others are simply written off or go straight to DVD. Given the movie industry's volatile nature, established actors will often choose safe options over a low-budget independent production. That said, the jury is out over whether a film's success is due to this or that star's presence. As a 2006 article in *The New York Times* points out, it is often hard to determine cause and effect: "*if a star-studded movie does well, it does not necessarily mean that the stars are causing higher ticket sales. In fact, it seems to move the other way around: stars select what they believe are promising projects. And studios prefer to put stars in movies that they expect to be a success […] Movies with stars are successful not because of the star, but because the star chooses projects that people tend to like.*"[11]

In life, as in business, we need to be able to identify the real causes of events, because it allows us to make decisions and reverse or replicate what happened. For example, if we know that a product that was intended to be innovative has not worked in a market, we try to find out the reasons for the failure, and not look for specious justifications. Spain's Philip II famously said when he learned in 1588 of the defeat of the so-called Invincible Armada, tasked with the conquest of England: *"I did not send my ships to fight against the elements,"*[12] referring to the bad weather conditions during the battle. A fallacious excuse if ever there was one.

Cause and effect have exercised philosophers since antiquity. In this regard, I find the work of David Hume, the Scottish Enlightenment philosopher, a useful guide. In his central work *An Enquiry Concerning Human Understanding*, he explains that all knowledge is divided into two categories: facts based on ideas, and facts based on experience, a simplification that has come to be known as "Hume's fork."[13] The former are based on relating abstract concepts, for example, mathematical propositions, which are governed by deductive approaches. The latter refer to judgments that we formulate when we relate experiences or observations, noticing some kind of connection between them. In this second category, we find inductive judgments, along with the rules or criteria that we form throughout our life, based on our perceptions or routines. For example, the proposition "the sun rises every day in the east" would be inductive in nature, because it is based on our direct experience and perception. Hume's conclusion to this classification places him in an orbit close to skepticism: The cause-effect relation only applies to deductive judgments, the associations of abstract ideas, but not inductive judgments, and he slips in a phrase that has become famous: From the fact that the sun sets every day in the west, I cannot deduce that it will also happen tomorrow.

I'm not about to enter into the scientific discussion of whether we can predict that the sun will set in the West tomorrow, and instead focus on Hume's concept of causality, because it seems to me to be particularly applicable to management. As the business environment is strategic, and management is not an exact science where deductive reasoning is possible, it is debatable whether causes and effects are produced automatically and evidently as a result of company's activities.

Even reasons that may seem to be proven and generally accepted are open to question. Have you ever encountered a case of groupthink, in which a team unquestioningly accepts a particular approach, which later proves to be wrong?[14] Although it may be in good faith, groupthink clouds reasoning and prevents the identification of the roots of a problem. If there is bad faith, the problem is greater.

The *Toyota 5 Whys* was invented by the Japanese carmaker to analyze business problems, regardless of whether there were seemingly irrefutable arguments to explain them.[15] The exercise started by posing the initial question, for example "why has the assembly line stopped for two hours?"; the immediate answer could be technical: "because the network has been down for that time." The second question would be: "why has the network been down for two hours?"; to which the answer might be: "because the electrical maintenance team only works an eight-hour shift"; to which the question would be asked: "why does the maintenance team only cover eight hours out of 24?" The answer could be: "to save personnel costs"; and now, the fourth question would begin to get to the heart of the real problem: "why was it decided to save on personnel costs?"; to which the answer would be prompt: "to balance the budget"; and finally, the fifth question would be of a truly strategic nature: "can savings be made on anything other than maintenance personnel?".

The virtue of the *Toyota 5 Whys* model is that the insistence, almost Confucian, ends up linking issues that seemed disparate, that would not have been probed had the analysis not been extended, that affect several departments or people, and even end up involving general management. Often, similar problems are not solved because either those directly responsible do not have the mandate to make executive decisions to remedy them, and therefore, they continue until top management intervenes; or because the questions, complaints and possible solutions get lost in the bureaucracy of the organization.

Toyota's persistent approach is more rigorous, because the analysis of a problem goes beyond the surface and touches other areas. According to Hume's approach, a necessary cause and effect relationship would still be missing that could be projected on to any future situation in which the assembly line stops because the network goes down, and he would be right. Business situations and episodes are human-made, and in events involving personal relationships it is not possible to apply mathematical rules, permanent criteria independent of circumstances or individuals. Our lives are not causal paradigms, such as the one that occurs when two balls collide and transfer the movement to a third one. There are many other unpredictable factors beyond such control.

As Yuval Noah Harari explains in his Sapiens: "*Newton showed that the book of nature is written in the language of mathematics. Some chapters (for example) boil down to a clear-cut equation; but scholars who attempted to reduce biology, economics and psychology to neat Newtonian equations have discovered that these fields have a level of complexity that makes such an aspiration futile.*"[16]

Hume's questioning of the causality paradigm in the use of intuition or inductive thinking does not prevent such reasoning from being part of our way of interpreting everyday events, analyzing business situations and making effective decisions. What Hume emphasizes is that causality in such reasoning is apparent, and need not necessarily always occur in the future. This relative skepticism leads us to be on our guard, especially in the face of momentous decisions in a company, and to avoid overconfidence based solely on previous experience. Again, a convenient prescription is to cultivate humility, possibly the best prism through which to see things in their best light.

## 3.3    Just How Rational Are We?

In the introductory session of my Strategic Management course, I often discuss with my Global Online MBA students the basic assumptions behind strategic analysis. One of them, which also underlies economic theory, is the assumption that business agents—managers, consumers, competitors, suppliers, among others—act according to the rationality paradigm. I then ask them what this paradigm consists of, and an entertaining debate ensues—not all MBA students are economists who have learned the technical answer to this question.

Some associate rationality with the satisfaction of selfish instincts—Adam Smith's butcher who makes the economy tick is a frequent reference;[17] others with the satisfaction of personal desires—in a more epicurean version. Increasingly, there are students who link rationality with altruism, reflecting the social commitment of the new generations, and even with the preservation of the planet, which makes enormous sense, given that in the absence of a sustainable environment there is no other personal goal to be achieved. Those familiar with economic science respond in a more canonical way, in the sense that acting rationally means maximizing utility, the pursuit of personal profit.

The next question that could be discussed, and which is a topic of controversy among economists, psychologists and philosophers, is the meaning of that personal utility or benefit. For example, some argue—in my opinion not very convincingly—that consistently ethical behavior maximizes long-term benefit, because the risk of acting immorally increases the risk of social reproach and exclusion, if not legal sanction. Similarly, systematic cooperation is the dominant strategy over time—one of the key contributions of John Nash's equilibrium theory—because it generates in most cases reciprocal behavior on the part of others, and ultimately everyone wins.[18] This is the basis, for example, for ruling out price wars, as a strategic option, because of their potential drawbacks not only for all competitors, but also for those who initiate them.

The rationality paradigm underlies strategic analysis, because without assuming this pattern of behavior, many of the models used to organize information and make decisions, structure sectors, evaluate competitive forces or anticipate scenarios would not work properly. For example, I will typically retain customers if I offer them better value for money than my competitors, because those users will be maximizing their utility function. These models and tools of strategic analysis allow us to formulate justified and convincing proposals, to put an end to the uncertainty that surrounds the activity of companies.

What happens, however, when economic agents do not conform to this pattern of rationality? For example, decisions based on ethical criteria do not conceptually fit this paradigm, even if, as we have seen, there are arguments that these ethical decisions are more profitable in the long run. It would require evidence, a causal relationship, which does not seem to have been convincingly demonstrated. As SDGs are now effectively obligatory for all companies, moral criteria have become part of the paradigm of rationality, and their noncompliance entails sanctions or social disapproval.

I have mentioned above, economists, psychologists and philosophers have questioned the rationality paradigm. Indeed, many leaders act irrationally, and it is precisely this anomalous, disruptive behavior that generates innovation and profit for their companies, as well as for themselves. It is often said that one of the attributes of the entrepreneur is to be misunderstood, to not act according to the patterns of their time. They have a precocious or advanced rationality, which does not fit in with that of their contemporaries, and which proves itself when they are successful and generally only bears fruit after a certain time.

The requirement to meet the standard of rationality becomes especially intractable during difficult times, especially when there is radical uncertainty and it is hard to predict how the situation will evolve. How can one act rationally under such circumstances? Although rationality is often associated with prudence, the advice to stand still seems undynamic and unbusinesslike. In reality, in order to stand still, it is still necessary to invest in maintaining customers, renewing products, defending territory and market share. Moreover, situations of uncertainty are also those that can provide the best business opportunities.

On other occasions, I have dealt with the uncertainty that is characteristic of the social and economic environment, which is not reduced today because we have universal access to a virtually infinite volume of information and data. Today, businessmen and managers are also aware that an abundance of information does not reduce the complexity of their decisions, and that uncertainty continues to exist. In their book *Radical Uncertainty*, John Kay and Mervyn King explain that: "*Business people, policy-makers and families could not even imagine having the information needed to determine the actions that would maximize shareholder value, social welfare or household utility. Or to know whether they had succeeded in doing so after the event. Honest and capable executives and politicians, of which there are many, try instead to make incremental decisions which they think will improve their business, or make the world a better place."*[19]

Kay and King review how economic science has been making proposals to provide reasonable proposals in uncertain environments, from Bayes—the theory of statistical probability—to Kahnemann, Nobel Prize winner, father of behavioral economics and one of the authors who has most emphasized the role of cognitive biases in decision-making, also in the field of business.

There are two proposals that seem to me to be sufficiently satisfactory to respond to this contradiction between the search for rationality and the solution to uncertainty, which I use in my strategy course: strategic models and narratives.

- The purpose of *strategic models* and tools is to simplify reality, to portray a situation in an accessible way, so that decisions can be made in accordance with the solutions they suggest. As they are simplifications, they are not the same reality, as is often explained in the concept of "the map is not the territory."[20] Logically, behind each model there are assumptions that must be understood and shared, otherwise the conclusions we draw from applying them may seem counter-intuitive or unacceptable. For example, in a business portfolio analysis model, we can introduce the growth expectations of a business unit, CapEx, OpEx, EBITDA and contribution margins, as well as other in line with the aspirations and objectives of the shareholders. The purpose of this type of model is to forecast and project growth, as well as the budgetary execution of part of the company.

The fundamental virtue of models and analysis tools is that they back up the arguments being presented to investors, shareholders, and other stakeholders. They make it possible to justify a decision according to approaches and reasons used in similar situations, provide peace of mind and reliability, and project rigor and professionalism. And as veterans often say, "paper can hold everything," meaning, as a cynical philosopher would do, that the opposite case could be articulated with similar facts and figures, and perhaps win over the same audience.

- Narratives are the crafting of consistent stories that substantiate a company's values and purpose, and can be retrospective in nature, if they are intended to account for the organization's past and history; alternatively, they can be forward-looking, framing prospective growth strategies. Organizations, and their members, need these narratives to generate a greater sense of identity, align their personal and collective interests and stimulate performance motivation. For this reason, senior management often periodically considers the formulation or renewal of these organizational narratives, which give meaning to collective activity and organize everyone's efforts.

Retrospective narratives are also those that give prominence and heroism to their protagonists. Figures such as Marie Curie, Winston Churchill or Steve Jobs have been elevated with the passage of time, as their biographers have enhanced their deeds. Their consecration as leaders of history does not occur during their lifetime, as a result of the ready recognition of their merits, but only with the elaboration and dissemination of the narratives that relate their profiles and achievements. Something similar happens with the singular lives of distinguished philosophers. For example, the narrative of the last hours of Socrates' life as told by his disciple Plato, which recreates reality to ennoble the master, is reproduced in multiple later chronicles.[21] Similarly, many authors highlight Immanuel Kant's daily routine, told by the writer Thomas de Quincey, who in turn used other sources and added his own considerations to improve the literary quality.[22]

Regardless of the cultural inclination of entrepreneurs and managers, of how rational they are or averse to uncertainty, their passion for philosophy or history, their job at the head of the organizations they lead is to make decisions that generate value, that guarantee the durability of their companies. To do this, they need to have a sufficiently objective view of their environment, and a proper diagnosis of what is happening inside their companies. As Kay and King explain, the simple question they need answers to is, "*What's going on here?*"[23]

The answer is often far from simple. Throughout my career as an academic manager, dean or university president I have had the opportunity to sit in on countless presentations of reports, financial statements, projected income statements and multiple similar studies. Like me, you too may have identified some figure that catches your attention, raises questions and requires clarification. Faced with an anomalous figure in the middle of a table, which arouses your curiosity, I usually add that there is always a first and last name, referring to the better or worse performance of some person or department, and avoiding attributing the causes of this result to exogenous factors or some crisis outside the company.

To answer the question "What's going on here?" we need to look inside the company, not outside. That is why reference to external elements should never be enough to those listening to the clarifications. Companies often deploy multiple systems of indicators, dashboards, scorecards, which provide timely information on the performance of departments, people and regions. But don't be fooled. To the key question that seeks to find out if there is a problem to solve, the answer, and the explanation, is inevitably qualitative, and not usually simple.

In *The Picture of Dorian Gray*, Oscar Wilde noted: "*knowledge would be fatal, it is the uncertainty that charms one. A mist makes things beautiful.*"[24] A world of certainties, where we knew what we were going to experience at every moment of our day, would be a life without surprises, in which there would be no admiration and so many other feelings related to the discovery of unsuspected sensations. Uncertainty makes our world more entertaining and interesting.

## 3.4   How to Keep Your Head in the Fog of War

As mentioned in Part Two of this book, one of the most common anecdotes used in business strategy to illustrate the concept of leadership is that of the Swiss police captain who used the wrong map to guide his unit to safety. We'll never know if the captain knew this, and therefore exhibited his leadership by keeping the secret and instilling confidence in the others; or if, on the contrary, he did not realize until it was pointed out to him, in which case we can only wonder at his luck and in general acknowledge the role of chance in critical situations.

One of the lessons of the anecdote, especially relevant for business strategy, is that in situations of radical uncertainty, when it is impossible to predict an outcome, any map serves as a reference to formulate a narrative that convinces the most relevant stakeholders, as long as the story is convincing and the leaders have the appropriate authority and prestige. During the recent pandemic, many companies and organizations experienced such a scenario. The most common measures companies implemented were to reduce costs, manage cash flow prudently, emphasize communication and convey trust and confidence. The idea is to create a map of measures intended to convey calm in times of extreme turbulence.

Uncertainty is a characteristic of strategic environments such as business or politics, where circumstances change and forecasts are indeterminate, sometimes volatile or completely unpredictable. Unlike a paradigmatic environment, in which evolution can be programmed—for example, a mathematical game—or there is no substantial change, in strategic scenarios multiple variables are all interacting simultaneously. One of the functions of management has been precisely to try to sort out this complexity in order to help managers understand the context of their companies and be able to make justified decisions.

Thirty years ago, when I studied for my MBA, one of the introductory courses in the program was *Decision Theory*. I remember the sessions devoted to learning how to meticulously construct decision trees, following the approaches of Bayes, the father of statistics. The fundamental assumption behind the course was that the risk of a given decision could be moderated by assigning probabilities to the various options in a business dilemma. For example, whether or not to launch a new product. Logically, after the two initial options, subsequent alternatives could be opened, which in turn were weighed up using our intuition, knowledge and previous analyses. For example, if the product were to be launched, it may have been accepted quickly and our sales and market share may grow; or development may be slow and we may encounter successful competing products. These options generated different effects, which in turn were weighted to calculate the respective potential returns. Although the analysis had to include qualitative elements—for example, estimating the entry of competitors—the emphasis of the model was quantitative, and I remember that the impression I got from this exercise was of a certain artificiality, even though the professor—an engineer—was brilliant.

Today, we have access to previously unimaginable amounts of information. Access to this abundant library of facts, ideas, opinions and figures is, moreover, simple and universal and relatively affordable. Nevertheless, the existence of so much data, well as the possibility of managing it, does not seem to resolve the problem of uncertainty so often highlighted by economic and business analysts. Perhaps the informative overload provided not only by digital media, but also by social networks, together with a tendency toward the hyperbolic, in search of larger audiences, contributes to spread a feeling of greater uncertainty, regardless of the facts.

At the same time, the digitization of all types of content, together with the standardization and centralization of search engines on the web, which is how we now look for information, has contributed to create increasingly homogeneous knowledge and opinion. In an encounter with thinker and writer Niall Ferguson during a conference before the pandemic, we commented on how nowadays most academic researchers browse Google to find sources for their intellectual output. Before this practice became widespread, for example, when I was preparing my PhD, it was normal to dive into library files, spend time "cherry picking," jumping from one topic to another, related or not, checking bibliographies cited in books, as well as asking professors and colleagues for suggestions. I have personally enjoyed such research in good libraries, and I have happy memories of hours spent at the shelves of the Bodleian Library in Oxford, consulting volumes of various journals, leafing through books, and inhaling the fragrance emanating from that formidable concentration of printed paper.

Another facet of automated research occurs when professors give assignments to their students, in different classes and independently of their experiences. Normally, they use the same sources, which are easy to digest due to the simplicity and speed with which they handle references in Google and other search engines. This process, however, greatly limits innovation and out-of-the-box thinking, and instead encourages a one-size-fits-all approach. The algorithm becomes the ultimate authoritative source of knowledge, or oracle, in establishing the order of links provided to the question posed by the user.

Paradoxically, although the feeling of uncertainty may be ingrained in the majority, search engines provide quick, almost instantaneous, and also consistent answers to their users' requests. These solutions are often very similar, and similarity or uniformity is a priority for users relying on the highest number of searches, for example, when choosing a certain expression or combination of words. This homogeneity and coincidence becomes redundant by the action of the algorithms themselves, in a circle that can be interpreted as virtuous, assuming that the questions we ask have only one correct answer.

But it can also be conceived as a perverse circle, if we value originality and uniqueness as attributes of good research, and even convenient to stimulate creativity in the work prepared by students. Education and research should not be conceived only as tasks of standardization, of studying what has already been proposed and shared, but fundamentally of presenting new ideas, questioning what has been learned and suggesting new avenues for progress.

Therefore, although there is a great deal of confidence—almost certainty—about what exists in the digital world, boosted by search engines, and to the extent that the management of big data and algorithms order research, determine navigation or prioritize certain options and preferences, uncertainty will nevertheless continue to exist outside the digital world. Interestingly, perhaps the digital world has the potential risk of being more finite and permanent than the physical world. To this drawback, the visionaries among us may reply that machine learning will produce the renewal of this digital space, that the intelligence that will be developed in the digital space has much more potential than human talent. But that's a topic for another discussion.

An important lesson, and perhaps the conclusion of this reflection on uncertainty, is that the enormous advantages offered by the digital environment should not diminish one's ability to develop a critical capacity, to seek information through alternative means, to adopt—at least methodologically—outlier or even contrarian positions when weighing important decisions, whether in business or one's personal life.

One of the classic works on military strategy, which has also had an influence on business strategic thinking, is "*On War*" by the Prussian military theorist Carl Von Clausewitz.[25] In one of its passages, he refers to the "fog of war" to describe the ambiguity of the battlefield. At such moments, as we see in Akira Kurosawa's monumental films, the confrontation between armies produces dust, death, and unimaginable terror. In such circumstances, as in situations of radical uncertainty, temperance and leadership are necessary qualities.

## 3.5    You May Not Know It, But You're Probably Guilty of the Naturalistic Fallacy

One of the most famous openings of any novel is Jane Austen's Pride and Prejudice, which begins: "*It is a truth universally acknowledged that a single man in possession of a good fortune must need a wife.*"[26]

I wonder if Austen had read *A Treatise of Human Nature*, the classic work of David Hume, published in 1740, some 35 years before her birth.[27] The Scottish philosopher's book was not initially received as well as he expected, as he himself recounts in his brief autobiography, so he rewrote many of the ideas in *An Enquiry Concerning Human Understanding*, in a more accessible style.[28]

One of the ideas expounded in the *Treatise* which has had most influence on later thinkers is contained in the following paragraph: "*In every system of morality, which I have hitherto met with, I have always remark'd, that the author proceeds for some time in the ordinary way of reasoning, and establishes the being of a God, or makes observations concerning human affairs: when of a sudden I am supriz'd to find, that instead of the usual copulations of propositions, is and is not, I meet with no proposition that is not connected with an ought, or an ought not. This change is imperceptible: but it is, however, of the last consequence. For as this ought, or ought not, expresses some new relation or affirmation.*"[29]

Hume's argument was later termed "naturalistic fallacy"; in other words, one cannot infer rules or prescriptive judgments about what ought to be done from observing facts or factual propositions. Returning to *Pride and Prejudice*, one cannot derive a moral obligation to marry upon coming of age, just because that's what most people did at that time. Fortunately, to everybody's benefit, things have evolved since then. Life expectancy has increased, women have more options about when, how and if they want to have children, and the idea of the good life is neither unique nor imposed, at least in advanced democratic societies. There are now any number of accepted family models outside the framework of traditional marriage. For this reason, Austen's opening paragraph jars with most readers' sensibilities, and one might wonder if she was not making an ironic wink to future generations, a criticism of the provincial society that she reflects in her narrative.

Reading Hume and understanding his naturalistic fallacy was a key moment during my doctoral studies at Oxford, which remain vivid in memory, my particular awakening from a sort of dogmatic sleep. Obviously, factual propositions, judgments about what happens in our environment, cannot constitute a moral or normative justification for action.

I will use an example to illustrate this. Imagine that you run a company that is considering investing in a country where corruption is rampant, and that your advisors have explained to you that the only way to do business is by paying bribes, including to members of the government. Does the existence of this corruption represent a moral reason to join in? The argument could be encapsulated in the sentiment: "if I don't do it, somebody else will."

In short, generalized immoral behavior is not sufficient moral justification for acting immorally. On occasions, when I discuss such ethical dilemmas with students, I express my understanding for the complex circumstances in which their companies often operate in countries with high levels of corruption, especially in sectors such as construction or infrastructure. However, we know that we must adhere to certain standards. Firstly, because the legislation in countries where corruption is rampant will nevertheless likely condemn such practices, and there is therefore a real risk of sanction—a prudential argument—even if the rules are not complied with. Secondly, because unethical behavior is rejected by external analysts and observers, as do most students, who censure it when we analyze them in class.

I will give another example to illustrate the accuracy of the naturalistic fallacy, this time taken from Carlos S. Nino, the Argentinean moral and legal philosopher.[30] Let's imagine a group of divers find a mineral with powerful properties at the bottom of a deep ocean trench, and hand it over to a team of academics made up of geologists, philosophers, chemists and physicists to analyze. These experts come to the conclusion that when an immoral act is committed in the vicinity of the stone, it turns red. For example, if a person is beaten, or someone says something insulting, or a coup d'état is being planned, the rock turns red. On the other hand, if a good deed is performed, for example, sharing resources with the needy or caring for the elderly, the rock takes on a green hue.

What would you do with such a stone? For me, it could become a kind of moral oracle, allowing us to know when an act is morally praiseworthy or when it is immoral and reprehensible. Imagine if we could all carry one in our pockets, to know whether to act in one way or the other when we are faced with a moral dilemma, especially those where the solution is not so obvious. Remember, the stone would change color not only when we did something immoral, but even when we expressed our intention to do so. Imagine your company is going through a difficult time, and you have to decide whether to lay off some less efficient workers, with the corresponding compensation, or even close the business due to cost overruns. Would you use the stone to guide you?

There would inevitably be complex situations, as with so many moral dilemmas, where one has to weigh up the lesser of two evils, which case, we might not agree with the stone's diagnosis, as happens sometimes with the decisions of supreme courts or the recommendations of experts.

The story of this fantastic stone recalls the question Plato posed in his dialogue Euthyphro: "*Is the good willed by the gods because it is good, or is it good because it is willed by the gods?*".[31] In this dilemma, the gods could be replaced by our prodigious stone. Similarly, the German philosopher Gottfried Leibniz posed an analogous question: "*It is generally accepted that whatever God wills is good and just. But the question remains whether it is good and just only because God wills it or whether God wills it because it is good and just; in other words, whether justice and goodness are arbitrary or whether they belong to the necessary and eternal truths about the nature of things.*"[32]

In reality, we already have our own ideas about what is good and evil. Some analysts of the dilemma presented in the Euthyphro explain that, conceptually, one could think of a malicious deity, in which case the argument that something is good because the divinity wants it would not be consistent. Greek mythology is awash with episodes where the gods of Olympus, including Zeus, behave even worse than humans.

Returning to the naturalistic fallacy, Hume would likely argue that to infer from the color of our stone any normative judgment, that something is good because it turns green, or bad because it changes to red, would be a logical transgression, and he would add that we assign that meaning because in many cases we associate them with our own intuition, but it cannot be inferred that it will always be so. In fact, as we saw earlier, one could imagine situations where we would disagree with the stone.

The naturalistic fallacy is one of the most effective criticisms directed at defenders of natural law, at those who argue that there are rules or principles embedded in human nature that must be observed. For example, the precept proposed by Austen at the beginning of her novel. However, as Hume insists, one cannot derive norms or commands from the observation of facts. We are not in the realm of the natural sciences, where, for example, there is certainty that water boils at 100 degrees Celsius, but in the territory of the social sciences and human behavior, where many questions require justification and argument.

The sea stone is an appealing idea, especially to excuse difficult decisions, but the truth is that the idea is flawed. Firstly, because decisions made in the face of moral dilemmas presuppose the autonomy of the agent. Otherwise one could not praise or reproach the person who had made a decision. On the other hand, because many decisions that are so obvious, genuine moral dilemmas, require discussion and the use of reason to others. We are in the realm of moral constructionism, the idea that there are no self-evident truths out there, to be applied automatically. Instead, we need to discern, infer, reason and try to make the decision we make the one that another well-intentioned person would have made in our situation. The best test to justify our decisions is to discuss them in the public arena.

One of the best analyses of the difference between what is and what ought to be was provided by Iris Murdoch in her book *The Sovereignty of the Good*, in which she outlines a moral philosophy rooted in Plato, who by then had fallen out of vogue with her colleagues at Oxford, more interested in applying the principles of science and logic to philosophical discussion. This prevalent trend involved analyzing moral judgments from an objective standpoint, principally focusing on the meaning we give to words and concepts.

Instead, Murdoch argued that our understanding of the world defines our moral behavior: In her opinion, science alone cannot explain our beliefs and hopes. Our moral behavior cannot be reduced to facts. Analytical philosophy is not much use either, argues Murdoch, describing it as simply "*the picture frame.*"[33]

To illustrate the importance of the "inner life," Murdoch uses the analogy of the mother-in-law's traditional animosity toward her son or daughter's partner. Murdoch argues that mothers-in-law can choose to focus on the positive qualities of their children's spouses, praising them and showing affection. Over time, the mother-in-law might change her opinion about her daughter- or son-in-law and end up loving and respecting her. For Murdoch, the only way to understand people or things is by loving them, by looking at them in the best possible light. "*We need a moral philosophy within which the concept of love, so rarely mentioned today by philosophers, can once again occupy a central role.*"[34]

In support of Hume, the existence of disruptors, of people who act against the tide, like entrepreneurs and innovators, is good evidence of the naturalistic fallacy's soundness, because they do not follow the dictates of the majority. Jane Austen's own life is a good example. Contrary to the maxim that opens her famous novel, she never married or had children.

## 3.6   Why Not All Prophecies Need to Be Fulfilled

Humans have always been fascinated by prophecies. In ancient Greece, no important decision was taken without first consulting one of the oracles, the most famous of which was in Delphi, next to Mount Parnassus, overlooking the Gulf of Corinth. It was there, for example, that King Laius of Thebes learned his unfortunate fate: *"your son will kill his father and sleep with his mother."*[35] The son was Oedipus and we know that he fulfilled the prediction involuntarily. The fate foretold by the oracle was always fulfilled; there was no use in trying to evade it.

In imperial Rome, omens and spells were also important. Eager to discover their destiny, Romans would disembowel animals and consult the sibyls, one of the most famous of whom Cumae, is usually represented as elderly woman. When Apollo, the inspirer of prophecies, promised her a wish, she took a handful of earth and asked to live as many years as grains she held, although she forgot to add that she also wished to maintain a youthful appearance. It is said she lived the equivalent of nine lives and wrote many books full of omens and prognostications, although she spent her final years locked in a cage.

Not far from Cumae, in Pozzuoli, near Naples, Cicero wrote *De Fato*,[36] a treatise written in haste due to the Roman senator's desire to return to political activity as soon as possible. Only the middle section has survived, which deals with the conflict between destiny and individual freedom. Cicero supposedly had access to the Sibyl of Cumae's few surviving works, and was able to read her predictions, which he doesn't seem to have found very convincing, perhaps because they clashed with his ideas about personal freedom, which contradicted the idea that we cannot avoid our destiny. Cicero was particularly focused on the concept of virtues, those beneficial daily habits acquired through the exercise of the will, which contribute to forge the desired personality, thus building one's own destiny. To the extent that people strive to live a virtuous life, they move away from a flat and dependent subsistence, which is not governed by their own will but by external circumstances. Cicero argued that even in the face of the most challenging adversities, we can employ fortitude and other virtues, thus retaining what we now call agency over our lives.

Nevertheless, his critics did not fall short when they said of him: "*Would that he had been able to endure prosperity with greater self-control and adversity with more fortitude!*" wrote C. Asinius Pollio, a contemporary Roman statesman and historian.[37]

I suspect that many of us are attracted by the idea of knowing something about our future, and may have been influenced by childhood predictions.

Growing up, my parents hired a musician to teach us to play the Spanish classical guitar. Over time, my two sisters became more than proficient, often entertaining the family and visitors at home. For my part, after two days of lessons, the teacher told my parents, "Your son may have other talents, but he will never be able to play any instrument."

The prediction was fulfilled. I love music, but I have never had the manual dexterity required to play an instrument, even the triangle. In fact, as a child I would frequently knock over glasses at the table. I tend to avoid having a glass of water on the podium when I speak, although on occasion the effects of my clumsiness at least help break the ice with my audience. Similarly, I have zero spatial intelligence, and have always failed shape tests. Over time I have accepted these shortcomings, recognizing that they also have their advantages.

Research shows that teachers' expectations of their students' performance can have a decisive influence on the outcome of the learning experience. When teachers believe that one of their students is especially capable or more intelligent than the others, they will probably pay more attention to their instruction, perhaps inadvertently generating an outcome in line with that expectation. One of the outstanding experiments that backs up this belief was carried out by Robert Rosenthal and Lenore Jacobson in several US elementary schools in 1968, later published in their book *Pygmalion in The Classroom*.[38] The pair used a simulated test that supposedly evaluated the intellectual capacity of students, and then randomly chose a group of students, assuring their teachers that they were the most gifted. Over time, the selected group of students improved their IQ test scores. Although the research was criticized from a methodological standpoint, educators know from experience that greater attention and dedication to students, as well as instilling the hope that outstanding results can be achieved, results in better performance. Unfortunately, as is the case in so many spheres of social relationships, teachers inevitably have their preferences. The challenge is to dedicate the same amount of attention and commitment to all students.

This takes us into the realm of the self-fulfilling prophecy, a concept introduced by sociologist Robert K. Merton, who explained that the belief that an expectation will be fulfilled, whether founded or not, can result in this happening.[39] Merton illustrated his concept with the example of a bank, which is well managed but that becomes the target of rumors about its solvency. When they hear the rumors, some wary customers withdraw their deposits, and as the rumors spread, more people withdraw their money, and the bank soon finds itself unable to meet its commitments. This is a collective behavior within the phenomenon known as behavioral finance, which is sometimes encapsulated in the saying money is fearful, to explain group reactions, instigated by alarm or irrational reasons.

Teachers who sense which students will be successful and dedicate more time to them, resulting in higher grades, or the analyst whose rumors provoke panic and a run on a bank, are examples of self-fulfilling prophecies. Our beliefs conclusively influence our actions and their outcomes. The philosopher Karl Popper called self-fulfilling prophecies the Oedipus effect, "*because the oracle played a most important role in the sequence of events which led to the fulfillment of its prophecy. [...] For a time I thought that the existence of the Oedipus effect distinguished the social from the natural sciences. But in biology, too—even in molecular biology—expectations often play a role in bringing about what has been expected.*"[40]

A self-fulfilling prophecy is not the same as divination or an oracle, because there is no certainty that something will actually come true. In any event, I don't believe in prophecy. The intuition or conviction that some experts possess about future events or trends is based on experience and knowledge of a sector, or the ability to associate phenomena, rather than a vision. That said, self-fulfilling prophecies resemble oracles in their anticipatory nature, as well as the desire to will others toward achieving an objective.

The business environment offers many opportunities to see self-fulfilling prophecies practiced, consciously or unconsciously, among them:

- Annual sales forecasts are often the occasion for clashes between the commercial and financial departments. Generally speaking, sales teams, with performance-related incentives, tend to set realistic and reasonably achievable targets, while finance teams aim for more ambitious goals. Setting modest objectives can be interpreted as predicting the self-fulfilling result of selling less, which is sometimes referred to as "satisfactory underperformance," while setting ambitious goals promotes growth beyond what could be expected.
- Meeting deadlines for product or service launches, even if they seem illusory. In hectic situations, when companies have to pool people and resources to meet tight deadlines, a sense of identity and unity is strengthened. I am

sure you know or have experienced cases in which incredible results have been obtained in record time under such circumstances.

- Trust or distrust in other people's performance, as in the case of teachers' dedication to their supposedly gifted students. This is what mentoring programs are for. In my experience, motivation and dedication to the people you work with produce positive results. On the contrary, systematic criticism, repeated negative comments about people either directly or behind their backs, ineluctably contributes to their failure, especially if manifested by members of senior management.
- Closely related to the above, stoking philias or phobias, preferences, or the creation of groups or "chapels" within the company contributes to the people who associate with them assuming the roles, affinities and enmities toward the others. This is why effective leaders know the importance of combating silos and factions, and try to create cross-cutting links between people in their organization, beyond the boundaries marked by departments, functions, business units, or even different generations of workers.
- Stereotyping, which focuses on people's culture, race, gender or other social or personal characteristics, is a highly negative version of self-fulfilling prophecy. Unfortunately, this is a common reaction, which needs to be banished through training and the promotion of diversity strategies.

In conclusion, our beliefs influence our behavior, especially if we lock in desire and will. Let me now ask you a question: Which oracle would you consult about your future? Before considering the answer, perhaps it would be helpful to remember the verse from Matthew's gospel: "*Beware of false prophets, which come to you in sheep's clothing, but inwardly they are ravening wolves.*"[41]

## 3.7   What Do Plato and Steve Jobs Have in Common?

Imagine a chocolate with the same kick as three dry Martinis, James Bond's favorite tipple. This is the unexpected brainchild of Jerry, a 1960s Madison Avenue advertising executive tasked with developing VIP, a product with prodigious attributes already being advertising, even if the campaign has yet to reveal exactly what it is.

This is the plot line for *Lover Come Back*, where Rock Hudson plays Jerry, with his perennial partner Doris Day in the role of Carol, who works at a rival advertising agency.[42] Carol loathes Jerry's sleazy approach to closing a sale, which usually involves the kind of junkets we saw in *Mad Men*,[43] so she reports Jerry to the advertising ethics board, accusing him of touting a product that doesn't exist. Forced to come up with something, Jerry shows the board a box of VIP chocolates, which everyone present tastes. Things get complicated from there, but needless to say, it all ends happily.

The screwball comedy, which earned writers Stanley Shapiro and Paul Henning an Oscar nomination, has many hilarious moments and is perfect for a rainy afternoon or when you need a lift. At the same time, it shines a light on the value of marketing and advertising, and the mission of these functions within business management.

Creating expectation without revealing the characteristics of a product before it's available is a far from new tactic: The surprise effect has long been a pillar of successful business strategies. Steve Jobs understood this well, and would announce the upcoming presentation of new Apple products without revealing many details. His product launches at the Moscone Convention Center in San Francisco were carefully staged events, bolstered by tight secrecy in the run up.[44]

A step further is announcing products or services while they're still on the drawing board. For example, a few years ago, at the height of the Covid-19 pandemic, Big Pharma reported on plans to develop vaccines. Remedies for other kinds of viruses existed, but no company yet had a specific solution or a timeframe, although fortunately for mankind a solution was found in record time.

There are similar assumptions about the progress of drugs to cure cancer and other serious illnesses, reflecting confidence that effective solutions will be discovered within the next few decades. The fact they don't exist yet encourages these companies to announce them, so as to make them seem more credible and hopefully boosting their share price and attracting further investment.

In general, R+D+I programs, whether financed by governments or companies, tend to be long-term, but again, announcing them early doesn't seem to make them any less plausible. When President John F. Kennedy announced in 1963 that the United States would put a man on the Moon within a decade, the technology to do so did not yet exist; but in doing so, he set in motion the space race.[45] Astronaut Neil Armstrong fulfilled his prediction within six years.

The aeronautics sector provides another example of a large research project with a long lead time. Airbus has announced that it plans to operate its first hydrogen-powered, zero-$CO_2$-emissions aircraft by 2035. The project is still in the concept phase, but based on past experience it is confident of meeting the deadline, and it is possible that some airlines will sign purchase contracts before the first prototypes are even flown, as happened with the A380.[46]

Buying off-plan properties is common within the real estate sector, a practice not without risks for the buyer. For example, some areas of Northeastern Brazil are awash with real estate developments, and when I'm there, I often see flags in front of vacant lots indicating developments of plots of land or homes, with no sign of construction year after year. Developers take special care to fill their sales offices with eye-catching and attractive artists' impressions that will probably bear no relation to the completed property, if indeed it is ever built. Anyone who has seen an apartment for sale on a real estate portal knows the impression generated by wide-angle interior photos.

In short, the value of marketing and communication (marcom) in preparing the market and the consumer before the launch of a product or service cannot be overstated. It focuses on generating expectations, on creating a narrative and positioning the product, on how to whet the appetite of potential buyers.

As said, many products and services do not exist at the time they are announced, so early communication is an important part of the pioneer's advantage. Marketing and communications departments act as companies' vanguards, creating expectations, driving the rest of the organization to conquer the market as soon as possible.

I sometimes encourage marcom teams to adopt this attitude. Their mission is to throw the ball forward, so that the production and sales teams run after it. Some people think that until they can touch the product and test all its features, it is unwise to launch it. I believe that innovation involves reversing the process: Many pioneers first communicate their intention and then build it, obviously with a clear and achievable concept beforehand.

One of the most famous passages in philosophy can help us understand the anticipatory function of marketing and communication: Plato's analogy of the cave. In his seminal work *The Republic*, the Greek philosopher uses this to explain the nature of our knowledge.[47] A group of men look at some images flickering on the wall at the end of a cave. In reality, these are the shadows of things that pass by a campfire behind them, which projects their silhouettes. The group cannot see what is behind them, and assume that the shadows they see are real. Plato argues that our knowledge is similar to the experience of those men: a poor expression of what ideas are. If one of the group were to turn and venture out of the cave, they would see things as they are and acquire proper knowledge. But Plato argues that if that were to happen, the others would likely kill him when he returned.

I have always thought that our experience in a cinema is a modern-day version of Plato's cave, and I like to use it to explain the function and meaning of marketing. When the lights go down in the theater and the projection begins, we watch the images with rapt attention, perhaps wishing that the real world could be like the one on the silver screen.

I have always been fascinated by movies, something I inherited from my mother. I remember a commercial from four decades ago for a well-known cigarette brand that was often shown before movies in those days, featuring a cattle drive through the American west. Today the spot is banned. The ingenuity of the advertisers consisted in associating the untamed life of the cowboys, driving herds of cattle through majestic countryside. At dusk, they would gather around the campfire where coffee was brewing to smoke a cigarette. The advertisement had no dialogue or messages, but the powerful images and the feelings they provoked were enough. That advertisement is my version of Plato's cave.

The challenge for advertisers is to create the best version of a product or service, to dream up ways to beguile their customers with the figures they will see projected on the wall of the cave. There is an additional resemblance to Plato's analogy, which is that products and services are constantly being renewed; similarly, the narrative, the profiles and shapes we see on the wall must also be transformed.

Marketing is all about anticipation, about creating an ideal. Which is why Plato's analogy is so powerful a way to explain how the essence of things largely depends on how we see.

In conclusion, allow me to share two quotations I find particularly appropriate for this reflection on the role of marketing and communication in business.

The seventeenth-century Spanish philosopher Baltasar Gracián: "*Things do not pass for what they are but for what they seem. To be of use and to know how to show yourself of use, is to be twice as useful. What is not seen is as if it was not.*"[48]

In short, it's usually best not to reveal all the qualities of a product or a service before its launch, and possibly not even afterward. Explanations, whether of people, products or services, do not enhance, instead, they tend to trivialize.

## 3.8    Who Wants to Live in a Goldfish Bowl?

In his novel *Men Like Gods* (1924), H.G. Wells, a pioneer of science fiction, tells the story of a group of people who find themselves traveling through time to a much more technologically and culturally advanced society called Utopia.[49] This is a place where the social and political upheavals, wars, inequality and selfishness typical of most societies are absent. The reason why Utopia is such a peaceful place is that its inhabitants have developed their communication and interpersonal skills to such an extent that they are able to understand each other without speaking. In one particularly entertaining scene, the natives try to explain their history and customs to their guests using telepathy, but they are largely unreceptive and hear nothing. Among the few who manage to pick up a few sentences is a character named Barnstaple, and the reason is simple: He has unconsciously connected his experiences and knowledge with his hosts'.

Imagine for a moment you had this powerful gift, and were able to read the thoughts of others just by looking at them. Some of us might be disturbed by the idea, but business leaders and would do anything to possess an ability that would allow them to undercut or preempt the competition just by looking at the faces of their partners or competitors. And what about jealous spouses, who want to know what is going on in the minds of their partners? We might do well to remember Othello: Suspicious people have enough problems; better not to burden them with additional information.[50]

I imagine you would agree that a society where we knew what others were thinking—and where everybody else knew what we're thinking—would be hellish. Only in a world where our souls were as pure as the driven snow would such transparency be bearable, and we well ask ourselves if such a scenario might not be tedious. Returning to Wells' Utopia, presumably the telepathy enjoyed by all was agreed.

Surely total transparency, the unwanted exposure of our thoughts, desires and imaginations, violates the most fundamental right to personal privacy, even regarding those closest to us, including spouses.

I imagine that, like me, you must have been charmed by central Amsterdam, its peaceful canals, its balanced architecture, the charm of the bicycles, its pulse. One of the features that most attracted my attention was the large windows on its facades, without curtains, which allow passersby and neighbors to see into the rooms within. When I asked about the origin of these wide openings without curtains, I was told that they reflected the country's Puritan history, the ideal of transparency, the belief that inside a house, in the intimacy of the home, there is nothing to hide, no need for screens. Malice lies not in the person who acts openly, without cover, but in those who hide their actions.

Over time, I also confirmed that the reason for those wide windows without curtains was primarily to provide more luminosity to the interior, given the scarcity of sunlight during the day. On the contrary, in Mediterranean latitudes, where there is an abundance of brightness, windows have traditionally been protected by screens and blinds.

Transparency, leaving ourselves exposed either physically or intellectually, is not instinctive. By living in society we train ourselves to dress, to restrain bodily excesses, to mind our language and to treat others with courtesy. We understand these patterns of behavior not as restrictions on some supposed natural freedom, but behavior that contributes to the collective good. That is why the ideal of mental or verbal transparency, in individual conduct, is likely to transgress basic civility, for example by saying the first thing that comes into our heads.

Similarly, from a psychological perspective, we might question the wisdom of acting consistently in a transparent manner. Sigmund Freud, the father of psychoanalysis, explained that many of our decisions are determined by subconscious desires we are often unaware of.[51] Psychoanalysis may have been largely superseded by other psychological techniques, but the concept of the subconscious continues to find acceptance, and calls into question whether most mortals, even if they set their minds to it, would be capable of unraveling and truthfully sharing their true feelings.

However, we live in an age where transparency has been elevated to an ideal, personally and institutionally, especially in some social media environments. In *The Transparency Society*, South Korean philosopher Byung-Chul offers convincing arguments as to how the ideal of transparency is fallacious, and its defense inadvisable. In his opinion, "*transparency is a systemic coercion that takes hold of all social events and subjects them to profound change.*"[52] It is a phenomenon that, far from favoring interpersonal relations, instead trivializes and hinders them. In his opinion, it is precisely the lack of transparency that makes it easier for relationships to endure.

Furthermore, he argues that "*transparency and truth are not identical (…) More information or an accumulation of information alone is not truth. It lacks direction, namely meaning. Precisely because of the lack of the negativity of the true, we arrive at an overcrowding and massification of the positive. Hyper-information and hyper-communication testify to the lack of truth, and even to the lack of being. More information, more communication does not eliminate fundamental imprecision altogether. Rather it aggravates it.*"[53]

Demands for greater transparency in society can be countered by arguments about our right to privacy, drawing on the work of two eminent early twentieth-century US jurists, Louis Brandeis and Felix Frankfurter.[54] In short, we have the right to manage information about ourselves. Today, in our increasingly hybrid lives combining the physical and the digital, the right to privacy has become much more meaningful and relevant. Here are some thought-provoking facts: A Microsoft report reveals that 75% of companies consult personal information about candidates on the internet when hiring, and in 70% of cases reject candidates based on that data.[55] Similarly, organizations can consult metadata related to social network profiles, along with analysis of the perceived behavior of their users, providing information on sexual orientation, religious or political opinions, race, intelligence and other areas. On a more worrying note, 5% of American teenagers aged 12 to 18 said they were victims of cyberbullying, according to a report published in 2017.[56]

There is also growing demand in the corporate sphere for transparency, which translates into the demand to know about performance, financial information and data referring to remuneration, minutes of meetings, decision-making and even future plans. The obsession with shining a light on the activities of companies, sometimes subjecting them to greater scrutiny than public bodies, constrains innovation and even raises doubts about the possible contravention of the right to freedom of enterprise enshrined in most democratic constitutions.

There is a reason inherent in the nature of business activity itself, which clashes with the paradigm of transparency. It is often explained that the environment in which companies operate is deliberately competitive, a circumstance fostered by the state itself through legislation and specific bodies that promote healthy rivalry. The aim is to avoid collusion, undesirable business concentration and other detrimental effects on consumers, workers, shareholders and the rest of society. However, the existence of competition entails a strategic attitude among the companies operating in a sector, understanding that the management of information and communication is a discretionary power, logically within respect for the law. For example, it would be absurd to require companies to share information on what products or services they plan to launch on the market at the time of making the decision, putting rivals on notice, or to publish the promotion plans of their executives for the next five years.

Similarly, the government of any country needs to keep certain things secret, information that is only accessible to a small number of decision-makers, who are also subject to the duty of professional secrecy. This is why the demand for complete transparency in all matters of state is fatuous and even dangerous, because it unnecessarily jeopardizes institutions and social coexistence itself. Obviously, the maintenance of state secrets does not preclude the healthy activity of the media which can uncover abuses in the exercise of these powers.

General Charles de Gaulle, father of the Fifth French Republic, once said that *"the essence of prestige is mystery."*[57] I could not agree more. Total transparency disappoints and trivializes people. Shadows, obscurities and angles provide depth and beauty, and also attract our attention and interest.

# Notes

1. D. Kahnemann, *Thinking Fast and Slow* (London: Farrar, Straus and Giroux, 2011) and 20 and N. Thaleb, *The Black Swan. The Impact of The Highly Improbable* (New York, NY: Random House, 2017).
2. https://www.britannica.com/event/dancing-plague-of-1518.
3. G. García Márquez, *Cien años de soledad* (Buenos Aires: Ed. Sudamericana, 1967); I. Allende, *La casa de los espíritus* (Barcelona: Plaza y Janés, 1982).
4. The term was coined by Herbert A. Simon, *Administrative Behavior: A Study of Decision-Making Processes in Administrative Organization* (New York, NY: The Free Press, 1997).
5. B. Caplan, *The Myth of the Rational Voter. Why Democracies Choose Bad Policies* (Princeton and Oxford: Princeton University Press, 2008).
6. S. Freud, *El chiste y su relación con el subconsciente* (trad. Luis López-Ballesteros) (Madrid: Alianza, 2012).
7. Z. Bauman, *Tiempos líquidos. Vivir en una época de incertidumbre* (Barcelona: Tusquets, 2022).
8. Though this quote is conventionally attributed to Charles Darwin, there is no such statement in *The Origin of Species*. The cause is probably the reference by Herbert Spencer in his *The Principles of Biology* (Edinburgh: Williams and Norgate, 1864), vol 1, part III: "*This survival of the fittest, which I have here sought to express in mechanical terms, is that which Mr. Darwin has called 'natural selection, or the preservation of favored races in the struggle for life*".
9. Aristotle, *Eudemian Ethics* (trans. B. Inwood and R. Wood) (Cambridge: Cambridge University Press, 2013), beginning: "*happiness, being finest and best, is the most pleasant of all things*".
10. G. García Márquez, *Love in the Time of Cholera* (London: Penguin, 2022).
11. E. Porter & G. Fabrikant, "A Big Star May Not a Profitable Movie Make," *The New York Times*, August 28, 2006.
12. C. Gómez-Centurión, *La Armada Invencible* (Madrid: Anaya, 1987).
13. D. Hume, *An Enquiry Concerning Human Understanding* (ed. T.L. Beauchamp) (Oxford: Oxford University Press, 1998).
14. S. Iñiguez de Onzoño, *Cosmopolitan Managers. Executive Development that Works* (London: Palgrave Macmillan, 2016), 10.1.
15. T. Ohno, *Toyota Production System. Beyond Large-Scale Production* (London: Routledge, 1988).
16. Y.N. Harari, *Sapiens. A Brief History of Humankind* (New York: Random House, 2011); Kindle ed. 4528.
17. A. Smith, *The Wealth of Nations* (London: Penguin, 1991), Vol. I.
18. J.F. Nash, "Equilibrium points in n-person games", 36 *Proceedings of the National Academy of Sciences* (1), January 1990, 48–9.

19. King, Mervyn; Kay, John. *Radical Uncertainty: Decision-making for an unknowable future* (Boston: Little, Brown & Co. 2020). Kindle edition, 2020, loc. 94.
20. A. Korzybski, *Science and Sanity. An Introduction to Non-Aristotelian Systems and General Semantics* (Brooklyn, NY: Institute of General Semantics, 1933).
21. Described in Plato, *Phaedo* (trans. R.S. Bluck) (New York: Routledge 2014).
22. T. de Quincey, *The Last Days of Immanuel Kant and Other Writings* (Miami: Hard Press, 2017).
23. King, Mervyn; Kay, John, op. cit.
24. O. Wilde, *The Picture of Dorian Gray* (London: Penguin, 2012).
25. K. Von Clausewitz, *On War* (trans. J.J. Graham) (London: Wordsworth Editions, 1997).
26. J. Austen, *Pride and Prejudice* (London: Penguin, 2022).
27. D. Hume, *Treatise on Human Nature* (London: Penguin, 1986).
28. D. Hume, *An Enquiry Concerning Human Understanding,* op. cit.
29. D. Hume, *Treatise on Human Nature*, op.cit., Book 3, part 1.
30. C.S. Nino, "Etica y derechos humanos" (Buenos Aires: Astrea, 2007).
31. Plato, *Euthyphro* (London: Oxford University Press, 20), 10 a.
32. G.W. Leibniz, "Reflections on the Common Concept of Justice" (1702), https://link.springer.com/chapter/10.1007%2F978-94-010-1426-7_60#page-1.
33. I. Murdoch, *The Sovereignty of the Good* (London: Routledge, 2001); Kindle loc. 807.
34. Ibid., loc. 1501.
35. Sophocles, *Oedipus Rex* (Cambridge: Cambridge University Press, 2006).
36. Cicero, *On the Orator: Book 3. On Fate. Stoic Paradoxes. Divisions of Oratory* (Cambridge, Mass.: Harvard University Press, 1942).
37. H.J. Haskell, *This Was Cicero* (Greenwich, Conn.: Fawcett Publications Inc., 1964), p. 296.
38. R. Rosenthal and L. Jacobson, *Pygmalion in the Classroom. Teacher Expectation and Pupil's Intellectual Development* (Carmarthen: Crown House Publishing, 2003).
39. R. Merton, *Social Theory and Social Structure* (New York: The Free Press, 1967).
40. K. Popper, *Unended Quest: An Intellectual Autobiography* (LaSalle, Illinois: Open Court, 1976), p. 346.
41. Matthew, 7: 15.
42. *Lover come back* (dir. D. Mann) (Universal Pictures, 1961).
43. *Mad Men* (M. Weiner) (Warner Bros, 2007).
44. W. Isaacson, *Steve Jobs* (New York: Simon & Schuster, 2011), Ch. 30.
45. J.F. Kennedy, "Address at Rice University on the Nation's Space Effort", 12 September 1962. https://www.jfklibrary.org/learn/about-jfk/historic-speeches/address-at-rice-university-on-the-nations-space-effort.

46. https://www.dw.com/en/at-airbus-a-hydrogen-powered-aircraft-takes-shape/a-55051579.
47. Plato, *The Republic* (London: Penguin, 2021), 7. 514a.
48. B. Gracián, *The Art of Worldly Wisdom. A Pocket Oracle* (Jersey City, NJ: Start Publishing, 1991), p. 53.
49. H.G. Wells, *Men Like Gods* (London: William Collins, 2021).
50. W. Shakespeare, *Othello* (London: Penguin, 2015).
51. S. Freud, The Interpretation of Dreams (New York: Basic Books, 2010).
52. *Byung-Chul Han, La sociedad de la transparencia* (Madrid: Herder, 2013), p. 6.
53. Ibid., p.13.
54. L.D. Brandeis and S.D. Warren, "The Right to Privacy", *Harvard Law Review*, IV, 1890–1.
55. J. Rosen, "The Web Means the End of Forgetting", The New York Times, July 19, 2010.
56. "What is Cyberbullying", stopbullying.gov., *24 September 2019. Retrieved 2 November 2021.*
57. Quoted in M. Lewis, *Liar's Poker* (London: Hodder & Stoughton, 2006), p. 73.

# 4

# Part 4: Vision—What Does the Future Look Like?

Among the philosophers frequently quoted by managers is Heraclitus, the ancient Greek thinker, nicknamed "the obscure" because of the difficulty of understanding the fragments that remain of his work *On Nature*.[1] Notwithstanding, his most famous idea is highly intuitive and simple: Change is a constant in our lives. To explain the idea, he used the well-known analogy that no one can bathe twice in the same waters of a river, because they are constantly flowing.

Never was a concept more applicable to business. Constant innovation in every business sector alters products and services, while disruptors and new competitors are always appearing, altering the rules of the game. Competition is the natural state of any industry, and when a leading player monopolizes their position, the authorities that oversee their activity will typically intervene to hopefully level the playing field.

In this volatile environment, the development of a strategic mindset and a vision of the future is particularly necessary. Business strategy is not about predicting the future or consulting oracles or crystal balls, although there are any number of tools and analysis models available to plan and establish contingency plans. "*Plans are worthless*," President Eisenhower once observed, drawing on his military experience, "*but planning is everything*."[2] Behind this paradox lies the unavoidable reality that we must always look ahead and constantly be trying to take into account any number of possible outcomes.

Technology has always impacted on business activity, but recent decades have seen unprecedented change wrought by digitalization. The potential

S. Iñiguez, *Philosophy Inc.*, https://doi.org/10.1007/978-3-031-20483-8_4

offered by the management of big data, the evolution of artificial intelligence and machine learning capture our imagination and raise important philosophical questions.

## 4.1    What Would Thomas Hobbes Made of Mark Zuckerberg?

Big Tech, with Facebook and Microsoft in the vanguard, is set to conquer the Metaverse, a place described by Merriam Webster as "*a highly immersive virtual world where people gather to socialize, play, and work.*"[3]

It's not a new concept, and was initially proposed by Neal Stephenson in his science fiction novel *Snow Crash*, where humans and avatars interact in a virtual environment.[4] You may also remember Second Life, a parallel world of clumsy avatars, and where IE Business School created an auditorium in a virtual tropical paradise where most users chose to act out their counterpart's lives anonymously.

The predictions that Second Life would revolutionize the world of education and social relationships never came to pass. In my career as an educator, I have witnessed similar unfilled prophecies of tsunamis that would sweep through the traditional world of university education. The impact of Second Life on education was minimal, although it served to ignite the imagination, while boosting the use of simulations, gamification and augmented reality (AR) in the educational environment.

As for personal relationships, dating portals have proven to be a more immediate remedy for finding a partner, and while some profiles do not fully match reality, they are more credible than avatars.

Mark Zuckerberg, founder of Facebook, announced that his company's future will be based on developing its own virtual universe, and changed its name to Meta Platforms, redefining its business strategy in bold terms: "*I expect people will transition from seeing us primarily as a social-media company to seeing us as a metaverse company.*" For Zuckerberg, the metaverse is "*a virtual environment where you can be present with people in digital spaces (…) an embodied Internet that you're inside of rather than just looking at. We believe that this is going to be the successor to the mobile Internet.*"[5]

There has been speculation as to whether Zuckerberg's announcement was merely an attempt to repackage Facebook in the face of growing hostility from governments and waning popularity among young people. That said, not all social networks are the same, nor have they experienced Facebook's problems.

LinkedIn, for example, has established itself as a platform that guarantees data privacy backed by robust protection and security mechanisms.

In any event, Facebook is not alone in seeing the social and business potential of the Metaverse. Microsoft CEO Satya Nadella has recently talked about an "enterprise metaverse" made up of digital twins, simulated environments, and mixed reality. "*With the Metaverse, the entire world becomes your app canvas*," he said.[6]

The appeal is clear: being able to live several lives or adopt alternative personalities without the risks we would face in the real world. Imagine, for example, being able to embark on the first voyage of the metaverse Titanic, and being assigned the role of the captain, or perhaps the ship's owner. On that adventure, you would interact with other passengers, some of whose profiles we know. We would know the course of past events, though perhaps there are multiple uncertainties and other factors we would be unable to foresee. We might change the final destination of the liner, or lessen the loss of life. In doing so, we might create an even more catastrophic outcome. It would certainly be a good test of leadership and a lesson in risk assessment.

The metaverse will allow us to experience all kinds adventures, allowing us, like James Bond, to live twice: once for ourselves and once to satisfy our dreams or to channel aspirations. Life in the metaverse could provide a deeper, more immersive experience than even video games or movies.

At the same time, the metaverse has huge potential in the educational world, offering an environment where learning could be more personalized, adjusted to students' tastes and hobbies, to their pace of study, more entertaining and perhaps with better results for the acquisition of individual knowledge and the exercise of certain interpersonal skills. Think for example of a role-playing exercise, with avatars assigned randomly based on different sexual identities or orientation. Imagine that in real life you are a 55-year-old male and you are assigned the avatar of a 22-year-old female, bullied by her boss, a situation condoned by your colleagues. This bullying would also have consequences for the emotional stability of your avatar, meaning you couldn't just sit the situation out. You would then have to discuss in class whether you would have been operating at your best.

The metaverse could also allow us to simulate political experiments that would otherwise be unfeasible or undesirable. For example, direct democracy, allowing us to assess whether these collective decisions generate the best results, whether users have sufficient information, whether the criteria for voting are justifiable, and if there are undesirable dysfunctions similar to those in the real world. By developing this exercise we would probably realize that representative democracy is the best possible system, with playful elements similar to those in a virtual world.

For me, the most appealing feature of the metaverse is how it enhances creativity and innovation, and by generating more options, increases our space of individual freedom. As we have seen, its application to multiple facets of social life is limitless: education, personal relationships, commercial activities, and work.

At the same time, the multiverse faces the same limitations as gamification: They both simplify reality; managers and other professionals operate in a much more complex world. It is also likely that behind the algorithms that make up the metaverse there are clear links between cause and effect, which, while useful for understanding the meaning of a given concept or model, are not a true reflection of the realities involved in managing a company, where the use of models and systems is limited.

The risks of the metaverse have been highlighted by various analysts and largely focus on lack of transparency, honesty, and the accountability of the people behind the avatars that will inhabit it. We are not only dealing with a playful or neutral environment. To the extent that the metaverse has any link with the real world, for example with the financial system through cryptocurrencies, there could be an incalculable impact on the life of social institutions. The same would happen with the activities that companies, organizations or individuals could develop in that environment: Could an avatar be held responsible for acts that in a physical environment would be considered fraud?

The seventeenth-century English philosopher Thomas Hobbes lived through a particularly turbulent period in his country's history, witnessing the consequences of weak governance, which sparked civil war, leading him to propose that the best guarantee of social peace is to locate the monopoly of force in the state. If power, and consequently the use of force to preserve it, is diluted, and there are no institutions and no rule of law to guarantee how to use it, society eventually becomes a war of all against all. In this circumstance, explained Hobbes, "*homo homini lupus*," man becomes a wolf to man.[7]

Were he alive today, I believe Hobbes would see the metaverse as akin to the state of nature, devoid of government, rules or principles, a place of perpetual confrontation. So, before we create this alternative parallel universe, perhaps we need to think about how it should be run, which institutions are going to be needed, which current practices should be replicated. Let's not deceive ourselves: Trusting in self-regulation to make up for the absence of a formal constituted power is at best a chimera, and at worst a malign fallacy. As Hobbes explained, political power is the repository of the social contract, that agreement of the individuals of a community about how they should live, their rights and duties. The social contract does not work in a leaderless and anarchic society.

We are also exposed to personal risks in the multiverse, if things are not properly managed. Without going into further detail, we know that the stress of experiencing multiple lives can result in schizophrenia, and of course some people would perhaps retire forever into a fantasy existence.

Finally, I have to say that I am intrigued about what would happen if our avatars were more successful than ourselves. Might we find ourselves living a back-to-front latter-day Cyrano, where Roxanne falls in love with the avatar?[8] Perhaps not. Emerging from the pandemic after lockdown and other restrictions, our love of the physical, real world, in education, at work and in social relationships, is deeper than ever, even among younger generations who are digital natives. That's why I think the winner of the contest with his avatar would still be Cyrano.

## 4.2    What Will Reality Mean When We're All Living in the Metaverse?

Imagine receiving an invite to some virtual activities on the metaverse: a walk around the Acropolis; a parachute jump; or joining the maiden voyage of the Titanic, in the class of your choice, of course. The invitation explains that the metaverse provides a faithful replica of reality: The visual, motor and acoustic technology is formidably immersive, the avatars, which have legs, look and sound like real people. The full-body suit you wear allows you to exercise not only your sight and hearing, but also your sense of smell, touch and even taste. For example, you feel the wind in your face, especially intense in the case of the skydive, and bracing while your promenade on the deck of the ocean liner.

Which would you choose? You could jump out of a plane and enjoy the thrill of the descent risk-free; if you opted for the Atlantic crossing, you could even reverse the course of history were you to play the role of the captain or the ship's owner.

In short, as mentioned before, the metaverse offers the chance to live any number of lives, allowing you to get to know people from faraway places you would never have had the opportunity to meet. Similarly, you could visit previously inaccessible corners of the world.

As the metaverse takes shape, we're beginning to see something of its potential positive impact on our lives. For example, in the field of education and learning, we could apply the flight simulators techniques that have long been used to train pilots.

And as well as developing practical or technical proficiencies, the metaverse could also be the place where we work on our interpersonal skills. Counterintuitive though it may seem, given that the digital environment has long been seen as a hideaway from the terminally shy, the metaverse is the ideal place to develop our ability to communicate, socialize, understand how to leverage a network, work in a team, or deepen bonds with others, at no risk to our self-esteem. Indeed, we can achieve these objectives if the skills we develop in the metaverse are interwoven with practices in the physical environment. As we know, skills are the result of habits, the repetition of actions that shape behavior.

The second area where the metaverse offers huge potential is diversity and inclusion: putting ourselves in the shoes of others who feel and think differently, who may have an alternative conception of the good life. Imagine that in a role-playing exercise in a professional setting you are assigned the part of somebody from a minority, where possibly the rest of the participants share the views, and prejudices, of the majority. In this situation, you would be asked to fully embrace your role, to try to play it to the best of your ability. As a result, you might begin to understand the importance of respect for different life choices and worldviews, celebrate diversity and innovation, and even support inclusion initiatives in the social environment. The results would be similar to those of other role-playing exercises that are implemented in many educational institutions.

That said, there has been opposition to these types of exercises being carried out by students in primary or secondary education, citing the risk of encouraging certain behaviors. I disagree: They offer the commendable opportunity to develop tolerance, an understanding of a complex world, along with a cosmopolitan spirit and recognition of the importance of innovation: In short, the ability to understand our fellow human beings and increase our personal leadership capacities.

The metaverse could enrich our lives by expanding our opportunities to experience new things far beyond what we could within the finite coordinates of space and time, allowing us to live different lives, alternative existences, thus broadening our personal freedom. Moreover, as we have seen, there are no physical risks, and we can even control the extent to which we engage with it mentally. In short, seen in this way, the metaverse, at least conceptually, is intrinsically good.

However, there are also some downsides to a life in the metaverse. Imagine that, after trying out different experiences in the metaverse such as a trip on the Titanic or parachuting out of an airplane, along with attending live seminars led by leading figures from the world of business education, you are given the opportunity to live in the metaverse for the rest of your life. This includes the possibility of enjoying a virtually immeasurable number of experiences, since the metaverse is being fed daily with new applications and experiences, while new people are signing up all the time. Imagine you are offered the chance to live in the city of your choice, work for the company of your choice, live in the apartment of your choice. And of course, you can spend your weekends—and vacations—in your favorite destinations; what's more, you can take your friends and family with you, assuming they wanted to join you in the metaverse.

Would you accept?

You can dismiss the proposal as currently beyond hypothetical, and while AI still has some way to go to make such a life possible, if we accept that everything imaginable can be realized—after all, German philosopher G.W.F. Hegel argued that what is rational is real, and what is real is rational[9]—I would argue that we can seriously consider it, at least in the context of a conversation about the kind of life we would like to live, and therefore with our idea of happiness and personal fulfillment.

In favor of accepting this radical proposal, one could point to the increased freedoms outlined above, but let's now consider the arguments against it.

In the first place, the proposal would be palatable if the metaverse we're going to live in is at least equal to or better than the real world. After all, we could end up with metaverse that's a human jungle. We need only look at some social networks to see what could go wrong. This danger has led me to propose in another article the need to establish principles or codes in the virtual environment, which by nature is extralegal and stateless.

Why should we believe that the virtual world in which we will live would be a fairer and more equitable place than the real one. In his book *The Metaverse*, Matthew Ball argues that the sector could end up being controlled by an oligopoly, governed by a few companies that would turn it into a "corporate internet." At the moment, the two companies that dominate this sector are Microsoft, which has won a $22 billion contract with the US Army to provide 120,000 HoloLens—the immersive glasses that provide sensory access—and Meta, formerly Facebook, which acquired the VR company Oculus and is investing more than $10 billion annually.[10]

An oligopoly might make it easier to monitor the metaverse, as well as providing guarantees; but it could also limit its development and innovation, as well as promoting asymmetry, to the detriment of users.

But I believe that control by a few companies, far from enriching the metaverse, would likely harm it. The tendency toward collusion would impose standardization and conservatism, possibly curtailing new experiences. Something similar to what the South Korean philosopher Byul-Chung Han explains when he compares beauty in the real and digital environments would happen: "The *natural beautiful contrasts with the digital beautiful. In the digital beautiful, the negativity of the different has been completely eliminated. That is why it is totally polished and smooth. It must not contain any tear. Its sign is complacency without negativity: the "I like it." The digital beautiful constitutes a polished and smooth space of sameness, a space that tolerates no strangeness, no otherness. Its mode of appearance is the pure inside, without any exteriority. Even to nature it turns it into a window of itself.*"[11]

Another potential problem with the metaverse is that it will be conceived and developed by others, meaning it may not be fully inclusive and therefore limiting in terms of personal freedom or choices, at least more so than the real world is. The counterargument to that is that in real life we are often unable to broaden our experience because we lack the initiative, knowledge or skills to do so. This is perhaps analogous to how cinema allows us to notice and discover circumstances and stories that we would not have anticipated on our own.

What is the nature of the experiences lived in the Metaverse?

The metaverse brings to mind Gilbert Hartman's analogy of a brain submerged in a bucket protected by an amniotic fluid. It is connected by electrodes to a computer that transmits a series of stimuli and information. For example, during the day the brain receives images and other sensory information pertaining to a regular working day, followed by some exercise, a few drinks with friends, and finally some time with the family at home, before enjoying a good night's rest.[12] The brain does not know that all the data and stimuli it receives are artificial, because the perceptions and vivid impressions it experiences make them real, even though it might be capable of asking itself whether everything it "lives" is real or invented. Similarly, we would never know we were living in the metaverse unless the computer we were connected to transferred images of us strapped to wires, or somebody found their way into our "world."

If we were to experience the same "sensations" of the brain in a bucket, we might not miss our alternative life. We would not realize that our brain is not biologically connected to the body, but to a computer. This deprivation of the relationship with the real world, the absence of a causal relationship with the external, according to philosopher Hilary Putnam's account, is what makes the experiences of the brain in a bucket different from those of a real subject.[13]

It would be something else to make an early decision to forgo that biological connection, and then to be shown pictures of the brain in the bucket and the electrodes connected to a computer. Surely this unexpected warning of our alienation would be too much to bear.

Perhaps the strongest argument against a life inhabited exclusively in the metaverse is the memory of sensations and sensory memories experienced in the physical environment. Our corporeal, animal nature—we are rational animals—requires the presential, the strength of material and somatic experiences. The hybrid work environment many of us experienced during the pandemic will have reinforced this feeling.

The advantage of the metaverse is that we don't have to abandon the physical world forever to take part in it. Perhaps this is the best of all possible worlds, the opportunity to live not just two lives, but many more. But I'm not convinced: A visit to the Acropolis on a warm summer afternoon, contemplating the play of light and shade on the marble around us, cooled by a Mediterranean breeze, is beyond compare with any virtual world.

## 4.3   Siri Would Certainly Have Given Wittgenstein Food for Thought

Two of the best-loved characters from George Lucas' *Star Wars* (1977), the first installment of the series, are R2-D2 and C-3PO, endearing droids with very different characters; cybernetic replicas of Sancho Panza and Don Quixote.

R2-D2 is an astromech droid, designed to repair spaceships and programmed to carry out multiple other tasks. Short, stocky, smart, and brave, he efficiently solves any number of problems and even flies as copilot to the movie's hero, Luke Skywalker. We are unable to understand the meaning of the sounds he makes, although he always seems to be right.

In contrast, C-3PO is a protocol droid, programmed to speak 6 million languages and forms of communication. Better proportioned and clad in golden armor, he is also pompous and petulant, too refined to engage in combat. Although he is capable of processing so many languages, he is nevertheless clumsy, fearful and impractical. He is frequently disabled or about to be chopped up among piles of scrap metal.

Star Wars envisions a world in which technology makes it possible to process and understand any language spoken in the universe, whether by humans, droids or other sentient beings. We have not yet reached that stage, although in recent years, language recognition systems like Siri, Alexa or Cortana have become part of our everyday life. The C-3POs of today are the translation solutions provided by Google Translate, used by millions of people to translate messages into other languages, which can then be turned into speech. There are other similar programs, such as Microsoft's LUIS, developed to make chatbots speak as close to the language we humans speak, or IBM's Watson, which can supposedly produce articles that are indistinguishable from those written by journalists.

Although these translation programs at our fingertips are imperfect, and far from the accuracy of C-3PO, they are sufficient. We use them to communicate in a rudimentary way, knowing perhaps that we run the risk of distorting our message or even saying the opposite of what we intend. But it is more than enough to say good morning in Chinese or to ask how somebody is in Arabic.

Over the past few decades, speech recognition and language translation technology has advanced by leaps and bounds, but it is still a science in its infancy. Using technical language, research has focused on developing natural language processing (NLP) programs based on large databases, multiple statistical resources, algorithms and artificial intelligence. However, the processing of words, sentences, whole texts, even if it can be done on an exponential scale, still cannot faithfully reproduce natural language understanding (NLU). Understanding a message depends on the context, on the people communicating, on the culture itself, on elements beyond the millions of pieces of data that are processed about the use and meaning of words. An example: enter a joke that you find particularly funny in Google Translate and put it into another language, then send it to a native speaker of that language. If your recipient finds it funny, you have a future in comedy.

The Italians have a saying *"traduttore, traditore"*: The translator is a traitor, highlighting the potential risk we run when conveying an idea or expression into another language. Google itself acknowledges that Google Translate does not reproduce NLU.

Walid S. Saba, founder of Ontologik.ai, explains in a recent article that in addition to the limited scope of the available technologies, scientists have not approached their task adequately: *"the advocates of the data-driven and statistical approaches to NLP were interested in solving simple language tasks—the motivation was never to suggest that this is how language works, but that "it is better to do something simple than nothing at all." The cry of the day was: "let's go pick up some low-hanging fruit" (…) The objective was to find "practical solutions to simple tasks by assuming that this Probably Approximately Correct (PAC) paradigm will scale into full natural language understanding (NLU)."* He concludes: *"Machine Learning and Data-Driven approaches are trying to chase infinity in futile attempt at trying to find something that is not even 'there' in the data. Ordinary spoken language, we must realize, is not just linguistic data."*[14]

I would suggest that a better understanding of the difference between NPL and NLU might be provided by turning to a thinker who emphasized the connection of philosophy with language: Ludwig Wittgenstein. In his 2008 book on the Austrian philosopher, British academic A.C. Grayling says *"he is regarded as quintessentially representative of twentieth-century philosophy, as if he exemplifies—not just in his work, but in his personality—what philosophy itself is like: difficult and profound."* Nevertheless, Grayling concludes: *"The journey through Wittgenstein's circuitous, metaphorical, sometimes opaque negations and suggestions is long; but the distance it takes is short."*[15] In other words, Wittgenstein is more important for what has been written about his ideas. With that caveat, I believe Wittgenstein's contribution can help us to understand the challenges facing AI researchers seeking technological answers to NLU.

Born into one of the wealthiest families in the Austro-Hungarian Empire, of Jewish origin but Catholic converts, the Wittgenstein household in Vienna was a meeting place for the most celebrated musicians, writers and entrepreneurs of the time, providing an enlightened environment and connecting Ludwig and his siblings with thinkers and artists from an early age. His parents decided that the children should be educated at home, and Ludwig's encyclopedic schooling showed itself in the house he designed for his sister, which still commands the respect of architects.

He initially traveled to England to study aeronautical engineering at the University of Manchester, but found his vocation in mathematics and especially in philosophy. His passion for philosophy possibly grew out of his contact with members of the Vienna Circle, who argued that anything that cannot be logically or empirically demonstrated is meaningless, the fundamental thesis of logical positivism. During World War I, he served in the imperial army, and was captured and held as a POW for nine months. This experience, together with the diffuse presence of religion, influenced his character more than his ideas, and he came close to becoming a monk on more than one occasion, as well as harboring a sense of guilt due to his repressed homosexuality.

Years later, he would meet Bertrand Russell, his mentor at Cambridge University, where he became a professor.

It seems that Wittgenstein was not a particularly happy man. His tortured personality is suggested in the photographs we have of him, and although he maintained a close and loyal relationship with his most direct disciples, such as G.E.M. Anscombe, he could be arrogant, intolerant and rude to his students. He would not be a good fit in most contemporary universities.

A distinction is often made between a "first Wittgenstein," associated with his first major publication, the *Tractatus Logico-Philosophicus*, and a "second Wittgenstein," associated with his posthumously published *Philosophical Investigations*, in which he rectifies the central theses of the first period.[16]

The "first Wittgenstein" harbors a disproportionate ambition. At the beginning of his *Tractatus*—structured in apothegms or sentences, many of them cryptic—he states that we will be able to solve all the problems of philosophy when we understand the logic of our language, no more and no less. Contrary to the belief of many thinkers, Wittgenstein saw the function of philosophy as having nothing to do with examining questions such as personal identity, the possibility of knowing, what truth is, or how we should act and behave. For Wittgenstein, these are illusory problems that arise as a consequence of not knowing the rules that govern language.

Language has a logical structure, which, if it can be unraveled and explained, will allow us to understand which ideas make sense. To this end, Wittgenstein dissects the basic elements that make up language—the propositions—and how they can be articulated logically. He also draws on the earlier contributions of Frege, Russell and the thinkers of the Vienna Circle. You will surely be familiar with this type of analysis: the logical rules, truth tables, deductive arguments, inferences and syllogisms that govern the reasoning of logic and that have had so much influence in other fields, such as programming and computation.

The conviction that any reasoning can be subjected to a logical analysis, that everything that is not explicable by this procedure is of no use, and that language has a structure that philosophy must elucidate, is a very similar approach to that taken by the architects of NLP. The programs developed under this rubric aim to identify the meaning of sentences from the complex analysis provided by statistics and AI. Any text could be translated into another language by applying the algorithms that have been developed using this procedure.

As you may have imagined by now, the "second Wittgenstein," the philosopher in now in his intellectual maturity, revisits and corrects his theses published in the *Tractatus*. His fundamental proposal is that the meaning of language is determined by its use, an idea that has been adopted by thinkers subscribing to analytic philosophy. An example: Advocates of the analytic theory of law argue that the best way to understand the meaning of concepts such as "obligation," "freedom" or "contract" is to see what meaning is given to them by legal operators such as judges or lawyers.

Wittgenstein uses an analogy to show the complexity of language and its meaning, disregarding his earlier belief that it was possible to solve all philosophical problems by addressing the structure of language. He explains that the meanings a group of people give to the language they speak resembles the similarities of the members of a family. When one looks at these relatives, one notices a certain resemblance, perhaps physical, but especially in the way they behave, gesticulate or speak. Something similar happens with language: The users of a language give a sense and meaning to words and phrases that is common to the group, and possibly very different from those of another collective.

This second Wittgenstein helps us to better understand NLU. Specifically, the difficulty of processing a language universally and translating all the phrases that its users may employ in a particular circumstance. Imagine again the example of translating a very short joke into another language. Or think how an AI mastermind would process a short comment made to your partner; for example, "bloody Mary never tires of talking," referring to a chatty table neighbor who happens to be drinking vodka with tomato juice. For the moment, AI's best minds typically translate the words literally. Similarly, if you ask Siri to play "that song I liked so much yesterday," it will ask you to repeat your request over and again.

As he grew as a thinker, Wittgenstein perhaps noticed how pretentious his original approaches were and how the great questions of philosophy are not reducible to a structured set of logical propositions, but are instead an dialectical, interactive, social and at times controversial exercise.

Perhaps the lesson is that, to solve real problems, and even to communicate effectively, it is not enough to know the words and phrases of all the languages of the world, to know the equivalences between the vocabularies of different languages, but instead to really understand the meaning of situations and of other people's intentions. In fact, even the most developed fictional droids still fall short of our expectations. It seems as if C-3PO speaks nonsense, even though he knows the meaning of the words. We stop trusting him and even stop believing that what he is telling us makes sense. Language is a human phenomenon, very human.

## 4.4    What Makes a Robot Tick?

Artificial Intelligence (AI) has a precedent in classical literature, when Homer tells in The Iliad how Hephaestus, the blacksmith of the gods, sculpts two maidens in gold whom he endows with understanding and speech, to keep him company in his celestial but lonely forge.

In the modern age, we also know that many developments in artificial intelligence are aimed precisely at overcoming loneliness or homesickness. Among the recent innovations that have attracted widespread attention are chatbots, patented by Microsoft, which generate a digital reincarnation of people, living or dead, from social data—images, voice, posts or emails, among others. Some people find these chatbots disturbing; others see them as an opportunity to relive memories of loved ones.

The protagonist of Klara and the Sun, the 2021 novel by Nobel laureate Kazuo Ishiguro, is a modern version of a robot: sophisticated, kind, observant and gifted with understanding.[17] She belongs to the AA category, whose role is to care for the minors assigned to them. In Klara's case, she is chosen in the robot store by Jossie, a chronically ill girl, for whom she becomes a friend, companion and caregiver.

How do robots feel and think? Ishiguro does an outstanding job of making Klara the first-person narrator and describing her one-way feelings, strong sense of duty, her mathematical perception of the external world, her candor and absence of malice. As some of the characters comment, Klara has developed an exceptional sensitivity for her nature: Some other specimens of the AA class have a more superficial understanding, and those of the more evolved B3 class can be downright perverse.

There are two clear traits in Klara's behavior that can be seen as manifestations of machine learning. The first is a quasi-religious obsession with the healing properties of the sun on people and robots. She arrives at this belief by association with circumstances she has experienced, for example, her robot companions that are powered by solar energy; or the awakening of a homeless man she thought dead at the first rays of sunrise. These episodes capture Klara's imagination and lead her to the conviction that Jossie will be cured if she is exposed to enough sunshine.

Klara's other robotic trait is the logic that underpins her reasoning, sometimes with philosophical depth. Well into the novel we learn that Jossie's mother has bought Klara to become a clone of Jossie when she dies, to learn to move, behave and think as her daughter would. Fortunately, this never comes to pass, because of Jossie's solar healing, but what is interesting is Klara's reasoning about how illusory the replacement would be. She explains that even if she had learned to copy every facet of Jossie's personality, spoke and thought like her, there would be something special that was impossible to imitate. However, that special something was not within Jossie, which could be replicated, but was within the people who loved her.

Klara's concerns bring to mind Iris Murdoch's *The Sovereignty of Good* and the importance of our inner life in understanding the world.[18]

This inner world is what gives meaning to our affections, to the affection we feel for other people, and what makes it difficult, if not impossible, to simply transfer love from one person to another. There is always a certain solipsism in any relationship of affection, that the love we profess for others is requited.

The allegorical style of *Klara and the Sun* is reminiscent of Antoine de Saint-Exupéry's *The Little Prince*, where the eponymous character ponders on how unique affection for a singular person or thing is. The Little Prince has just encountered some roses, and realizes that "his rose" is not unique. Nevertheless, he turns to them and says: "*To be sure, an ordinary passerby would think that my rose looked just like you—the rose that belongs to me. But in herself alone she is more important than all the hundreds of you other roses: because it is she that I have watered; because it is she that I have put under the glass globe; because it is she that I have sheltered behind the screen; because it is for her that I have killed the caterpillars (except the two or three that we saved to become butterflies); because it is she that I have listened to, when she grumbled, or boasted, or even sometimes when she said nothing. Because she is my rose.*"[19]

## 4.5   Let's Not Forget: Robots Are Neither Good Nor Bad; They're Our Creation

Scientists and writers who speculate about the future of Artificial Intelligence (AI) and how it will impact our society usually foresee scenarios based on two extremes: utopias, where technological progress improves the quality of life for all; and dystopias, where the development of machine learning leads to repressive societies and much human misery, and perhaps even our extinction.

Our expectations of the future are in large part based on the assumption that machine learning will continue to grow exponentially in the coming years. Machine learning is the enhancement of autonomous forms of artificial intelligence not programmed by their designers, which together with deep learning—the nonlinear association of data and information—will create cyborgs capable of knowing, innovating and even sensing. This is a plausible argument, because experience shows that reality has always surpassed fiction, and that human ingenuity has created products that exceed our imagination.

The question on many people's minds is whether the computer overlords we're creating will be intrinsically good or evil.

Among the defenders of the prevailing goodness of artificial intelligence are Ray Kurtzweill, director of engineering at Google, Peter Diamandis, founder of Singularity University, whose motto is "*the best way to predict the future is to create it yourself,*"[20] and Peter Thiel, cofounder of PayPal.

Those who fear its potential results include Bill Gates, founder of Microsoft, Elon Musk, creator of Tesla, or Stephen Hawking.[21]

Max Tegmark of MIT explains that AGI (artificial general intelligence) is evolving at a speed that not even its creators could foresee. In the fictional story that opens his latest book, *Life 3.0*, a group of scientists create a prodigious machine, Prometheus, whose intellectual capacity grows exponentially as it functions.[22] In the early stages, Prometheus delivers global political and economic control for its creators, given the way that data and information controls and influences key decisions and value distribution. To keep Prometheus under control, its owners can disconnect it and thus prevent its access to external networks and uncontrolled development. However, through learning, Prometheus manages to overcome these barriers and achieve full autonomy from its owners, eventually taking over the world.

Tegmark's dystopian vision is disturbing, and recalls similar episodes in literature and cinema, such as HAL (Heuristically programmed Algorithmic computer) from Arthur C. Clarke's novel *2001: A Space Odyssey*.[23] HAL is the central computer in charge of managing all the vital functions of the Discovery spacecraft, and its behavior changes during the voyage.

What will make these machines become good, normal or evil intelligent beings? I believe it will depend on the moral disposition, or beliefs, of their creators. Since they are products created by human beings, they will try to project their image or likeness—to borrow from Genesis[24]— and will want to reproduce themselves intellectually through their inventions.

If humans want to propagate themselves through their works, and we are interested in anticipating whether the result will be good, bad or otherwise, perhaps we should take into account two great visions that philosophers have formulated about human nature.

For Jean-Jacques Rousseau, the father of Contractualism, man is good by nature and is only corrupted when he enters society.[25] His philosophy fueled the myth of the noble savage, the belief that humans who have grown up outside of civilization are innocent and pure. This model was recreated in novels such as *Tarzan* or *The Jungle Books*,[26] where the state of nature is the fullness of human life, and integration into society is a source of frustration. Society, in Rousseau's opinion, curtails the freedoms of individuals and increases inequality.

Rousseau's distrust of the benefits of the community can be explained by his life, which was a sequence of fiascos and contradictions. For example, he handed his own children to the care of a foundling hospital because his wife's family could not provide them with a better education, and argued constantly not just with his detractors, but his friends.

As mentioned earlier, for Thomas Hobbes, man is a wolf to man and it is only through law and the state's monopoly of power that human survival is guaranteed. The alternative to society is disorder and violence.

Hobbes' arguments were rooted in history. He lived through the nine years of the English civil war that began in 1642 and fled to Amsterdam with other supporters of King Charles I, where he wrote his classic work *Leviathan*.[27]

If humans have an inclination toward perversion or evil, so will their creations. HAL is regarded as the archetypal evil robot who over time takes over the mission and decides to dispense with the crew.

Hal's behavior is alarming, given that one of the key attributes of any form of intelligence, artificial or otherwise, is survival, and in case of conflict with other life forms would opt for its own survival. Technically, moreover, they would be tougher than fragile human beings.

A third view could be that technology is morally neutral. Robots are neither angels nor demons. As Daniela Rus, Director of the MIT Computer Science and Artificial Intelligence Lab, explains, "*It is important for people to understand that AI is nothing more than a tool. Like any other tool, it is neither intrinsically good nor bad. It is solely what we choose to do with it. I believe we can do extraordinarily positive things with AI, but it is not a given that it will happen.*"[28]

From an analysis of two differing interpretations of human nature, provided by Rousseau and Hobbes, we should ask which is the closest to reality. For example, why not ask yourself about the legacy you would like to leave behind. When you think about who should replace you in your position, would you try to select better people than yourself?

## 4.6    The Remote Working Debate: It's Not Just About Productivity and Convenience

In our ever-expanding knowledge economy, a growing number of tasks no longer require people to be in a specific place or time. Additionally, the past pandemic has changed the workplace, as well as professional relations, irreversibly. This has resulted, for example, in companies have moved their meetings and interviews to the virtual environment, so that almost all activities can now be carried out online.

Therefore, a relevant question facing employees and employers is: Which is the most efficient and sustainable hybrid environment, combining teleworking and attending the office, to ensure productivity, security and durability?

First of all, before deciding whether to work remotely or to continue spending our week in the workplace, we must be happy with our work, regarding it as an opportunity for personal and professional development, and also enjoy collaborating with our colleagues at work. In this context of job satisfaction—although Gallup polls show that the majority of people are dissatisfied with their jobs[29]—absenteeism is still rare, while measures to force people into the office are counterproductive.[30]

Studies show that most people's ideal situation is to telework at least part of the time. The proportion varies according to the circumstances, ranging from one to three days of working from home and two to four days in the office.[31] Obviously, positions requiring face-to-face contact with customers or other stakeholders, as well as jobs in infrastructure, maintenance, representation and senior management, typically demand more time in situ. My experience suggests that younger generations seem more predisposed to teleworking, perhaps due to their familiarity with relationships in digital environments. Similarly, people who live far from the office, or in large cities, appreciate working from home.

In any event, recent research shows that once telework is implemented in an organization, making it mandatory is preferable to keeping it voluntary.[32] When teleworking is optional, it tends to benefit employees who continue working from the office, supposedly reflecting their dedication and commitment and enhancing their career opportunities.

The experts say that there will be fewer business trips and in-person attendance of conferences in the postpandemic period.[33] Similarly, a significant percentage of in-company meetings will continue to be held on digital platforms like Zoom and Teams. Some companies have started using online meetings as part of a strategy to help break down silos between departments, encourage integration within the organization, as well as fostering innovation by inviting coworkers from other units.

That said, online meetings do not provide the basis for the kinds of informal exchange that often take place during face-to-face meetings. In response, some companies are now organizing meetings with a social component, inviting a wider range of stakeholders to take part as a way to share knowledge and information, create cross-cutting opportunities and structure the organizational culture.

Traditionally, attendance has been an important part of how our performance has been measured, starting with clocking in and out. But as the digital revolution spreads, performance can now be measured better by activity completion, goal achievement or impact measurement. However, older generations still attach special significance to their time in the office. But if a physical presence is no longer important, innovative systems of continuous performance appraisal will have to be developed and more timely objectives will have to be set.

Nevertheless, we should remember that for many people going to the office every day means provides an opportunity to talk face-to-face with colleagues, as well as being able to share information and news. If we are no longer going to spend our days in the office, we will need to improve internal communication through effective channels.

Similarly, remote working means a greater need for in-company training programs to update knowledge and develop skills, as well as to foster greater corporate identity, while helping to disseminate the culture and values of the organization.

Finally, working from home may be more comfortable and facilitates a better work-life balance, but it can also produce the opposite effects: more stress, a sense of detachment, and even isolation and depression. Organizations need to think about implementing health and well-being programs.

During the pandemic lockdowns, we have seen how it is possible to work from anywhere (WFA).[34] From now on, we could think about spending part of the year in a completely different location, provided we have good connectivity and for those with families, educate our children partly online. Can you imagine spending the winter in South Africa and the summer in Iceland?

## 4.7    Why Have So Few Philosophers Written About Work?

Given how it shapes our lives, it is perhaps surprising that so few philosophers have given much thought to work. And the few that have, they have tended to look at the values and principles we bring to our jobs, or the way labor is organized and implemented, rather than its impact on our personal development. Left-leaning philosophers like Jean-Paul Sartre have explored work in relation to the means of production. Sartre argued that the *"golden age of work for philosophy" was due to the "tenacious presence, from my viewpoint, of the working masses, that huge and grim body that lived Marxism."*[35]

Simone Weil, the French mystic, social philosopher and political activist, also criticized the lack of interest in the topic in classical philosophy: Writing in the 1930s, she noted: *"A philosophy of work has yet to be created. It is perhaps indispensable. It is perhaps more particularly needed in this age."* She added: *"Art/science/work/philosophy first. Plato said no more than half."*[36]

Weil's ideas are particularly interesting at a time when traditional large companies are struggling to attract and retain talent. As seen in the previous section, in today's digital and knowledge economy, there are any number of occupations where we no longer need to go to an office to do our job, at the same time, more and more companies are holding meetings in virtual environments, thus increasing productivity while saving time and costs.

Teleworking is about flexibility, which is why more and more people working in professions who can, are moving out of expensive cities either to smaller towns or the countryside, where they can purchase a bigger property and enjoy a better life.

In my interviews and conversations with executives from several large and medium-sized companies, I realized that most companies have kept some form of teleworking: Employees have returned to the office, typically working from home for one or two days a week, but with plenty of flexibility.

Proponents of teleworking say it could reduce the working week, giving us longer weekends or shorter working days. But the trade-off is that employees tend to spend more time connected to the office, even outside traditional working hours. So while working from home can improve the work-life balance, giving us more time with our families, it can also blur the boundaries between work and our private lives increasing stress, producing feelings of detachment and isolation, and even depression.

Furthermore, I would argue that working online deprives us of those vital informal connections, unplanned conversations, surprise meetings, spontaneous comments and essential exchanges that only occur in the workplace. Work is a social activity, and all those face-to-face encounters spread knowledge, foster camaraderie, strengthen corporate culture and can help identify new business opportunities.

One of the concerns managers have shared with me during recent interviews is the effect of the pandemic on attracting and retaining talent; the so-called *Great Resignation*, which has seen huge numbers of professionals quit their jobs. First detected in mid-2021, it coincided with the lifting of lockdown in the United States, a country that still enjoys close to full employment. Analysts initially associated this exodus with the rise of entrepreneurship and freelancing, a result of the experience of many professionals of working from home, being able to interact directly with suppliers and clients online, as well as taking initiatives on their own account.[37] Certainly, in confined situations, dealing face-to-face with bosses or subordinates was impossible, and decisions had to be made independently, which increased people's sense of autonomy.

However, closer observation and examination reveals other priorities than the work-life balance. A 2021 Pew Research Center study showed that the four most important reasons for the Great Resignation were low pay (63%); lack of promotion opportunities (63%); lack of respect at work (57%) and spending more time with children (48%).[38]

In light of these revealing results, it is worth offering some advice, both to individuals considering joining the Great Resignation and to companies experiencing it.

- *Advice to individuals*

First, it's a good idea to see one's career as a marathon, a long game, rather than a series of sprints. This allows us to make decisions based on the values that we want to shape our personality. Sometimes they will lead us to adopt significant changes; at others to remain in a company for long periods, even for life.

Let me use a personal example. Years ago, when I graduated, I became an associate professor of Philosophy of Law at Madrid's Complutense University. Initially, I saw my career panning out with the institution, but after returning from doctoral studies at Oxford University and finding, on more than two occasions, that I had no chance of rising up through the ranks, I decided to change careers and do an MBA. I was extremely fortunate to be recruited by IE Business School, where I have stayed for the last three decades.

Loyalty to the company has its rewards, as long as there is reciprocity. For some reason, many young professionals believe that if they aren't promoted every three years, it is better to leave the company. Some organizations, especially in consulting and auditing, have enshrined this as a rule, and their employees are obliged to go along with it.

But research shows that, statistically, the majority of CEOs in the United States and Europe have worked in at most three different companies, and a quarter have always stayed with the same one.[39] This shows that in many cases the most valuable people for a company are those who recognize its corporate culture, the values of its stakeholders and who have developed a valuable network of contacts within their industry.

It's best not to take oneself too seriously, and to cultivate personal modesty. Humility is not a reflection of lack of ambition, it is closer to the truth than hubris. We have all been hurt at some time by comments about our performance, or about our ideas, mainly due to misunderstandings and overreactions. In some cases, I have seen people resign or threaten to because they felt offended. I have always thought that such pressures can only be applied once, and with one's back well covered.

The truth is that we continue to learn throughout our careers, and the best attitude is to accept criticism and try to understand if there are objective reasons for feeling offended. The best recourse in these cases is to consult true friends, who will offer constructive advice. And above all, we should take decisions coldly, allowing ourselves at least 48 hours to mull the matter over; we may well see things differently once we have had time to think things over.

Innovative companies with ambitious missions, high growth rates, social commitment and a global presence attract the best talent. Generally these companies tend to be on sites such as *The Best Companies to Work For*, although their position on these rankings is not guaranteed unless they maintain their innovative drive. These organizations generate collective enthusiasm and inspire the passion of their employees and managers, in addition to having an attractive and original narrative.[40]

There is no doubt that salary increases and regular performance-linked pay improvements are a necessary prerequisite for talent retention, although on their own they not sufficient. It could be that the many financial and operational difficulties caused by the pandemic have made it difficult for many companies to pay their employees more. On top of that, the war in Ukraine has extended the previous crisis, sending inflation through the roof, further increasing the cost of living. Under these circumstances, and especially in competitive sectors or regarding key posts, failure to increase pay inevitably leads the most-sought after talent to look elsewhere. Good talent is always a scarce resource and this is a significant challenge for many companies, which are still recovering from the economic effects of the pandemic.

The best professionals, who look to expand their skills and play a key role in their companies, prefer to work for organizations where there is a career plan. These nurture good expectations, generate fairness in employee relations, along with a sense that merit will be rewarded.

Directly linked to the above, training programs, upskilling and reskilling, reflect the company's commitment to improving the employability of the workforce, generating trust and loyalty in return. Given the permanent change underway in every sector of the economy, both companies and employees need to know they can make a long-term commitment.

We often say that people are a company's most valuable asset. With the return to normality, and the migration resulting from the *Great Resignation* and subsequent similar trends, it is necessary for companies that want to retain their talent to move from words to actions.

## 4.8    Let's Remember That Education Is Not Just About Transferring Knowledge, It's a Journey

Imagine we were able to create a machine using AI that revolutionized education and personal development. Dubbed the *Educatron*, it is able in seconds to transmit knowledge that once took a lifetime to acquire.

Shaped something like an old telephone booth, with a burnished titanium exterior, there is a silent automatic door that gives access its interior. The device is operated digitally from an internal control panel and can impart all the knowledge contained in the world's libraries, including virtual ones, in about two minutes. In addition, the user can program the machine to teach five languages, four if Chinese is selected, in a few moments. Such is the rigor and extent of this newly acquired expertise that the user would be accepted at any university; in fact, some prestigious institutions have already signed contracts with the company that designed the Educatron.

What's more, the Educatron provides a painless learning process with no side effects. The company that has launched the device has not disclosed the technology behind the device, although it claims it has been exhaustively tested and is safe and reliable.

Imagine reading about this one morning over breakfast. Would you be interested in using this machine, knowing about its formidable and immediate effects, assuming you were able to afford it?

I sometimes put this fictitious case to my audiences at conferences. To my surprise, few people raise their hands when I ask who would use the Educatron, although I suspect this is due more to the fear of attracting public attention than risk aversion, since the typical profile of my audience tends to be composed of executives and entrepreneurs, more prone to adventure.

The Educatron might seem like science fiction, but we should remember that reality often surpasses fiction, and what we imagine can end up coming true if the right means are put in place. As Archimedes, the ancient Greek philosopher and scientist, used to say, with a sufficiently long lever and the right fulcrum, the entire globe could be moved.[41] The challenge with the Educatron would be to find the right lever and the right fulcrum.

In short, the Educatron does not yet exist, but its conceptualization brings it into the realm of the possible. Over the years, any number of novels and movies have anticipated reality by exploring the idea of immediate learning. From Ovid to Kazuo Ishiguro, it's clear that the literary imagination sometimes falls short, and that many of these inventions and fantasies are implemented with the advance of technology and the passage of time.

My inspiration for the Educatron was Woody Allen's Orgasmatron, one of the high points of his 1973 movie, *Sleeper*, set in a future world where people no longer engage in sexual intercourse and instead achieve satisfaction jointly in ten seconds through the aforementioned machine.[42] Allen never showed what went on inside, but moans and screams of pleasure could be heard, and the users emerged perfectly dressed, as if nothing had happened. From the plot of the film we can deduce that the use of the Orgasmatron has solved the problem of overpopulation while providing our descendants with a few moments of pleasure periodically.

The second question I usually ask my conference audience is about the idea of being able to acquire so much knowledge in such a short time.

Some reply that the Educatron misses the point of learning, the essence of the learning process. Making the effort to learn is a fundamental part of human happiness, our development and the formation of a personality. We study, attend classes and lectures because the experience of knowing, thinking and understanding is a demanding, but satisfying activity.

The so-called culture of effort, that is, the view that personal success and happiness depend on the individual, on the exercise of will, on the practice of habits that shape character and perseverance, has its advocates and detractors. As described in Part I of this book, those who are committed to equal opportunities emphasize effort as a fundamental factor in achieving personal goals. Those who believe that meritocracy and inequality impede social mobility detract from the value of effort, and think that not even the most willing are capable of achieving their goals. Both sides use facts and data as the basis for their diagnosis and proposals. As with other polarized debates, there are compelling arguments on both sides.

One of the earliest proponents of the importance of effort in education was Aristotle. In his *Politics*, writing about teaching children music, he notes: "*Now it is not difficult to see that one must not make amusement the object of the education of the young; for amusement does not go with learning—learning is a painful process.*"[43] Aristotle justifies the study of music not for its usefulness or for the purpose of practicing a profession—except in the case of musicians— but for its contribution to the development of character and to enable young people to enjoy their leisure time in a better way. His point is that all learning requires effort, especially in the early stages of a discipline or career, not that the learning process is fundamentally painful in and of itself.

The learning curve illustrates this very well: When we start studying, for example, a new language, we need to spend a great deal of time and effort, but, as time passes and we acquire more knowledge and skills, the amount of effort required decreases until the next stage begins and the process is once more arduous and we have to spend more time on it. We have all experienced difficulties when starting a new course, until a moment comes when we become comfortable with the concepts being used. At that point, we feel satisfaction, a healthy sense of happiness with the knowledge acquired.

One of the most influential thinkers in the world of education was the American John Dewey, who is considered both an educator and a philosopher. Dewey's work can help us understand why devices such as the Educatron are no substitute for the learning process that takes place in schools or universities. For Dewey, the purpose of education is not solely and fundamentally to transfer knowledge, and much less to indoctrinate. Its fundamental purpose is to integrate us into society: "*the school, as an institution, should simplify existing social life; should reduce it, as it were, to an embryonic form.*"[44]

To achieve this, the educational environment must be a replica of what students will find after graduation. Dewey explains that education is a social process, and as such requires interaction with other individuals and the creation of relationships. Through an interactive methodology, one can learn as much from the teacher as from the other students. Therefore, education alone, or the acquisition of knowledge or even the development of skills, as could be done for example in a simulator, would not be sufficient to replicate the social life which takes place in the educational space.

This function of education and learning is also inferred from the teacher: "*The teacher is not in the school to impose certain ideas or to form certain habits in the child, but is there as a member of the community to select the influences which shall affect the child and to assist him in properly responding to these influences.*" This applies to the methodologies and the meaning of evaluation systems and examinations: "*Examinations are of use only so far as they test the child's fitness for social life.*"[45]

As in other sections of this book, I would like to formulate some takeaways from this analysis:

We live in an era characterized by quick, effective solutions. For example, we talk about knowledge pills, summaries and synopses to tackle the understanding of new concepts and ideas. So why reject the Educatron?

- First of all, there are many ways to learn. As opposed to a traditional, uniform and standard educational formula, new technologies and methodologies facilitate the personalization of learning. This is truly the challenge for educational institutions: the personalization of learning, how to adapt teaching to each student, to extract the greatest potential and develop each person according to his or her talents. The Educatron would simplify this process, unless it could also be adapted to the uniqueness of each user, something virtually impossible to pre-program.
- Secondly, one of the characteristics of genuine knowledge is access to the original sources of knowledge. The point of reading Shakespeare's plays directly, rather than the children's summaries of Charles and Mary Lamb, is to experience firsthand the emotions his language arouses, to work on one's own to makes sense of passages or words that stimulate new and unusual thoughts; producing experiences that are difficult to predict.[46]

You may have noticed that books in Kindle format have underlined passages, the most popular with readers. But surely you will bookmark different ones, and in any case, I imagine that you would not be satisfied with reading only the passages marked by others. What's more, any author worth their salt would not want their work to be encapsulated in a few quotations.

Similarly, while I think Blinkist-type reviews have their use, which I might consult in deciding which works to buy or read, the experience of reading the original work is unmatched by skimming a summary.

- Finally, you may have wondered why a college degree takes three or more years. My answer is that learning is a social process, one of sharing, discussing, agreeing or disagreeing. Furthermore, my experience is that knowledge, like good wine, matures with time, becomes more moderate, consistent and complete.

An analogy I often use to explain the ongoing, incessant, iterative nature of learning is the story of Odysseus in Homer's Odyssey. What gives meaning to the Greek hero's journey is not his arrival in Ithaca, his homeland, but his adventures during his voyage. It's the experiences, lessons, the setbacks and disappointments during study that contribute to the development of the personality, and to our life. As Dewey explained: *"I believe that education, therefore, is a process of living and not a preparation for future living."*[47]

# Notes

1. Heraclitus, *The Fragments of The Work of Heraclitus of Ephesus on Nature* (Whitefish, MT: Kessinger Publishing, 2007).
2. L. Freedman, *Strategy* (Oxford: Oxford University Press, 2015), p. 609.
3. https://www.merriam-webster.com/words-at-play/meaning-of-metaverse.
4. N. Stephenson, *Snow Crash* (London: Penguin, 2011).
5. https://www.newyorker.com/culture/infinite-scroll/facebook-wants-us-to-live-in-the-metaverse.
6. https://hbr.org/2021/10/microsofts-satya-nadella-on-flexible-work-the-metaverse-and-the-power-of-empathy.
7. T. Hobbes, *Leviathan* (London: Penguin, 2017).
8. E. Rostand, *Cyrano de Bergerac* (London, Penguin, 2006).
9. G.W.F. Hegel, *Outlines of the Philosophy of Right* (Oxford: Oxford University Press, 2008).
10. M. Ball, The METAVERSE, and How It Will Revolutionize Everything (New York: W.W. Norton & Co., 2022).
11. Byung-Chul Han, *La salvación de lo bello* (Barcelona: Herder, 2015), p. 27.
12. G. Hartman, *Thought* (Princeton, NJ: Princeton University Press, 2016), p. 5.
13. H. Putnam, "Brains in a VaT", In S. Bernecker & F. I. Dretske (eds.), *Knowledge: Readings in Contemporary Epistemology* (Oxford: Oxford University Press, 1999), pp. 1–21.
14. W.S., "Machine Learning Won't Solve Natural language Understanding", The Gradient, 7 August 2021 https://thegradient.pub/machine-learning-wont-solve-the-natural-language-understanding-challenge/.
15. A.C. Grayling, *Wittgenstein: A Very Short Introduction* (Oxford: Oxford University Press, 2001), p. 131–3.
16. L. Wittgenstein, *Tractatus Logico-Philosophicus* (introd. B. Russell) (Garsington: Benediction, 2019); and Philosophical Investigations (ed. A. Ahmed) (Cambridge: Cambridge University Press, 2010).
17. K. Ishiguro, *Klara and the Sun* (London: Faber and Faber, 2021).
18. Op.cit., part 3 of this book, n. 33.
19. A. de Saint -Exúpery, *The Little Prince* (London: William Heinemann Ltd., 1966), p. 68.
20. https://www.youtube.com/watch?v=1KxckI8Ttpw.
21. https://analyticsindiamag.com/10-well-known-personalities-fear-rise-artificial-intelligence/.
22. M. Tegmark, *Life 3.0: Being Human in the Age of Artificial Intelligence* (London: Penguin, 2018).
23. A.C. Clarke, *2001: A Space Odyssey* (London: Penguin, 2000).
24. Bible: Genesis 1:27.

25. J.J. Rousseau, *Of The Social Contract and Other Political Writings* (London, Penguin, 2012).
26. E.R. Burroughs, *Jungle Tales of Tarzan* (London: Penguin, 2015); R. Kipling, *The Jungle Books* (London: Penguin, 2013).
27. T. Hobbes, op.cit.
28. https://www.forbes.com/sites/robtoews/2020/12/13/8-leading-women-in-the-field-of-ai/?sh=282877035c97.
29. https://www.gallup.com/workplace/313313/historic-drop-employee-engagement-follows-record-rise.aspx.
30. P. Hemp, "Presenteeism: At Work But Out of It", Harvard Business Review, October 2004, https://hbr.org/2004/10/presenteeism-at-work-but-out-of-it.
31. https://www.ft.com/content/887085b5-00b7-44f4-832c-c8e9d5f9da5f.
32. https://static1.squarespace.com/static/5cfdf6cb8acf8600012f8920/t/60628737923dcc75455e10e9/1617069883400/WFH_Will_Stick_V7%2C+22+March.pdf.
33. https://www.wsj.com/articles/covid-19-pandemics-impact-on-business-travel-hitting-local-economies-11610879401.
34. https://hbr.org/2020/11/our-work-from-anywhere-future.
35. E. Bea (ed.), *Simone Weil. La conciencia del dolor y de la belleza* (Madrid: Trotta, 2010), Kindle, loc. 3283.
36. Ibid., loc. 3289.
37. https://www.cnbc.com/2022/03/22/great-resignation-continues-as-44percent-of-workers-seek-a-new-job.html.
38. https://www.pewresearch.org/fact-tank/2022/03/09/majority-of-workers-who-quit-a-job-in-2021-cite-low-pay-no-opportunities-for-advancement-feeling-disrespected/.
39. https://store.hbr.org/product/job-hopping-to-the-top-and-other-career-fallacies/r1007q?sku=R1007Q-PDF-ENG.
40. https://www2.deloitte.com/us/en/insights/topics/marketing-and-sales-operations/global-marketing-trends/2020/purpose-driven-companies.html.
41. https://www.jstor.org/stable/24540769.
42. *The Sleeper* (United Artists, 1973).
43. Aristotle, *The Politics* (London: Penguin, 1981), Book VIII, Part V.
44. J. Dewey, *Moral Principles in Education and My Pedagogic Creed* (Morham, ME: Myers Education Press, 2019), p. 39.
45. Ibid., p. 41.
46. C. and M. Lamb, *Tales from Shakespeare* (London: Penguin, 2007).
47. J.Dewey, op.cit., p. 41.

# 5

## Part 5: Honesty—How Should I Behave?

Is it possible to be evil, selfish, a hypocrite, to swindle and lie your way to being a millionaire, and at the same time project an image of virtuousness, honesty and generosity, to appear a model citizen? Plato asks a similar question in *The Republic*, a dialogue between Socrates and one of Plato's brothers, Glaucon, who argues that being virtuous is arduous and often not valued, while vice can go unnoticed by others and generate immediate benefits.[1]

To illustrate his point, Glaucon retells the myth of Gyges' ring. After a powerful earthquake, a shepherd discovers a cave where he finds a ring that renders him invisible when he puts it on. Initially, he considers the number of positive actions that can be implemented by taking advantage of his good fortune, since it grants superpowers. He could prevent theft, perform good deeds and correct some injustices. But instead, he travels to the city and, taking advantage of his invisibility, seduces the queen, with whom he conspires to assassinate the king.

At the end of the story, Socrates asks Glaucon what might dissuade the shepherd from acting justly, rather than for his own illicit gain. The argument Socrates makes is that the truth will out, and that when discovered it has a negative and indelible impact on one's reputation.

Plato's argument is not entirely convincing. For one thing, the justification he proposes for acting rightly is essentially one of caution, and lacks the force of a genuinely moral justification. If it could be shown that most people who act immorally get away with it and are not found out or denounced, the Platonic argument is weakened. There are cases of corporate scandals in which the guilty lost their reputations and their wealth. Perhaps the best known is Bernard Madoff, who, after defrauding his clients of $65 billion through a

S. Iñiguez, *Philosophy Inc.*, https://doi.org/10.1007/978-3-031-20483-8_5

Ponzi scheme, died in prison at the age of 82. A judge even denied him permission to be released for humanitarian reasons. His family also experienced misfortune. His eldest son committed suicide and his other son died of cancer. His brother Peter was sentenced to nine years in prison and his wife dispossessed of his entire fortune. However, while the Madoff case shows that white-collar criminals sometimes suffer punishment during their lifetime, we also know that in many other cases they live to enjoy their ill-gotten gains.[2]

In any case, as we have seen in several passages of this book, the reasons for trying to be a good person are the result of combination of prudential approaches, appealing to the likely consequences of one's conduct, but also to a sense of duty, or to the attractiveness of a virtuous life. This chapter addresses the question of why it is makes sense for managers to behave ethically.

## 5.1   What Makes the Best Strategic Mindset: Business First, or Ethics Above All Else?

Over the past 25 years, I have had the enormous good fortune to teach a course on Strategic Management at IE Business School. Thanks to my contact with my MBA students and managers attending executive programs, and in recent years with participants in our Global Online MBA—which is delivered through a hybrid model, alternating synchronous sessions, in person or by videoconference, with asynchronous sessions in a forum format—I have learned a lot, arguably more than they have from me, particularly how to better understand and use analytical tools, exercise critical thinking skills, and the art of developing a strategic vision.

Over the last quarter of a century, many strategic analysis tools have been perfected and used for decision-making in companies. At the same time, as companies continue to undergo transformation, many other models, paradigms and concepts have also emerged. As in most areas of academic knowledge, golden rules and best practices have been consolidated, while many assumptions and received wisdoms have been discarded.

The traditional foundations of strategic analysis are still valid, which is why most strategy courses focus on them. First of all, companies and managers must have the will to win. Mere survival, sadly the most frequent reality for many companies during the pandemic, does not encompass strategy. In contrast, a winning attitude means achieving different objectives for a company, such as becoming a sector leader, being the most innovative, having the largest market share or achieving the biggest geographical presence.

Companies must embrace the reality of operating in a constantly changing environment, which often means questioning beliefs or even dropping them. There's no denying the value of experience and intuition, honed over time, but evolution and disruption forces us to rethink the validity of convention. Think, for example, of the impact of the new hybrid work environment, new ideas about the office, the relationship between workers and the company, or the shift regarding how globalization now functions.

Another important aspect of strategic analysis is the need for stakeholders to behave rationally, and therefore predictably. If managers make decisions without thinking them through, then no amount of strategy will help. At the same time, decisions based on altruism or that prioritize respect for the environment at the expense of short-term profit may be justified on the basis of long-term profitability, reputational returns or customer loyalty.

However, as we have seen in Part 3 of this book, some of the assumptions behind strategic analysis are open to question. For example, that the behavior of stakeholders conforms to the rationality paradigm.

In the first session of my strategy course, I also discuss a number of key questions with my students that have a philosophical underpinning. For example, defining in some way the commitment of managers to certain ethical principles, a sort of Hippocratic oath encapsulated in a synthetic, clear, intuitive and universally accepted formula. Milton Friedman's classic assertion that the commitment of managers is to maximize the value of shareholder investment, nothing more and nothing less, is questioned by most students.[3] They all recognize the fiduciary commitment of managers to the owners of a company, and their duty of loyalty to them, but they also open up another set of perspectives that are part of what is now understood by good management. For example, the link with the ideal of sustainability, taking into account the social impact of a company's activity, and in general the search for a balance between the competing interests of stakeholders.

Another question I raise is based on the dilemma posed by Machiavelli in *The Prince* as to whether a manager should be either feared or loved.[4] Some of my students answer that it is preferable to be respected, an option that seems to elude the question: Respect is sometimes based on a combination of fear and love.

In any event, a balanced reading of The Prince provides a less diabolical interpretation of what has traditionally been attributed to Machiavelli. His purpose was that heads of state must have the support and respect of their subjects.

Another classic, and often cited by business leaders as providing unique insight into strategic analysis is *The Art of War*, attributed to the fifth-century

BCE Chinese military tactician Sun Tzu.[5] Reprinted every year, it's to be found on many bookshelves, albeit often unread.

Works such as *The Prince* or *The Art of War* are guides on how to conduct oneself in strategic, competitive contexts, and are not moral guides. The world of business has its own specific rules, as is the case, for example, with the gaming environment.

For example, many of Sun Tzu's maxims are easily recognized by most managers. "*A great strategist communicates nothing before its time.*"[6] Applied to business, the key question, in my opinion, this means what is meant by the right time to announce something, for example the launch of a product, the purchase of a company or the decision to enter a new market. We shouldn't forget the importance that Steve Jobs, the cofounder of Apple, placed on secrecy in the run up to the launch of the iPad or the iPhone. The drama of this secrecy was part of Apple's marketing strategy, which gave a great deal of prominence to the on-stage presentation by Jobs himself.[7]

That said, I don't believe in waiting until every aspect of an initiative is tied up before announcing it. Sometimes it can be advantageous to anticipate the launch of a product or service even if it is not yet fully configured. Recent events have shown us that the race between different multinationals to offer effective vaccines against COVID-19 has been, to a large extent been about communication.

Another piece of advice is: "*In battle, victory must be quick.*"[8] The key question here relates to how one interprets victory, or as a consultancy firm might ask: "how would you define success?" Perhaps this could be answered as something like "in quantifiable and measurable terms in an expeditious time." Victory is not about annihilating the competitor, because, as Sun Tzu explains in a later chapter, preserving the system and avoiding total confrontation is necessary for the survival of the contenders.

The issue here is about the advantages generally associated with time to market, the lead time a company has for being the first to act. Being a frontrunner means, for example, being able to develop experience curves, reduce operating costs, increase volume and generate the virtuous circle that can lower prices and increase market share.

Being a pioneer does not imply being governed solely by a preordained plan. Sun Tzu says one must be the first to arrive on the battlefield, but also that victory is achieved when one has the ability to change and to cultivate what Sun Tzu calls "mystery," perhaps referring to the magical characteristics of leaders, which gives them control over their people.[9]

Sun Tzu also writes that controlling a large force is the same as controlling a few men: It is merely a question of dividing up their numbers. As with most aporias, the theory is fine, the practice is more difficult. It is attractive and suggestive, because leading small groups includes those involved more closely, is more entrepreneurial, and possibly generates better results.

However, if we divide the top management of a large company into small groups in search of these desired effects, how many people would report directly to the CEO? Logic and experience dictate that the greater the number of people reporting to the CEO, the harder it is to coordinate and involve managers.

One of the key challenges facing large businesses is matching the advantages of a broad structure, covering all management functions—with diversified activities and a presence in different sectors and countries—with the dynamism of a start-up. Some organizations separate some of their divisions and give them autonomy to innovate. Would Sun Tzu's approach of dividing activities into smaller groups result in more diligence, inventiveness and excellence?

In another passage, Sun Tzu states: *"No ruler should put troops into the field merely to gratify his own spleen; no general should fight a battle simply out of pique."*[10] Sadly, international current affairs offer us situations in which some leaders seem motivated by just such primal instincts. In the business world, hot-tempered reactions are usually restricted by the checks and balances of corporate governance. That said, we've all seen managers make decisions in the heat of the moment, based on their opinion of other people, often on the basis of misunderstandings.

As I have commented on several occasions, misunderstandings, especially when put down in writing, are often at the root of disputes in companies. Overreacting can often result in undesirable and unforeseen problems. *"Every intelligent man is prudent. Every good general is careful,"*[11] explains Sun Tzu. Recommendation: If you are not calm when making contentious decisions, it is better to hold off until you are.

As with The Prince, it's best to read The Art of War judiciously. The aim is not to apply its maxims to the letter, but to gain inspiration so as to improve our strategic vision.

The best way to define the strategist, according to Sun Tzu, is as a "master of deception," because in war, as in business, very different rules apply than those we follow with friends and family, or with those to whom we have a professional commitment, such as stakeholders in our company.[12]

To better explain this divergence between business, professional, and moral issues, I usually refer to the following two levels:

- *The business case.* This is when we make decisions based on reasons related to profitability, to efficiency, to the success of an initiative and in general to the growth of the company and its sustainability. Building an institution, or in Machiavelli's case a state, means addressing complex dilemmas, often having to choose the lesser of two evils, or sacrificing the interests of some in favor of the organization. In general, the business case is usually utilitarian, based on the consequences or results of actions, which is why works such as The Prince or The Art of War are popular.
- *The moral case* is the justification of a decision or an action based on ethical criteria, which do not necessarily have to do with profitability, nor with its consequences. In its extreme expression, some would say "fiat iustitia, pereat mundus" (let justice be done and the world perish), meaning that sometimes the right decision can have devastating consequences.

It is desirable to seek a balance between the business case and the moral case, but often the two spheres conflict. The fundamental test of resilience will be to be able to justify the decision in the public arena with reasonable arguments, which, although controversial, can ideally convince the majority. We are in the realm of moral constructionism.

## 5.2    Kant and Appiah, Two Routes to Cosmopolitanism

Growing up, there was probably an atlas, a globe, or a map of the world at home that your parents would sometimes sit you down in front of to point out the continents, the oceans, or the capitals of this or that nation. For many of us, this childhood experience will have sparked a love of travel, inculcating in us a certain cosmopolitanism.

The origins of cosmopolitanism date back to antiquity: Diogenes of Sinope, an early Cynic, is cited as one of its precursors, although the first globe was not built until the sixteenth century, in the German city of Nuremberg.[13] Before that, although world views were partial, an adventurous and enterprising spirit led explorers and traders across oceans and continents to learn about different cultures and contact with other civilizations. Even then, distances and orography were not precisely reproduced, and much of the planet terra incognita.

The industrial revolution, followed by the conquest of the poles, literally broadened our horizons, opening up the world as never before. Jules Verne's

*Around the World in Eighty Days* followed the adventures of Phileas Fogg and his hapless companion Passepartout, launching the age of global travel.[14]

German philosopher Rüdiger Safranski believes the moon landing in 1969 and the subsequent images of our planet from space awakened in us a truly global awareness.[15] Today, heightened understanding of sustainability and the threat posed to life by the climate emergency have arguably strengthened our cosmopolitanism and the conviction that collective action is the only way to save the planet.

Cosmopolitanism refers to those of us who feel they are citizens of the world, part of the human race: We may identify with our place of birth, our culture, but this is balanced by a certain sense of belonging to a wider community.

In 1795, at the age of 71, the German philosopher Immanuel Kant wrote *To Perpetual Peace*, a proposal on how to end warring between the nations of the world.[16] Published as Napoleon launched his attempt to conquer Europe, the book epitomizes the cosmopolitan spirit and is one of the first calls for the creation of a global government, along the lines of today's United Nations. Kant argues that world peace requires two conditions: the replacement of national armies with a single global force; and the creation of international legislation applicable to all countries.

As we know, Kant's ideas have only been partially implemented: Military alliances such as NATO see themselves as global peacekeepers, and national armies still persist. At the same time, the multilateral organizations created in the last century such as the United Nations have a system of governance that prevents the effective resolution of military conflicts: the veto system of the countries that make up the Security Council. Even the European Union, the political structure with the greatest cession of sovereignty of its member states, has weights and counterweights that limit the scope of the most sensitive decisions, especially in the international arena.

From Kant's writing we can infer that there are at least three tendencies that drive a degree of moral progress, favoring a degree of global peace. First, the spread of democracy in most regions of the world—although in recent years the rise of populism has led some analysts to doubt whether we are facing an involution. Secondly, the civilizing power of world trade, which Kant described as the commercial spirit, which cannot coexist with war, and which prevails over time. This phenomenon has led me to repeat one of my favorite maxims: The best antidote to bad international politics is good business. And thirdly, the growing importance of public opinion, which two centuries after Kant predicted it, is a consolidated trend with the universal presence of social networks.[17]

One of the most interesting contributions to our understanding of cosmopolitanism has been made by the Ghanaian-born philosopher Kwame Anthony Appiah, professor at Princeton University. His book *Cosmopolitanism: Ethics in a World of Strangers*, is a classic that addresses many of the issues raised by globalism.[18] I will focus on two issues he addresses, the permissibility or condemnation of customs that may clash with the dominant ethical sensibilities of Western democracies, and whether there is a moral obligation to help disadvantaged individuals or communities in developing countries.

Appiah starts by recognizing cross-cultural diversity in customs, usages and practices in all kinds of social spheres, taking in the family, the community, politics, and the workplace. There are common principles, but the level of agreement is relatively generic. Beyond the "golden rule" that can be stated in terms of "do unto others as you would do unto yourself," many rights and duties, authorizations or restrictions, differ according to region or culture. One example is the treatment of other living beings, and what constitutes animal cruelty. Those who are not familiar with rodeos or bullfighting, for example, see these practices as obvious cases of mistreatment, reprehensible and doomed to disappear in an advanced society, whereas there would be greater divergence of opinion over banning farms or the consumption of meat.

There are many other examples of customs and norms that can be criticized from a Western perspective. For example, opposition to the death penalty, especially when carried out by stoning and for offenses that many do not consider crimes, such as adultery. Similarly, bans on homosexuality or abortion are considered by most people in Western democracies as anachronistic and unacceptable. What to do then, when a nation is locked into its ancestral customs and refuses to evolve?

In my experience, it is never advisable to adopt a paternalistic attitude of moral superiority. The evangelical phrase is particularly appropriate in this case: "*Let the person who is without sin cast the first stone.*"[19] Most countries, even the most democratically advanced ones, could be the target of many criticisms, for example of lack of solidarity with the rest of the world, and in recent times we have seen the rise of populism and collective irrationality even in supposedly civilized communities.

I would argue that among the most effective remedies to encourage a democratic and moral evolution of global society are those proposed by Kant. On the one hand, public opinion pressure has a decisive influence, and perhaps the most emblematic example is the suppression of apartheid in South Africa through international and corporate pressure.

In addition, trade and business relations are undoubtedly a catalyst for rationality, freedom and equality. In today's multipolar environment, where questionable barriers have been imposed on trade, the open flow of talent, and the promotion of orderly migration, there is an urgent need to encourage international bodies to re-establish free international exchange. Good business fosters profitable relations between peoples. This is by no means a question of reviving imperialist or colonialist initiatives, but instead of devising the best version of international economic integration.

Another question Appiah addresses is whether there is a moral obligation to help people in need in other countries. In his view, a cosmopolitan spirit entails such an obligation, but the relevant question is what degree of involvement it would entail. For example, the philosopher Peter Singer uses the metaphor of the duty to provide relief to our global fellow human beings.[20] Just as if we saw an accident victim in a ditch at risk of death, we would have an obligation to assist them, he explains, we have a similar duty to people at risk of death from hunger or starvation in other latitudes. Another American thinker, Peter Unger, takes this further, arguing that any citizen of an advanced society with the available resources has the duty to share their wealth with the poor, even if they are from other countries.[21]

Appiah, aware of the differences between peoples, weighs these arguments and tries to reach conclusions that are acceptable to the majority, for example, the heroic behavior of the missionary does not seem plausible today. In *The Theory of Moral Sentiments*, Adam Smith writes that a person "of humanity in Europe" would be moved to know that there has been an earthquake in China and that there many victims, but that if he had no other more personal and selfish concern, he would sleep peacefully that night. Indeed, remoteness from other communities makes us more insensitive to their problems or calamities, and although considering ourselves cosmopolitan citizens should move us to contribute to just causes outside the domestic horizon, for example in favor of the Ukrainian people, the sense of commitment and urgency is lesser than that we feel toward our relatives, friends or acquaintances.[22] The French philosopher Simone de Beauvoir illustrates this in *Les Belles Images*, where a mother prevents her son from watching news footage of a catastrophe on television, lest he be traumatized.[23]

Cosmopolitanism is a sentiment and an attitude that will continue to spread as the ideas Kant explored continue to evolve. This is where education can raise awareness of the predicaments of people in other countries. We do not live in a perfect world, but the least we can do is to work toward creating a more tolerant, integrated and just society.

## 5.3    Speaking Truth to Power: The Pros and Cons

An abiding illustration of the dilemma we sometimes face between indulging in flattery or speaking truth to power can be found in Hans Christian Andersen's moral fable *The Emperor's New Clothes*.[24] We all know the plot: The pompous ruler parades naked before the people, who cheer him on, convinced that he is wearing the finest suit made by the best tailors, but who in reality are fawning impostors. It takes a young boy in the crowd, in his innocence, to expose the truth and shout out that in reality, the emperor is in the buff.

Few of us are immune to flattery or adulation, and the powerful are no exception. Inevitably, it seems that the exercise of power, in both the public and private spheres, all too often confuses and blinds us to the truth, instilling vanity and even arrogance.

Some CEOs and other senior figures like to focus on the symbols associated with their position, insisting on protocol and receiving the reverence they believe they are due. This might be because lauding the CEO reflects well on the company: The prestige of bosses is in direct relation to the reputation of the institution they head; they are the face of the organization, and to a certain extent they and their post are inseparable. The problem arises when bosses believe these honors are being bestowed on them for who they are rather than for what they represent.

One situation where this overreaching pride is often displayed is when a CEO is introduced at a public event. Some expect a eulogy, laden with accolades, but my experience is that genuinely important people, by virtue of their position or track record, tend to need no introduction. In contrast, ambitious or recognition-hungry leaders tend to have long, detailed resumes, lingering on this or that achievement or position.

To be honest, I do not consider myself much of an example of humility, but I believe that one creates a better impression by being discreet regarding introductions. An early mentor of mine—who despite his many achievements always shunned praise—taught me that when one finds oneself the object of adulation, it's a good idea to ask: "who are they talking about?"

Similarly, if the person introducing you mispronounces your name, which happens to me frequently, or forgets some of your achievements or relevant positions, it's always best to avoid making a big deal and accepting that they were acting with the best intentions. Overreacting in these cases can backfire.

Interestingly, the pomp we often associate with senior positions is not only found in business or administration; there are many striking examples in the academic world. During my first year as president of IE University, I wanted to visit several colleagues from US universities to present our project and establish relationships. Logically, I did not expect them all to open their doors to me, and some politely declined my request. We were a young university and the academic world is generally conservative and not very receptive to newcomers. What shocked me most was the agenda prepared for me by the president's staff of a prestigious institution that explicitly stated, "11.00–11.05 am: Brief greeting at the door of the president's office." I still joke to this day with my personal assistant about the protocol on that occasion. Fortunately, over time I have been able to establish a closer relationship with that president, and eventually we even had lunch together.

As a result of that experience, I resolved to pay the same level of respect to everybody I meet, regardless of their status, and of course to avoid even the appearance of condescension that some people perceive in authority figures. Using our sense of humor always helps in these circumstances.

Unfortunately, I often do not have the time to respond directly to the requests or messages I receive, and instead I sometimes delegate to my colleagues. On other occasions, I respond directly, because I think it is a good idea, and even healthy, to maintain open communication channels with people inside and outside the organization, from different levels and generations, for example through LinkedIn.

Returning to the emperor's new clothes, and specifically to the question of how honest to be with one's boss, from a deontological perspective, in terms of best managerial practice, the answer should be: completely. After all, managers are employed to give their honest professional opinion, especially if they believe it is relevant to the company, even if it bothers the boss. It is a matter of compliance, of professionalism.

However, many of us know from experience that as a rule, bosses do not like to be disagreed with and take criticism, or opinions contrary to their judgment, especially if it occurs in a meeting with other people, badly. In general, bosses see contradiction as questioning their authority.

When I ask my students during the first session of my Competitive Strategy course at IE Business School's MBA program—who are usually executives with more than five years of management experience and from different countries—about the ideal attributes required of a CEO, one of the most frequent responses is that they should be a good listener. I think this indicates a desire for a more open approach on the part of their bosses, to be able to talk honestly with them. The response also reflects an understanding that decision-making requires listening to a wide range of views. As happens in other contexts where the highest authority does not have all the information or specific knowledge on a topic, and needs advisors, CEOs would clearly benefit from listening more and talking less.

After posing this question, I engage in a conversation with my students about whether they tell their bosses what they think in meetings or if they are encouraged to contradict the opinion of their superiors. There is always one participant who argues for the need to be candid and to be able to speak one's mind in a reasoned, polite manner, regardless of the consequences. However, most of them recognize that it is not easy to disagree with their bosses, let alone in public.

Benjamin Franklin, one of the fathers of American Independence, was in favor of caution and not speaking one's mind, because in his experience any kind of criticism always offends the recipient. Franklin was his newly constituted nation's first ambassador to Paris, and possibly his diplomatic experience led him to be cautious in form and words. Walter Isaacson explains in his excellent biography, that "*the older he got, the more Franklin learned (with a few notable lapses) to follow his own advice. He used silence wisely, employed an indirect style of persuasion, and feigned modesty and naïveté in discussions.*"[25] In his autobiography, Franklin explains that "*When another asserted something that I thought an error, I denied myself the pleasure of contradicting him,*" adding a recommendation to keep in mind when defending an argument, "*For these fifty years past no one has ever heard a dogmatical expression escape me.*"[26]

Franklin's restraint reminds me of an observation made by a coach who had worked for the CEOs of several Fortune 500 companies, who told me that, in his experience, negative feedback, even if it was constructive, justified and tactfully communicated, was usually turned down. Only in a very low percentage of cases, below 5%, did those who received it react positively and were grateful for it, demonstrating significant emotional intelligence on their part.

This is consistent with our own experience. We may say we want the unvarnished truth, and even beg our friends to correct us when we get something wrong, but let's be honest, criticism always leaves us feeling a little ruffled.

Isaacson explains that as he gained in his knowledge of people, Franklin understood the wisdom of developing his "*velvet-tongued and sweetly passive style of circumspect argument that would make him seem sage to some, insinuating and manipulative to others, but inflammatory to almost nobody. The method would also become, often with a nod to Franklin, a staple in modern management guides and self-improvement books.*"[27]

The possibility of contradicting or criticizing the boss, even if privately and well-intentioned, can be further complicated by cultural factors. One of the variables proposed by Geert Hofstede to measure cross-cultural diversity was "power distance," the set of characteristics that define the relationship between

bosses and subordinates, such as treatment, formalities, interaction in meetings and relationship protocols. Japan is arguably the benchmark for maximum power distance, while the United States and the Scandinavian countries
are examples of minimal power distance. Unsurprisingly, the culture in countries with shorter power distance encourages open debate, and even criticism
or dissent toward superiors.[28]

Validating Franklin's approach, contemporary studies show that going
along with one's superiors, even flattering them, can be good for one's career.[29]
On the other hand, relying exclusively on performance or personal worth is
no guarantee of promotion. Flattery may be better received by recently
appointed bosses, who may lack confidence and need support. In a crisis or
emergency, such as the pandemic we have been through, there is also an
understandable tendency to keep one's own council, for fear of losing one's
job. However, the research also reveals that serial sycophants are often criticized by their colleagues, something that can also eventually turn against them.

The results of this research, as well as my students' comments on the characteristics of a good CEO, suggest to me that flattery is not just an issue for
those lower down the food chain, and that at least half of the responsibility
lies with bosses themselves. Of course, the emperor shares responsibility for
his nakedness, even if he wants to blame others. It's the same with CEOs who
encourage flattery. On the one hand, they distort the nature of the debate at
management meetings, where "nothing personal, it's just business" should be
the guiding principle. In addition, the running of the company itself, the
objective examination of its performance, the identification of faults and their
causes, and the remedying of these faults are compromised.

In this respect, a particularly recommendable thinker is Niccolò Machiavelli,
whose mentioned *The Prince* has been a reference manual for many leaders,
including CEOs, over the last five centuries. His philosophy is an expression
of the absolute pragmatism required to stay in power, regardless of any moral
concerns. Therefore, his suggestions on how to obtain the best advice from
subordinates and avoid flattery are useful from a technical perspective, albeit
devoid of any deontological consideration:

Machiavelli explains: "*The only way to guard yourself from flatterers is to let
people understand that to tell you the truth does not offend you. However, when
everyone feels free to tell you the truth, respect for you goes down. Therefore a wise
prince ought to follow a third course by choosing the wise men in his state, and
giving to them alone the liberty of speaking the truth to him, and then only of those
things of which he inquires and of none others. However, he ought to question
them about everything, and listen to their opinions, and afterwards form his own
conclusions. With these counselors, separately and collectively, he ought to behave*

*in such a way that each of them should know that the more freely he speaks, the more he will be preferred. Outside of these, he should listen to no one, pursue the thing resolved on, and stick to his decisions. He who does otherwise is either beaten by flatterers, or is so often changed by varying opinions that he is laughed at.*"[30]

With experience and age, some managers can become closed to the ideas of others, although there are also impetuous and arrogant young leaders who refuse outside assistance. Machiavelli was right: Being open to the advice of the wise increases the chances of success in power.

## 5.4   Why Keeping One's Council Is Often the Best Course of Action

*When an artist cannot be attacked for his style or technique, his detractors will resort to personal attacks or spurious arguments.*[31]

This is how Giorgio Vasari, the sixteenth-century Italian biographer of Renaissance artists, explains the story of Francesco Botticelli's *The Assumption of the Virgin*, now in the National Gallery in London.

The painting was commissioned by Matteo Palmieri, a Florentine merchant later accused of heresy because he believed that in the course of the Biblical battle between the army of the Archangel Michael and the hordes led by Lucifer, a third group of angels declared themselves neutral.[32] These lofty non-aligned are supposedly represented in the painting along with the rest of the angels, something expressly condemned by the ecclesiastical authorities of the time, whose dogma made it clear that all those present at the celestial showdown had taken sides for good or evil, for all eternity. What were these "neutral" angels thinking? Couldn't they see which side would emerge victorious?

In contrast to events in heaven before the creation of the world, the evolution of earthly conflicts, especially over the last two centuries, has seen the development of the concept of neutrality. The United States was a pioneer in this respect with its declarations of neutrality in 1793 and 1794 during the European revolutions, as well as with the enactment of its *Neutrality Law* in 1818. Today, the position of nonalignment in the event of war is of international law and in the norms adopted by the United Nations.

Alfred Verdross, the renowned scholar of international law, argued that since the eighteenth century, wars have been conceived as duels between states, even if others supported them. Neutral countries were traditionally islands of peace and might act as arbitrators between disputants, and even benefit in terms of trade and finance for staying on the sidelines.[33]

The second half of the twentieth century saw the creation the "Non-Aligned Movement," in part due to the widespread belief that wars of aggression constitute a violation of international law, and therefore require a collective response from other states. That said, the inevitable internationalization of armed conflicts calls into question the viability of neutrality, which can be seen as encouraging warmongering countries to throw their weight about.

My interest in neutrality stems from its usefulness as an analogy for business. Battles between companies are common, an environment in which there are groups of stakeholders with diverse interests, limited resources and a permanent dispute for power and control.

Below I refer to three episodes that I have had the opportunity to experience first-hand, and which reflect business situations in which wars may arise, more or less open or declared, and in which one or more parties might adopt a position of neutrality:

- *Mergers are a common way to channel growth*, especially in highly competitive sectors. Some entrepreneurs overvalue mergers, failing to look ahead to the years of hard work involved. Mergers do not really occur at the time of the agreement, but only over time, when the two companies have been integrated, at least relatively successfully. Furthermore, experience shows there is no such thing as a fair merger, a perfect equilibrium between two parties. Over time, the shareholders or the management team of one of the companies always prevails. Until that victory is achieved, there is usually a power struggle, whether hidden or open.

A few years ago, I was given the inside story of the first years following the merger between two companies directly from their respective CEOs who consecutively led the merged organization, as well as senior executives. As typically happens with mergers, the management team of one of the companies ended up dominating the other. As with other situations where two parties have competing interests, the prospective narrative of some episodes and decisions differed, sometimes radically. For example, each of the CEOs recounted the merger as being their own idea, which had been opposed by the other CEO.

Outwardly, the merger was proceeding peacefully, but behind the scenes, there were major differences about strategy, vision, and many day-to-day aspects. Finally, a corporate governance incident anticipated the replacement of one CEO by another, as well as the replacement of most of the board members and senior management of the former's company. Interestingly, the winning management group did not belong to the smaller or less valuable company prior to the merger.

Under these circumstances, a small group of managers from the "losing group" considered remaining neutral in the face of these developments. In the view of the outgoing CEO, this neutrality—his exact words were "this betrayal"—helped the change in power and changed the direction of the company for the worse. In the opinion of the triumphant CEO, the consistent attitude of this group of managers who did not follow the dictates of their former boss promoted both a better climate within the company as well as the consolidation of the merger.

What became of the managers who remained neutral? Although some were subsequently promoted, most lost rank and visibility in the merged company, and a good number chose to move on. In the words of one: "It is very difficult to gain the trust of a boss when you have faithfully served your main enemy for years. And if you also betray the trust of your former boss, the new boss will always be wary of you being a repeat offender."

- *Another recurring instance of corporate belligerence are decisions to innovate and launch new products and services,* which can create two long-lasting camps over time, represented by the innovators and the conservatives. At the risk of generalizing, a relatively frequent organizational pattern is that commercial teams—especially when the products or services they sell are performing satisfactorily—often tend to be conservative, while marketing, operations or strategic development units are more prone to innovation, renewal and experimentation.

In many cases where there is tension between conservative and innovative departments—which is healthy because it promotes dynamism—the finance team often plays a neutral role. In interviews with CEOs from various industries, I have tried to understand the role of arbitrator that many of them give to the CFO to resolve these interdepartmental conflicts related to innovation or launching new initiatives, which always have budgetary implications. This intermediary role, or the CFO's neutral position, is often reinforced in times of budgetary restraint or adjustment.

In any case, there do not seem to be any functional aspects to CFOs' role or in their training or background that would indicate they make better negotiators or are more impartial than their colleagues in the C-suite. Their neutrality is sometimes mandated by the CEO, and my experience is that most CFOs tend to be conservative, a consequence of their obligation to optimally manage risk.

- *Family businesses, particularly when one generation is handing over to another,* are also subject to internal wars. It is difficult for family members to remain neutral under such circumstances, except in the more exceptional case of having no interest in the ownership or management of the company.

In these family struggles, professional managers from outside the family should remain neutral. Firstly, because on many occasions outsiders do not fully understand the seriousness of the confrontation, while those who have taken sides or are seen to have done so may be sidelined when a peace agreement is signed. We should remember that in family businesses, economic criteria are not the only basis for agreements. Feelings, sensibilities and emotions come into play, and this should always be remembered by outsiders.

Consultants from outside the company may appear neutral: When dealing with the company's executives, they usually emphasize their independent and disinterested position on the company's current affairs. But the truth is that most consultants are hired by the CEO or the relevant department head, in most cases with a clear mandate. My experience is that the clearer their mission is formulated in a particular project by the contractors in the client company, the greater the relative success of their work. Therefore, one cannot speak of neutrality in these cases, but rather of a specific mandate.

A different question is the role to be played by the board of directors of companies with a large number of shareholders, especially those listed on the stock exchange. In this case, we should speak of the board's function as guarantor of the interests of the shareholders and of the company's compliance with the law. A certain degree of independence is required to perform this function, and codes of good corporate governance are becoming increasingly demanding with regard to the duties of board members. However, this does not, in my view, equate to neutrality. Defending the interests of shareholders, or ensuring the sustainability of a company, requires a decided bias in favor of the winning team or proposals.

A number of practical conclusions can be drawn to better understand the advantages and disadvantages of neutrality in key situations within the company:

- First, it seems intuitive that adopting a broad vision about the company and being open to different opinions and teams is the dominant strategy. That is, a cooperative and systematically collaborative, rather than confrontational, attitude generates better aggregate results in the long run. However, this is not the same as maintaining a neutral position in the face of conflict.

Systematic neutrality is more likely to come over as amateurish or reflecting a lack of commitment.

- Second, although taking sides in key debates may be riskier than remaining neutral, it also generates greater chances of success, of promotion, in the event of being part of the winning group.
- Third, as seems obvious, the ideal is not simply to take sides, but to lead. The concepts of leadership and neutrality seem opposed. Neutrality connotes passivity, laissez-faire, abstention from judgment or opinion. Leadership implies initiative, action, will, courage. Leaders are only neutral when they are preparing for an assault on power.

In any case, as with other situations over the course of one's career or in one's personal life, the fundamental criterion for action is integrity and staying true to one's values. Sometimes the most consistent position with values is to remain impartial. However, the absence of an opinion or view does not seem sufficient justification for neutrality, since we live in an increasingly unpredictable, uncertain and changing environment. On the other hand, the risk of a third party incurring harm may be sufficient grounds for remaining impartial.

Did neutral angels deserve a place in Botticelli's painting? If they had existed, they would probably have played a relevant role, perhaps not so much in the conflict itself, but later, in recounting what really happened. Perhaps somebody has to stay out of the fray so as to objectively narrate the decisive episodes of history.

## 5.5  Pay Credit Where Credit Is Due and You'll Be Seen as a Better Leader

Few natural disasters have captured the collective imagination down the centuries like the eruption of Mount Vesuvius on August 24, AD 79. In the space of a few hours, the twin cities of Pompeii and Herculaneum were buried in ash or burned to the ground as they were showered with molten rock. Anyone who has visited the ruins of these Roman enclaves in the Bay of Naples cannot fail to have imagined the terror the victims buried there must have felt.

The best direct account of the cataclysm is contained in a letter from Pliny the Younger, who was with his mother and uncle—Pliny the Elder—at their home in Misenum, a small town at the northwestern end of the bay.[34] The first alert of the impending disaster was given by his mother, who noticed a large, unusually shaped cloud. Pliny the Younger explains, "*its general appearance can best be expressed as being like an umbrella pine, for it rose to a great hunk on a sort of trunk and then split off into branches.*"[35] The description is so accurate that to this day, eruptions with these characteristics are called Plinian.

Pliny the Younger's letter was in reply to a request from the historian Tacitus about the death of his uncle. Therefore, rather than detailing his own experiences and feelings, or how he dealt with the catastrophe, he recounts the last hours of his uncle, based on his own and other people's testimonies. He explains how Pliny the Elder, as soon as he saw the suspicious cloud and received a request for rescue from a friend in Pompeii, led the triremes under his command—he was commander of the Roman fleet—along the coast. Having reached his destination, he exhibited extraordinary calm, encouraging those around him. "*He was quite cheerful, or at any rate he pretended he was, which was no less courageous,*" wrote Pliny the Younger.[36] So calm that he even took a nap in the middle of the eruption.

After several hours exposed to the fumes and heat, Pliny says his uncle asked for a glass of water, and returned to the fray. His body was found two days later, intact, as though he had fallen asleep.

The courage of Pliny the Elder and his crews helped save the lives of a good number of Pompeiians. Archaeologists believe that most inhabitants were incinerated, despite the many corpses found in molds of lava that had enveloped and burned the victims.

After recounting his uncle's deeds, Pliny the Younger concludes his letter with the words: "*Meanwhile my mother and I were at Misenum, but this is not of any historic interest, and you only wanted to hear about my uncle's death. I will add no more.*"[37]

Historians wish he had expanded his report, providing more details about the eruption, an experience that some of his countrymen considered the end of the world. But his story focuses solely on his uncle's exploits, prompting Umberto Eco to write almost two millennia later: "One wonders whether Pliny the Younger would have preferred a reader who accepted the glorious conduct (merit of the Old Man) or one who understood the lionizing tale (merit of the Younger)."[38]

Leaving Vesuvius behind and moving forward to the present day, many of us will know someone who, when they tell a success story, whether personal or professional, give others the credit, playing down their own contribution: a noble, altruistic attitude, not unlike Pliny the Younger's.

Paying tribute to the people who have preceded us in a position or who have worked with us shows generosity and magnanimity, important qualities for leaders, albeit ones that are rarely recognized, perhaps because many people consider them a reflection of naivety. But I believe that praising others, especially our predecessors, exhibits a finesse that allows us to connect with people and generate greater empathy, while at the same time projecting authenticity and grace.

In contrast, the inability to praise, or taking credit for the efforts of others, makes colleagues wary. In my experience, it is a negative character trait that is quickly noticed by those around us. Given the speed with which we sum up and label people, a reflection of our defensive personality, failing to recognize the achievements of others or appropriating undue credit generates rejection and distrust in the workplace.

Sadly, praising our predecessors is rare, especially so by those who follow them into the highest positions in an organization. A characteristic of some newly appointed managers, which to me denotes a certain inferiority complex, is criticism or denial of what has been achieved prior to their arrival. I call this the Messiah syndrome, which in large and complex organizations is unfounded, unless the new manager comes in to resolve a truly chaotic situation. However, even then, if the entrants are smart, they will know that discretion is the better part of valor.

The clean slate approach, putting everything that has been done before on hold, is a healthy exercise that can help generate new ideas, stimulate innovation, question prejudices or preconceived ideas, as well as encouraging "out of the box" thinking. However, in large organizations, where tradition and inertia are powerful forces, newcomers should be wary of throwing the baby out with the bathwater. Few large companies have survived dramatic reversals of strategy.

Sigmund Freud believed that the Oedipus and Electra complexes drove young men and women to symbolically "kill" their fathers and mothers. In *Totem and Taboo,* he uses the examples of tribes that had established rules to contain parricidal and incestuous tendencies, in his opinion rooted in the sexual impulse. Freud's work has been questioned over the years, but in the organizational environment it is common for people promoted to senior positions to emancipate and dissociate themselves from their predecessors.[39]

Newly appointed CEOs often change the corporate logo or the mission and vision statements, along with the organization of the C-suite, as well as making their own new appointments. That said, such changes are often superficial, and everybody in the organization knows it.

At the other extreme is the Rebecca syndrome; anybody who has read Daphne Du Maurier's novel or seen Hitchcock's film of the same name will know what I mean.[40] In the movie version, Joan Fontaine marries Laurence

Olivier—a taciturn, widowed aristocrat by the name of Maxim de Winter. The newlyweds move into Manderley, the family home, but the second Mrs. de Winter is overwhelmed by her predecessor's imprint on the house, which is maintained by the intimidating housekeeper, Mrs. Danvers, who refuses to allow her new mistress to change anything, undermining her confidence at every turn.

Younger managers may undergo similar experiences, especially if they succeed a prestigious, recognized professional who has left a mark on their organization. The important thing is not to give importance to any feelings of insecurity, which are normal, and above all avoid trying to emulate their predecessors, and much less to try to annul their memory.

"*Gratitude is the sign of noble souls,*" wrote Aesop.[41] In the long run, this approach always results in better personal development and recognition of leadership by those around you.

The eruption of Vesuvius in AD 79 took place the day after the feast the Romans celebrated in honor of Vulcan, the god of fire; a macabre coincidence. In those days, people hung their clothes under the sun, symbolizing the theological connection between Vulcan and the sun, lit candles at night to perpetuate the fire and continued the revelry with wine and food. The only consolation we are left with is that the victims of the eruption at least enjoyed life on the eve of its extinction.

## 5.6  What Schopenhauer Can Teach Us About Respect

We may not like to admit it, but the fact is that most of us care about other people's opinion of us; it's inherent to life in society. We may sometimes wish we lived in a bubble, but since we are fundamentally social animals, we accept that our identity and reputation are formed through contact with our fellow human beings.

The judgment of third parties about our worth, our merits or our performance is decisive at key moments in our personal and professional lives. Friends who recommend potential partners, talent managers who decide on a job, bosses who evaluate their professional colleagues and how much they're going to be paid in their new position, panelists who decide the winners in competitions, and countless other situations are not only assessed on measurable facts, but also on the prestige we project, on the opinion others have formed of us or that someone has passed on.

I'm sure that from time to time you've asked trusted colleagues or close friends for their opinion on something you have written, their verdict on a presentation, or an assessment of a decision you are considering making.

But if you were to ask somebody you trust about their general opinion of you, assuming they would answer honestly, how would they rate you on a scale of 0 to 10, from worst to best, compared to other people they know?

Obviously, our happiness shouldn't depend on such a summary evaluation and, in fairness, it would be futile and even perverse to issue an appraisal of people in such terms, as if it were an abbreviated final judgment. Gauging the quality of a person is a nuanced exercise, and a good friend would rarely venture to formulate such a diagnosis. Nor would I recommend that you put them in that position.

However, despite the complex and even unfathomable nature of our personalities, we still make judgments about others on an ongoing basis, educationally, professionally, politically, socially and emotionally. In addition, we also ask other people for their opinion about a mutual acquaintance.

CEOs and senior managers are particularly reluctant to ask others for an overall assessment of their personality. Doing so, many believe, would expose their vulnerabilities, and bosses must project security and full self-confidence. But this kind of solipsism in senior positions can also generate a vicious circle, leading to distancing and a certain cognitive dissonance on the part of CEOs, which is sometimes alluded to as the loneliness of leaders, but which is really the result of self-isolation. In my experience, one of the most frequent reasons why boards of directors hire a CEO coach is to help them avoid the ivory tower syndrome.

Many organizations practice 360° feedback involving people from different areas, but its scope and effectiveness has been questioned, as well as the undesirable effects it can produce.

Some years ago, a colleague with extensive experience in management coaching, who has taught at several prestigious business schools, told me that, from his experience, less than 10% of us know how to accept negative feedback and draw conclusions for personal improvement. Unfortunately, vanity, resistance to change, stubbornness, mistrust and even fear cause most of us to ignore such advice, even if they openly accept it.

On the other hand, although we ask others their opinion about our behavior or works, many times we do not want to know the truth, we seek acquiescence and praise. When we fall short of our expectations or fail in some endeavor, we do not want them to compound our disappointment.

Among the many works of Arthur Schopenhauer is a short treatise entitled *On the Art of Being Respected*, a compendium of maxims on honor and respectability.[42] The German philosopher argued that: "*honor is the opinion that others have of us, and especially the general opinion of those who know something about us. And more specifically still, it is the general opinion of those who are qualified to give an opinion about us, who know our worth in any respect worthy of consideration.*"

I'm not sure how one would go about identifying the right person to give an opinion about someone. If we were asked to select such a figure, we would probably think of our parents, spouses, children and close friends, who generally adore us.

In many situations, however, we are under scrutiny by more detached people, and as a result, their assessment is likely to be more neutral. Their opinion is especially relevant because, as Schopenhauer explains, it determines decisions that affect us and their own behavior toward us.

To illustrate how an opinion about someone is formed, Schopenhauer turns to the Spanish Golden Age thinker mentioned elsewhere in this book, Baltasar Gracián, who insisted that "*things do not happen because of what they are, but because of what they appear to be.*"[43] Appearances, as many think, are the basis on which we form a judgment about others. After all, we still do not possess the means to know what is really going on inside other people's minds when they act. The problem with judging by appearances is of course that they can be false. In response, Schopenhauer explains that "*a false appearance may deceive someone, but it will hardly ever deceive everyone,*" a belief I share, although one sometimes suspecting that the time it has taken to see through somebody has been used by the deceiver.[44]

Schopenhauer distinguishes between honor and fame. The former is made up of the qualities that others expect of us, which most of us possess, and therefore, we are "no exception" to the majority of people, about whom a similar degree of honorability is presumed and taken for granted. Therefore, in this sense, it takes on a negative character.

However, fame is of a positive or proactive nature, because it denotes attributes others lack.

It is remarkable that Schopenhauer, who wrote his book at the height of the Romantic period, rejected the chivalric notions of honor that led many of his German contemporaries to settle disputes by means of duels. For Schopenhauer, honor has a fundamentally practical meaning, for example in the professional sphere: It is the opinion that others have of us.

Understood in the sense proposed by Schopenhauer, honor provides us with that assumption of trust that others have in us, the minimum required to participate in society, maintain personal and commercial ties or develop a profession.

Needless to say, honor is reciprocal in nature, and to the extent that we arouse respect in others, others will also expect us to be worthy of their trust. Most social institutions are based on this ideal of mutual trust, of the presumption of honor. The guarantee offered by honor is enormously profitable, and is the basis of any personal or professional bond. Logically, this honor can increase or decrease depending on the vagaries of a relationship.

Schopenhauer's idea of honor may seem outdated, which is why some business schools prefer to focus on fame, which is arguably closer to excellence. Attempts are made to identify and teach the paths toward fame, related to tangible achievements such as acquiring money, power, position and awards, as well as distinction in certain skills like intelligence, eloquence, honesty, generosity, or our impact on the environment by creating companies or civic alternatives.

However, there can be no fame without first gaining the respect of others.

Building honor is a task we must undertake alone, depending on our circumstances, our vision of the world, values and ideas about relationships. Schopenhauer explains that the idea of honor that others have of us is immutable, regardless of whether we change, provided of course that we do not disappoint others' idea of who we are.

So what can we do to safeguard our honor?

- Since appearances are so important, minding our manners plays a vital role in the opinion that others form of us. Politeness, humor, and a willingness to openly recognize the achievements of others, while avoiding flattery, will strengthen the reciprocity mentioned above.
- Being positive in our relationships, with a wide range of people, will garner the best personal and professional results, and will strengthen our prestige with other people. Dividing the world into friends and enemies is a mistake and tends to make us more unhappy, as well as weakening our honor and undermining our chances of achieving fame.
- Avoiding misunderstandings prevents friction in relationships with others, both at work and in the private sphere. Many interpersonal conflicts arise from errors that, if cleared up quickly can help instill trust and friendship with those around us. In particular, written misunderstandings can be the most destructive: It is best to resolve them face to face.

Charles de Gaulle is attributed as having said: "*There can be no prestige without mystery, for familiarity breeds contempt.*"[45] The general was right in the sense that in order to maintain leadership, given the importance of appearances, it might be preferable reveal something of one's inner workings than one's defects. But as Schopenhauer explained, in the final analysis, honor will always shine through.

## 5.7    Where to Draw the Line on Lying?

"*Lie is so unmusical a word*," muses Downton Abbey's caustic Dowager Lady Grantham—played by the brilliant Maggie Smith—when challenged on the veracity of one of her judgments.[46] Nobody likes being called a liar, although the data suggests we lie more than we admit.

And while the Oxford Language Dictionary is clear enough on the matter: "*to say or write something that you know is not true,*"[47] we have come up with any number of euphemisms to justify or mitigate our untruthfulness. There are "white lies," when our intentions are good; "half-truths" to back up less-than honest statements; "whoppers" to reinforce the scale and impact of a full-scale deception; similarly, we can be "economical" with the truth when seeking to avoid a full and frank explanation of events; which others might simply dismiss as "bullshit"; along with myriad other categories of falsehood, all with their own subtly aggravating and extenuating interpretations.

The profusion of terms to designate what are simply lies not only confirms our capacity for complex mental acrobatics, but also exposes the assiduity of our mendaciousness. A well-known study by US psychologist Robert S. Feldman shows that we lie on average of two or three times every 10 minutes.[48] That may seem shocking, but only because we lie to ourselves about it. The reasons are varied: the need to express self-esteem; to boast to colleagues; to avoid conflict, especially at work; the desire to be right; to project solvency; and of course to manipulate those around us so as to achieve our goals.

Contrary to the belief that childhood is a time of innocence, research shows that we develop our ability to deceive from as young as six months. Obviously, our environment, education and the example of our elders vital factors if we are to avoid becoming compulsive liars from an early age.

Some people think that lying is a cultural issue, more common, for example, in Latin countries than in the Anglo-Saxon world. I disagree, based on my experience in academia, where cheats are to be found on every continent. Perhaps the difference lies not so much in how often people from one part of the world or another lie, but in the social disapproval it arouses. In the United States or the United Kingdom, it used to be that when a politician was found to have lied or breached the rules, he or should would automatically resign: Bill Clinton lied about his extramarital affairs with an intern, was impeached, but refused to stand down, even though his political career was over. In other countries, however, voters show more leniency in the face of personal entanglements. Sadly, lying in politics is now perceived by voters to be widespread and blatant; in response, sociologists and political scientists are trying to understand the phenomenon.

Interestingly, research shows that few of us are able to recognize when someone is lying to us: Estimates suggest that only 50% of deceptions go unnoticed. The old saying, "the liar is sooner caught than the cripple" no longer seems the case. Experts explain that it is easier to see if somebody is lying by studying their nonverbal language: Gestures, facial tics or refusing to make eye contact are some of the best-known indicators.[49]

Perhaps lying is simply an integral part of what it means to be human, even if philosophers have long argued against it, albeit with nuances. Plato, for example, justified concealing the truth in the public interest, an approach similar to that formulated centuries later by John Stuart Mill, as an application of utilitarianism: Certain lies can be seen as being for the greater good if they benefit the maximum number of people.[50]

One philosopher who would have no truck with lying was Immanuel Kant, who was categorical in his condemnation of any kind of lie, putting forward an argument that has been the subject of widespread jokes. He explains that the command to tell the truth is so categorical that even if a murderer were to knock on the door of one's house with the intention of killing one of the inhabitants, one should not lie by saying that his potential victim is not to be found. The example contradicts what any well-meaning person would do, especially if we want to save family members. After World War II, the intrinsic perversity of the Kantian approach was alluded to in reference to the Nazi searches of houses in which Jewish citizens were sheltering.[51]

Some analysts of Kant's work have tried to explain what he meant by this inflexible adherence to telling the truth, in my opinion with little success. Benjamin Constant, the British philosopher who had an exchange with Kant on this subject, threw common sense on the dilemma, illustrating the folly of categorical approaches: "*The moral principle that it is one's duty to speak the truth, if it were taken singly and unconditionally, would make all society impossible. We have the proof of this in the very direct consequences which have been drawn from this principle by a German philosopher, who goes so far as to affirm that to tell a falsehood to a murderer who asked us whether our friend, of whom he was in pursuit, had not taken refuge in our house, would be a crime.*"[52]

Constant argues that there is a duty to tell the truth only when two conditions are met: The counterparty has a right to know the truth; and when there is no harm to third parties—and perhaps one could even include oneself in some cases: an example of enlightened self-interest.

Two environments where this approach might be applicable are personal relationships and the work space, where I will refer mainly to the company, excluding other professional habitats such as politics or other nonprofit institutions.

A commonplace in American movies dealing with relationships is the breakup of the couple: One party has lied to the other, which is seen as a betrayal and sufficient reason to end things. The thesis behind this moralizing narrative is that when it comes to love, anything other than total transparency is a deal-breaker. Typically, even if the guilty party fesses up, shows contrition and commits to changing their ways, the outcome is always rupture, because the offended party considers that the lie is reason enough to end things, however painful. As a narrative pattern, it seems to me an overreaction and inconsistent with reality. In many couples, as long as there is respect and affection, reconciliation can usually be rekindled.

Contrary to the present, in the 1960s and 1970s, bad behavior was common among characters on the big screen. For older movie fans, the change in narrative is surprising, although it is probably a reflection of the times we live in.

As Greek mythology shows, forgiveness is a gift reserved for the gods. But I believe that practicing it both elevates us and rather than divine, makes us more human.

Beyond the duty of loyalty and sincerity, I think we also have a right to what we might call our own space, indeed it is often a requirement for the survival of the relationship itself.

- *Dishonesty in business*

Senior management has a special duty to be candid with the company's shareholders. What's more, failing to be transparent will often be perceived as fraud or fraudulent, which can have serious legal consequences.

More nuanced is the duty of timely and complete transparency with other stakeholders, whether employees or suppliers, customers, or even competitors. Lying is obviously wrong, but I wonder if there really is an obligation for complete transparency, but that's a topic I will discuss in detail in another article.

Sun Tzu, whose *The Art of War* has inspired military and business strategy, argued that all warfare is based on deception, and details false maneuvers, feigned attacks, contrived orders of battle, and the creation of apparent indications of strength or weakness to influence or wrong-foot the enemy.[53]

Steve Jobs was a master of stretching the boundaries between reality and the imaginable. Bud Tribble, the company's chief software engineer, described how his boss would create a "reality distortion field," a term borrowed from Star Trek: "*In his presence, reality was malleable. He could convince anyone of virtually anything. This disappeared when he wasn't around, but it was hard to make realistic plans.*"[54] Jobs' intransigence had a very simple goal: to get his people to produce the best possible product, and sometimes that meant meeting seemingly impossible deadlines or double-checking information and data in search of perfection.

In conclusion, a few takeaways on the merits or otherwise of complete candidness.

1. As the old saying goes, honesty is the best policy, and in the long-term it will garner the respect of the people who count. Trust based on the openness of relationships, truthfulness and the reasonable expectation that this is the direction of travel, are the basis of trade and business. We need only remember the prisoner's dilemma to see how systematic cooperation is the preferable strategy for all parties.

That said, there are similarities between business and gaming, where simulation, secrecy, deception and even trickery are accepted and practiced, especially between competitors, often driving innovation and other benefits to the market.

However, we should always remember that knowingly lying and harming third parties is not only morally reprehensible, but often punishable under law. However, there are situations and circumstances where it is appropriate to weigh up the degree of truthfulness, or concealment, that can be justifiably employed.

In sum, while outright lies are deplorable, as with other situations, there are many nuances to be taken into account before concluding that somebody's conduct is deceitful. As Algernon says in Oscar Wilde's theatre play *The Importance of Being Earnest*, "*the truth is rarely pure, and never simple.*"[55]

## 5.8    Why Teaching the Humanities Is the Best Way to Improve Management Studies

The governing bodies of many universities and business schools have been debating for some time the problems of implementing DIEB (diversity, inclusion, equality and belonging across all their stakeholder groups, from faculty and staff, as well as students or boards.

Here I focus on business schools, suggesting that they should not only explain what companies are, but what they can do to become fairer, more effective and sustainable organizations. In my view, they should focus on developing research that is prescriptive, not merely descriptive. Most of the dilemmas academic institutions are wrestling with, such as inclusion or equality, are essentially contested concepts: We agree on their generic formulation, but disagree on how to implement them. In conclusion, I argue that when there is a diverse range of beliefs in a community, conventions become especially important.

Not long ago, during a class on strategy as part of the Global Online MBA at IE Business School, I was asked by one of my students, why all the CEOs of the companies I was using in my case studies were white men. Realizing this deficiency, I immediately set about making the program more inclusive.

But the problem was that when I looked for case studies on General Management and Strategy with female CEOs, I found that a Harvard Business Publishing survey showed that only 11% of the case studies in its directory had a female CEO or director, and most of them were about the glass ceiling syndrome. I could only find one name, Ginni Rometty, the former CEO of IBM.[56]

Admittedly, there's been some progress in the interim, but the disappointing reality is that the reason there are still not enough case studies, teaching materials or academic research that reflect diversity in companies is because most companies themselves are not diverse enough.

Notwithstanding, that student, a middle-class, white male in his thirties, was highlighting the need for business schools to play a more active role in opening students' eyes to the need for a more inclusive approach to business. Just because there are not enough women heading multinationals, doesn't mean we shouldn't teach the kinds of values and principles we want to instill in the business leaders of tomorrow.

I agree: Business schools must do more than simply explain how companies work; they have to develop models to inspire entrepreneurs, creating models to make organizations fairer and more effective.

It is precisely because there are still so few female CEOs that business schools should design programs that will inspire young women and help balance senior management.

However, a prescriptive approach of this nature will require business schools to look beyond merely describing today's business environment, and instead play an active role in driving change and helping create companies that are sustainable and address the needs of all their stakeholders.

Sumantra Ghoshal is among the academics who have called out business schools for pushing the same management practices that they now condemn. He also believed that most business school teaching is based on false criteria.

The roots of the problem are deep: Business schools like to see their activities as part of the social sciences. While the physical sciences are governed by cause and effect, social sciences is essentially about how individuals behave. Ghoshal argued that no amount of scientific theory explains company's "organized complexity" or more importantly, the type of companies we need.

Ghoshal's view was that including management in the social sciences reduced human behavior to the satisfaction of our most basic instincts. Which is why so much business theory has traditionally lacked a moral or ethical perspective. In short, theories in the social sciences tend to be self-fulfilling.[57]

I agree with Ghoshal in that the first step is to accept that management thinking is as ideological as any other, meaning that business schools carry an even greater social and moral responsibility than institutions that teach the physical sciences.

The way to drive the kind of change Ghoshal have called for is by bringing management research into the humanities. The Carnegie Foundation's 2011 report, *Rethinking Undergraduate Management Education: Liberal Learning for the Profession*, recommends that the BBA (Bachelor in Business Administration), follow the lead of undergraduate programs in the liberal arts and strengthen the humanities' presence in business schools' curriculum and in their research.[58]

In recent years, more and more business schools have begun to introduce the liberal arts into their curricula. It is to be hoped that modules on, say, critical thinking will help students to challenge unethical decisions made by their bosses. In short, it is high time business schools benefited from a classical education.

Bringing management studies into the humanities and adopting a prescriptive approach to business research will first require important clarification of the debatable nature of many values and ideas used in business.

Many of the ideas used in the social sciences are open to interpretation, with different meanings depending on the background and worldview of the individual discussing them. Equality, freedom and justice can be considered and applied in different ways. We are in the presence of what Walter Bryce Gallie identified as "essentially contested concepts" in the 1950s.[59] He pointed out that we might all say we are in favor of freedom, but opinions on how to realize it will differ, especially when different values or rights coexist in a society; for example when the right of freedom of expression seems to clash with somebody else's belief that they have the right not to be offended.

In most cases of essentially contested concepts, there is general agreement on the generic concept itself, for example, the right to freedom of expression, the right not to be offended. But there are also different conceptions about which there is potential disagreement.

For example, we would all agree with the principle of feminism, which at its most basic level holds that men and women should enjoy the same rights. Which is why it is surprising that there are people who consider themselves liberals but disavow feminism. The disagreement is over how to implement the ideal of feminism. There are people who defend affirmative action, because they think it is the fastest and most effective method to transform society, even if it generates tensions in the short term, while others believe that any form of discrimination, even if an argument can be found to justify it, is expendable.

The dilemmas managers often face mean confrontation between different ways of understanding a principle or value, such as freedom, justice, equality, the concept of merit and so many others. The best way to resolve these conflicts is constructively, through reasoned discussion, as other difficult issues in the company are decided.

Today's MBA class will be more diverse than it would have been 25 years ago, a reality that requires more awareness and respect for others, regardless of one's personal affinities. To enforce respect, a business school community should set down in writing its principles and practices regarding the fundamental duties and rights of its members. This may be done through a code of ethics that comprises norms related to the academic community's behavior, as well as the basic principles guiding interpersonal relations.

The beliefs that underpin most business schools' codes of ethics do not reflect a specific ideology, religion or morality, and instead constitute what we might call cosmopolitan ethics. In fact, in today's multicultural classes, composed of people with diverse views of the world or personal morality, a code of ethics should only cover the core rules, seeking to guarantee a constructive coexistence among participants, a sort of minimum common denominator that balances diversity and respect for others with the adherence to common rules of behavior.

Besides beliefs, conventions—understood as the customs shared throughout a community—also play an important part in facilitating relations among a business school's stakeholders, as in society at large. Indeed, the more diverse are the personal convictions among the members of the academic community the more important is respect for agreed conventions.

Conventions, although the result of arbitrary choices by members of a given society such as driving on a certain side of the road, are fundamental for coexistence. Examples of conventions include dress codes, forms of greeting or etiquette at the table. Conventions do not rely on values or moral principles—like beliefs—and being "a well-mannered person" is not the same as being "a good person." It's easy to imagine somebody who is both exquisitely polite and utterly immoral. But somebody with bad manners, however well-intentioned, will likely encounter rejection from the group.

In recent decades, many educators have argued for the need to encourage spontaneity in students, so as to spark their creativity. But taken to its extreme, this could lead to relaxing conventions—on the basis that they inhibit students from freely developing their personality. In contrast, I would argue that observing conventions is, precisely, a requisite to nurture students' personalities since it facilitates the integration of individuals in a community.

Conscientious managers proactively cultivate the conventions that make business relations with people from different cultures not only possible but fruitful. A golden rule is to treat others as they want to be treated. This is a lesson that business schools' educators cannot omit. Indeed, it is an exciting challenge for those who aim at molding cosmopolitan citizens.

## Notes

1. Plato, *The Republic* (London: Penguin, 2021), 2, 359a.
2. B. Masters, "Bernard Madoff, criminal financier", 1938–2021, *Financial Times*, August 16, 2021. https://www.ft.com/content/df7263ef-31a5-487e-af76-8df4af8afa2d.
3. M. Friedman, "The Social Responsibility of Business Is to Increase Its Profits", *New York Times Magazine*, September 13, 1970.
4. N. Machiavelli, *The Prince* (London: Penguin, 2013), cap. VII.
5. Sun Tzu, *The Art of War* (London: Penguin, 2009).
6. Ibidem., P. 1.
7. S. Iñiguez de Onzoño, *Cosmopolitan Managers. Executive Development that Works* (London: Palgrave Macmillan, 2016) pp. 223–224).
8. Sun Tzu, op.cit. Ch. 3.
9. Ibid., Ch. 6.
10. Ibid., Ch.12.
11. Ibid., Ch.4.
12. Ibid., Ch.1.
13. R. Safranski, *¿Cuánta globalización podemos soportar?* (Barcelona: Tusquets,), p. 20.
14. J. Verne, *Around the World in Eighty Days* (London: Penguin, 2021).
15. R. Safranski, op. cit., p 25.

16. I. Kant, To Perpetual Piece (Indianapolis: Hackett Publishing, 2003).
17. R. Safranski, op.cit., p.55.
18. K.A. Appiah, Kwame Anthony. Cosmopolitanism (London: Penguin, 1997), p. 156.
19. John, 8:7.
20. P. Singer, "Famine, Affluence and Morality", Philosophy & Public Affairs, Spring 1972, p. 231.
21. P. Unger, *Living High and Letting Die: Our Illusion of innocence* (New York: Oxford University Press, 1996), p. 56.
22. A. Smith, *The Theory of Moral Sentiments* (ed. K. Haakonssen) (Cambridge, Mass.: Cambridge University Press, 2002), p. 157.
23. S. de Beauvoir, *Les Belles Images* (Paris: Gallimard, 1964).
24. H.C. Andersen, *The Emperor's New clothes and Other Stories* (London: Penguin, 1995).
25. W. Isaacson, *Benjamin Franklin: An American Life* (New York: Simon & Schuster, 2004), p.56.
26. B. Franklin, *The Autobiography of Benjamin Franklin* (New York: Random House, 2005), p. 73.
27. W.Isaacson, op.cit., p. 57.
28. https://www.hofstede-insights.com/fi/product/compare-countries/.
29. https://www.latimes.com/archives/la-xpm-1989-07-04-fi-3279-story.html.
30. N. Machiavelli, op.cit., Ch.23.
31. G. Vasari, *The Lives of the Artists* (trans. J. Conaway Bondanella and P. Bondanella) (Oxford: Oxford University Press, 1991), p. 226 and 546.
32. Bible, Revelation, 12, 9–12.
33. A. Verdross, *The permanent neutrality of Austria* (Vienna: Verl. f. Geschichte u. Politik, 1978).
34. Pliny The Younger, *The Letters of the Younger Pliny* (trans. Betty Radice) (London: Penguin, 1969).
35. Ibid., pp. 166–7.
36. Ibidem.
37. Ibidem.
38. D. Dunn, *The Shadow of Vesuvius. A Life of Pliny* (New York: WW Norton, 2019), p. 48.
39. S. Freud, *Totem and Tabu* (London: Routledge, 2001).
40. D. du Maurier, *Rebecca* (London: Penguin, 2003).
41. Aesop, *The Complete Fables* (trans. O. Temple) (London: Penguin, 1998), p. 52.
42. A. Schopenhauer, *El arte de hacerse respetar, expuesto en 14 máximas* (Madrid: Alianza, 2011), p. 11.
43. B. Gracián, *The Art of Worldly Wisdom. A Pocket Oracle* (Jersey City, NJ: Start Publishing, 1991), p. 53.
44. A. Schopenhauer, op.cit., p. 26.

45. Quoted in M. Lewis, *Liar's Poker* (London: Hodder & Stoughton, 2006), p. 73.
46. *Downton Abbey* (creat. J. Fellowes) (Carnival Films, WGBH-TV, 2010).
47. https://www.oxfordlearnersdictionaries.com/definition/american_english/lie2_1.
48. R. Feldman, Liar: *The Truth about Lying* (London: Virgin Books, 2010).
49. https://www.businessinsider.com/how-to-tell-someones-lying-by-watching-their-face-2016-1.
50. https://www.britannica.com/topic/lying/The-morality-of-lying.
51. H. Varden, "Kant and Lying to the Murderer at the Door…One More Time. Kant's Legal Philosophy and Lies To Murderers and Nazis" 41 *Journal of Social Philosophy* 4 (Winter 2020), pp. 403–21.
52. Ibidem.
53. Sun Tzu, op. cit.
54. W. Isaacson, *Steve Jobs* (New York: Simon & Schuster, 2011), p. 117.
55. O. Wilde, *The Importance of Being Earnest* (London: Penguin, 2011), First Act.
56. L. Symons, Only 11% of Top Business School Studies Have a Female Protagonist, *Harvard Business Review*, March 9, 2016. The author suggests that "*Clearing houses should publicize and reward cases with diverse characters. If you can measure it, you can start to change it. Data in this area is crucial. Case clearing houses, such as the Case Centre or Harvard, can assist by actively bringing the topic into the open. They could start by tracking the gender—and ethnicity—of the protagonist and making this information visible on their websites.*" An interesting contribution providing data on women in business and analysis: C. Criado Pérez, *Invisible Women: Data Bias in a World Designed for Men* (New York, NY: Abrams Press, 2019).
57. Ghoshal, S., "Bad Management Theories Are Destroying Good Management Practices", 4 *Academy of Management Learning & Education* (2005), 75–91.
58. Iñiguez de Onzoño, S. *The Learning Curve: How Business Schools Are Re-Inventing Education* (London: Palgrave Macmillan, 2011), p. 126.
59. W.B. Gallie, "Essentially Contested Concepts", 56 Proceedings of the Aristotelian Society (1955–6), pp. 167–198.

# 6

## Part 6: Optimism—Is Happiness Attainable?

When we congratulate family, friends, colleagues or acquaintances, we may wish them luck, good health or express our love and gratitude; for those with a more material outlook, perhaps success in a new business venture or job. And all these aspirations can be summed up in one goal: happiness, because Aristotle was right: "*happiness is the meaning and purpose of life, the whole aim and end of human existence.*"[1]

Notwithstanding, each of us has our own understanding of happiness. For some, it might be as straightforward as watching their favorite sports team once a week; for others a concert, an evening at the movies, or a lengthy chat over dinner with friends.

Similarly, philosophers have also differed in their answers as to what is meant by happiness.

For the Epicureans, happiness lies in the pursuit of pleasure and the avoidance of pain. The founder of this belief, Epicurus of Samos, lived in the fourth century BCE in Athens. Epicureanism is sometimes misunderstood as debauchery, excess, self-gratification and vice, but rather than being about the pleasure of eating it is more about not going hungry.[2] Epicurus thought that the goal in life was to avoid pain, and for this, the key was to cultivate mental pleasures, which in Greek was known as "ataraxia" or imperturbability, something that is achieved through philosophy, knowledge, education.

Another ancient Greek philosophy was Stoicism. Essentially, the Stoics believed that self-control was necessary to achieve perfection, along with subjecting the senses to the mind, along with acceptance of nature and the given state of things. Its representatives include Marcus Aurelius, whose book *Meditations* has long been a key text for executives and managers. In it, the

S. Iñiguez, *Philosophy Inc.*, https://doi.org/10.1007/978-3-031-20483-8_6

Roman emperor proposes: *"Begin the morning by saying to yourself: I shall meet with the busybody, the ungrateful, arrogant, deceitful, envious, unsocial [...] I can neither be harmed by any of them [...] for we are made for cooperation, like feet, like hands, like eyelids, like the rows of the upper and lower teeth."*[3] This is good advice for those of us who have to deal with a wide range of people every day. The Stoics establish a distance with the world and understand that happiness lies in strengthening our will, in not taking things personally, in temperance and achieving our objectives.

Another major current of classical thinking was represented by the Cynics. Their founder, Diogenes of Sinope, is considered one of the fathers of modern cosmopolitanism. The Cynics are the forerunner of moral relativism, in that they believed that no moral proposition can be demonstrated, so they defended one idea and its opposite, showing dialectical brilliance. This position did not imply that everything was simply relative; instead, they proposed a return to nature, while respecting existing rules and customs.

In this section, I'll explore some of the major ideas about what is understood by happiness and how we can try to achieve it.

## 6.1    If Life Is a Comedy, Why Not Laugh More?

*"Joy, beautiful spark of the gods,"* wrote the German poet Schiller in his justly celebrated ode, augmented by Beethoven in his Ninth Symphony and subsequently adopted by the European Union as its anthem.[4]

Surely we all yearn for that spark of joy; melancholy holds little appeal for the majority of us. Yet as Schiller writes, living in a state of joy would be a divine gift; at some time in life, most of us will endure personal, family, health or economic difficulties, as many of us can attest from the experiences of the past pandemic.

Sadly, there are those among us who interpret the joy of others as some kind of toxic positivism. It is not uncommon, for example, for upbeat comments on social networks to prompt criticism and ridicule. There's little to smile about, given the state of things, is a recurring sentiment. Or perhaps, as Adam Smith suggested: *"It gives us the spleen (...) to see another too happy or too much elevated (...) with any little piece of good fortune. We are disobliged even with his joy; and, because we cannot go along with it, call it levity and folly."*[5]

Perhaps some conceptual precision would help us to better understand the object of our analysis here. Joy is usually considered a fleeting condition, associated with immediate experiences such as a celebration, although a positive outlook is required to be able to enjoy such events. When somebody is mostly to be found in a good mood, we regard them as a happy person, indicating a character or disposition that is carefree, positive and sociable.

On the other hand, while good humor is often employed as a synonym for joy, its nature is ephemeral, associated with episodes of joking and fun. This meaning has been consolidated in the Elizabethan and Jacobean playwright Ben Jonson's comedic theater of characters or "humors"—in the biological sense of the term. Humor was conceptually linked to comedy, a dramatic form that intentionally seeks laughter.

Finally, when we speak of happiness we are referring to a vital state that covers a long period of time, generally a lifetime. As we will see in more detail in the next section, at the same time as happiness reflects a certain degree of achievement or realization in life, it also includes an important aspirational component that makes it a state of permanent search, of incomplete satisfaction, an ongoing project.

Having established these brief definitions, I should also acknowledge that most people use the concepts of joy, good humor and happiness interchangeably, perhaps because when they experience them in the first person they feel something so similar that it is very difficult, not to say impossible, to differentiate one from the other.

As we have seen, most of us are open to good times, which is why those who aren't, are saddened and may even feel envy or bitterness when they see others enjoying themselves. Envy is sadness for the happiness of others, especially when our personal goals have not been achieved.

A scene from Woody Allen's 1997 movie *Deconstructing Harry* captures this perfectly.[6] The protagonist sits in a railway carriage occupied by crestfallen, gray, silent passengers as the train slowly lurches forward. From his window, Harry can see another train alongside where a riotous party is underway, the black-tied guests knocking back champagne, and in the midst of it all, a dazzling Sharon Stone notices him and blows a kiss, leaving a lipstick imprint on the window as the two trains move in opposite directions. Our hero's face is a portrait of despair. Needless to say, if we were offered tickets on either of these two trains, provided our choice didn't result in undesirable consequences, we would unhesitatingly opt for the party Pullman.

In classical antiquity, comedy was as important a theatrical genre as tragedy. Playwrights like Aristophanes in Greece or Plautus and Terence in Rome enjoyed the same recognition and prestige as their "tragic" counterparts, and inspired later writers. Terence's Adelphoe—a topical comedy that asks which is better: a liberal education or a strict and severe upbringing—was in large part the basis for *School for Husbands* by the French comic playwright par excellence, Moliere.

Comedy was also an important part of the culture of other major civiliza-tions such as China, where the genre flourished during the Zhou dynasty between the eleventh and third centuries BCE, influenced by the teachings of Confucius. The aristocrats of that time also employed jesters, later introduced into the courts of Western monarchies.

In the Middle Ages, however, comedy as a theatrical genre disappears. The Middle Ages in the West are still seen as a barbaric era, with no room for humor, although some historians, such as Johan Huizhinga, argued that social and cultural life at that time was more complex and colorful than we tend to think.[7] Nevertheless, we tend to remember works of literature and cinema that focus on the repression of fun during this era, such as Umberto Eco's emblematic *The Name of the Rose*, where a few monks in a remote Italian abbey succumb to the temptation of reading a lost work by Aristotle, *The Poetics*, hidden away in the most recondite part of the library, dedicated pre-cisely to humor. For their sins, they are ingeniously poisoned.[8]

Over time, comedy has returned to occupy a relevant place in all artistic forms. Even so, it is still largely considered a subordinate genre to tragedy, for example in theater or cinema, perhaps vestiges of that collective repression rooted in religion. For example, far fewer Oscars have been awarded to come-dians, and some critics simply ignore comedy all together. Only established actors are able to move between drama and comedy without risking their careers.

The presence of comedy around the world reflects the universality of humor as an indisputably human phenomenon. We tend to laugh in the same way, regardless of race, beliefs, culture or age. Different things may provoke laugh-ter depending on gender or culture, but the right jokes told in the right way can provoke laughter among the most varied audiences, breaking the ice, bringing people together and strengthening group feeling. I have experienced this as a teacher in multicultural and diverse classes. Even when putting in writing the expression of laughter, the same interjection is usually used in most of the messages: ha-ha. Nowadays, the use of emoticons, which signify joy, has displaced conventional words. LOL!

In conclusion, three takeaways:

- First, maintaining a positive and cheerful outlook tends to make others more receptive to what we say and do, and is also more rewarding to the person who cultivates it.
- Second, the benefits of cultivating comedy, possibly throughout life. This can be done in different ways: reading—the best literature always has shades of humor—and watching good comedies at the theater or the

cinema. What's more, there's little personal risk here, compared to stand-up comedy: As a spectator, you're not exposed to being the butt of jokes.
- Third, try to empathize with others by applying good humor, especially in the family or at work. Laugh at jokes, as long as they aren't offensive, and respond with similar jokes. This will help you improve your relationships and cultivate personal confidence.

## 6.2 Aristotle, a Man Who Understood Happiness

Few would argue that Aristotle remains one of the most influential philosophers in the Western canon; Plato's pupil, his ideas nevertheless differ substantially from his master's: an early example of "killing the father," a frequent practice in the field.

While Plato's proposition is essentially that human knowledge grows from ideas, and that philosophical speculation about those ideas gives us a better understanding of things, Aristotle believed that it is experience which helps us to comprehend the world. This discrepancy is illustrated in Raphael's famous Vatican fresco *The School of Athens*, which you may have been lucky enough to see in person, and if not, it will be familiar from any number of reproductions. The center of this masterpiece is occupied by the walking figures of Plato, older and white-bearded, pointing his finger to the sky, indicating the empyrean and ethereal nature of ideas, while a younger Aristotle, to his left, points to the ground, signifying the importance of reality and empirical verification in philosophical reasoning.

In my capacity as an educator, after sharing this brief summary of both thinkers with executives and business people, they typically align themselves with Aristotle. After all, which action-oriented worldly person would deny the importance of practical evidence for any kind of thinking or decision making? However, as we will see in another section, Plato's proposition has relevance for other areas of social life and business: for example, marketing and communication, or evaluating intangible assets.

Aristotle's "realism" has particular implications for his conception of ethics, because his interest lies not in discovering or unraveling the meaning of the good, delving into the concept of the good, or providing a rounded definition of it, but rather how we can be better people; in short, how to live a good life through our actions.

At the beginning of his *Nicomachean Ethics*, dedicated to his son, Aristotle recalls the inscription on a stone on the sacred island of Delos, which read: "*The three most important goods in life are justice, health and satisfying personal desire.*"[9] He then argues that the fundamental purpose of life is to be happy, and to achieve that, we must each develop our potential, mold our character, so as to realize the best version of our own life and personality. Identifying how to achieve this happiness is a rational exercise, which presupposes the autonomy of individuals as moral agents, our ability to identify how we should act.

In some cases, however, this autonomy is undermined. For example, Aristotle questions whether children can really be happy, since they do not have experience, they have not lived enough to understand and make sense of what a good life is as a whole. However, most people believe this statement contradicts common sense. In fact, people talk about happy children and sad children, and good parents are concerned that their children's childhood is a time of happiness, sometimes too much, forgetting the need to learn what hard work and discipline are.

Another external factor that Aristotle says limits happiness is bad luck, arguably the greatest threat we face. The contemporary example he uses is that of Priam, king of Troy and immortalized in the Iliad, who loses all his sons and dies cruelly on the altar of his own city. All this without being directly responsible for what happened or deserving that punishment. Unfortunately, life also provides us with many examples, on a daily basis, of undeserved human suffering: wars, pandemics and calamities that destroy families and deny people the opportunity to even think about enjoying a good life.

In *Eudemian Ethics*, Aristotle outlines how we can achieve a good life by developing his proposition on the virtues, which are the pillars on which excellence rests.[10] Virtues are good habits, not innate but instead acquired through repeated exercise. The Aristotelian golden rule to reaching excellence is "in medio virtus," in other words, that the best degree of implementation of a virtue is between two extremes, both of which are undesirable because of their excess or defect. For example, self-esteem as a virtue lies between the poles of vanity—the excess of self-love—and inferiority complex. Temperance, on the other hand, is the point of balance between licentiousness and insensitivity; or patience the proper balance between irascibility and lack of courage.

Equilibrium, balance, the middle ground, has a dynamic nature that depends on each situation and brings to virtue ethics a sporting spirit very much in line with some theories of self-improvement, and also with the ideas of positive psychology.

Aristotle was the tutor of Alexander the Great, one of the most famous conquerors in history. Among the virtues listed in the Eudemonia is courage. Like the others, it is a balance between two extremes, recklessness and cowardice. Reading Plutarch's biography of Alexander, one can only wonder if the boy soldier was paying much attention to his teacher about maintaining this balance, or if he disregarded him, or if his conception of courage was simply beyond any comparison.

The purpose of living a virtuous life is not selfish, in the sense of being proud of being virtuous, of simply measuring personal progress by pride, conceit or arrogance. To be sure, practicing the virtues generates personal satisfaction, and it is this self-esteem that represents the source of genuine happiness for Aristotle, but not by being on the road to perfection, but by doing the right thing. Moreover, we live in society, and the exercise of virtues impacts on others.

Virtue ethics is an approach to ethical thinking based on the character of the individual involved rather than a set of rules or consequences. Virtue ethics was the prevailing model in the ancient and medieval worlds. It emphasizes the character of the individual rather than rules. In this sense, it places responsibility and accountability firmly with the conscience of the individual rather than the interpretation of law or regulations. This is very different to the approach of consequentialism, which argues that the outcome or consequences of a particular action determine whether it is morally acceptable or not. It is also different to deontology, which asserts that the rightness or wrongness of an act is determined by the character of the act itself. In practice, the difference in these three alternative views of morality tends to lie in how issues are approached rather than the conclusions reached. For example, a consequentialist may argue that stealing is wrong because of the negative consequences produced by stealing—though a consequentialist may allow that certain consequences might make stealing acceptable. A deontologist might argue that stealing is always wrong, regardless of any potential "good" that might come from it. A virtue ethicist, however, would focus less on stealing in any particular instance and instead consider what a decision to steal says about a person's character and moral behavior,

Developing virtues, understood or routines that form our character—and not necessarily in the religious sense—has been a core aspect of teaching in all societies throughout the ages. In Ancient Rome, young men were taught the virtues of dignitas, pietas et virtus. Dignitas meant adopting greater decorum as one assumed more responsibility. Pietas involved respect for the family, law, and tradition. Virtus included a bundle of skills such as bravery, trust, and moral courage. Military training throughout the ages has also involved developing virtuous habits. Jeffrey Pfeffer, for example, suggests that business schools could learn from military academies, where humility is an important part of the code of conduct, as is discipline, along with punishment for failing to observe the rules.[11]

The concept of virtue has been further developed by contemporary thinkers such as Elisabeth Anscombe and Alasdair McIntyre, who have developed a theory of morality that attempts to go beyond the rigid principles of most ethics, based as they are on Kant's categorical imperative or John Stuart Mill's principle of the greatest happiness. Anscombe and McIntyre argue that the key questions related to how to live and how to behave are best answered by identifying and then practicing virtues, rather than through a rational exercise based on the principles outlined in other philosophical models. I would say that this approach is the way to teach and learn what constitutes good management.[12]

## 6.3    Why It's Best to Accentuate the Positive, Within Reason

Economists, when reproached for making gloomy forecasts, will sometimes reply that pessimism is simply optimism tempered by reality. And while it's true that their predictions tend to be conservative, prioritizing risks and contingencies, when all is said and done, an economist's job when making their calculations is to take into account uncertainty, a factor never to be underestimated.

Entrepreneurs, on the other hand, are generally seen as compulsive optimists. And even within companies, certain clichés are often associated with particular functions: CFOs tend to see the glass as half-empty, while strategists, sales and marketing teams are typically glass-half-full types.

How would you describe yourself: optimistic or pessimistic? Philosophy can lend us a hand here, from two thinkers who held very different views of the world, the German Gottfried Wilhelm Leibniz and the French François-Marie Arouet, better known by his pseudonym Voltaire.

Leibniz is one of the fathers of modern logic and a reference of rationalism. One of the central tenets of his philosophy is "metaphysical optimism," the thesis that God has created the best of all possible worlds.[13] This is so because one of the attributes of divinity is perfection, and therefore, logically, any of the Creator's works must be perfect. According to this approach, calamities such as earthquakes, epidemics or floods, while regrettable, can only be understood in the broadest of contexts, difficult for human beings, with our finite capacity, to grasp.

You may know people who share this alacrity in the face of the events that humanity experiences, both happy and tragic. The existence of hardships and disasters, their unpredictable character and the absence of justifiable reasons, from a moral point of view, is one of the most difficult challenges for believers to understand.

And it is precisely metaphysical optimism that Voltaire turns his sights on in his novel *Candide*, whose title expresses the candor and innocence of its protagonist.[14] In his youth, Candide experiences disappointment in love, after which he embarks on a journey around the world during which he undergoes many experiences, accompanied by Dr. Pangloss, a wise man who sees everything that happens on their travels as opportunities to transfer a unique lesson to his disciple. Parodying Leibniz's thesis, Pangloss concludes at the end of each adventure that we live in the best of all possible worlds. In their travels, they witness myriad deaths, wars, calamities, religious persecution and slavery. And in every instance, Pangloss sums up the situation with the mantra that, despite all these evils, we live in the best of all possible worlds.

One of the episodes in the book takes place in Lisbon, coinciding with the earthquake that hit the Portuguese capital in 1755, followed by a tsunami and widespread fires, which devastated the city and left thousands dead. It is likely that this event prompted Voltaire to questions his own religious convictions. While a skeptic, Voltaire did not consider himself an atheist, instead preferring deism, the belief that divinity is to be found in nature, which at bottom is not far from Leibniz's view.

At the end of his wanderings, Candide meets his youthful love again, both older and disillusioned with life, and they decide to rebuild their lives and run a farm. Another of the characters, Martin, states that the best way to make existence bearable is to stop philosophizing and devote oneself to the tasks that provide a livelihood. Pangloss again drones on about how all the experiences they have lived through make for the best of all possible worlds, to which Candide responds expeditiously: "*il faut cultiver notre jardin*" (let's cultivate our garden), which in modern parlance might be rendered as "let's cut the crap."[15]

It is easy to sympathize with Candide's mature pragmatism, particularly in light of what he has lived through, along with Pangloss's banal positivity. At the same time, we know the advantages of philosophy in our lives, and how, as Socrates pointed out, a life without scrutiny is meaningless.

Candide's proposal recalls a maxim enshrined as a principle of life in the Benedictine monasteries in the Middle Ages: *ora et labora* (pray and work). The abbots wanted to prevent their monks from spending too much time praying and to also focus on tasks that supported their community such as working in the library or the apothecary, preparing meals, gardening and tending to the animals. Ora et labora represented the balance required between reflection, analysis and philosophizing, and action, work and daily life.

Reading Candide, we inevitably feel antipathy toward the insensitive redundancies of Pangloss, and instead identify with the protagonist, a model of sanity and realism. And while it seems as though the optimists are deluded and we should be content to live from day to day, thinking only of our material needs, in all honesty, Leibniz's argument of the best of all possible worlds is based on logic, not on a justification of the morality or fairness of the things that happen in the world, for which we rarely find reasonable explanations.

I would argue that the caricature of Pangloss in Voltaire's work misrepresents the advantages of being optimistic, of being happier or living better. Over the course of the pandemic we have seen the benefits of exercising hope, optimism and resilience. Without hope, it is difficult to think of new projects or make plans for the future. Hopelessness leads to apathy, and although it can sometimes appear closer to pragmatism and realism, as seems to be the case with Candide, it has the pernicious effect of generating indifference toward what is valuable, what is difficult to achieve, and that gives meaning to life.

We know from experience the benefit of hanging out with optimists, and most of us have learned to avoid pessimistic and mistrustful people.

Like other habits that shape our character, I believe that hope and optimism are virtues that are best developed through repeated actions, and therefore, constancy and sportsmanship—knowing how to start over again and again—are essential. But optimism is also an attitude toward life. It leads us to see the positive side of things, not because we repeat it insistently as Pangloss did, but because it teaches us to learn from setbacks, preparing us to face the next trial better prepared.

Daniel Kahneman, Nobel Prize-winning economist and psychologist, is very clear: "*If you were allowed one wish for your child, seriously consider wishing him or her optimism. Optimists are normally cheerful and happy, and therefore popular; they are resilient in adapting to failures and hardships, their chances of clinical depression are reduced, their immune system is stronger, they take better care of their health, they feel healthier than others and are in fact likely to live longer.*"[16]

How to cultivate the healthy mental athleticism of optimism without falling into the cloying and unconscious platitudes satirized by Voltaire? Below are a few helpful, practical tips.

- *Avoid negativity*. Some people think that saying "no" is a virtue. However, systematically rejecting new opportunities, refusing to take part in initiatives or being closed to different approaches mean, we end up doing little else than tending our own garden, like Voltaire's Candide. In contrast, keeping an open attitude to new options and proposals, and believing that the default answer is affirmative makes you a more positive and optimistic person.

- *Cultivate a sense of humor.* In several articles published on LinkedIn, I have explored the thaumaturgical effects of a sense of humor in all areas of our life. Good humor is the little brother of optimism, and practicing it generates a favorable state of mind, mentally and physically.
- *Socialize more frequently.* Closing oneself off and avoiding contact with other people tends to make us more self-absorbed, which is a breeding ground for pessimism. On the contrary, meeting other people, widening our circle of acquaintances, worrying about their problems, sharing their ambitions or participating in their joys, and also in their failures or misfortunes, develops their humanity and the understanding that many of our problems are common and perhaps less serious than those endured by others.
- *Set yourself ambitious challenges*, as long as they are imaginable and achievable, even if they are difficult to reach. Entrepreneurs, by nature dreamers and visionaries, tend to be optimists. Conformism, on the other hand, breeds apathy and results in paralysis.
- *Avoid criticizing people.* It's a good idea to practice constructive criticism, particularly at work. The use of critical capacity—one of the most highly valued professional skills—helps combat groupthink and enables us to challenge preconceived ideas and promote innovation.

That said, criticizing people, rather than what they say, tends to create an unsettled working environment and potentially can turn you into an unhelpful and unreliable colleague.

I remember the title of the title song of a Broadway musical about the American comedian Will Rogers, which went *Never met a man I didn't like*, taken from the title of his memoirs.[17] In other words, look for the positive side of everyone you meet.

- Exercise humility, a quality that has nothing to do with weakness, but as Socrates said, with understanding: in reality, we know nothing; there is still much to learn and to rectify, regardless of age, experience or the position we occupy.[18]

Lack of humility leads some intelligent people who have not met their expectations, generally due to their own responsibility, to feel resentment, a close relative of pessimism. They blame others for their failures, believing they have not received the recognition they deserve. Resentment is avoidable, because there is always time to start practicing humility.

Finally, while there is no denying that luck plays an important role in our lives, it seems that optimists enjoy better luck, I wonder why that might be?

## 6.4   Solitude, Plus Contemplation, Equals Happiness

One of my favorite poems is W.B. Yeats's *The Lake Isle of Innisfree,* in which the great Irish poet evokes one of his best-loved places, somewhere he was happy maybe, where perhaps he was inspired to write, or even fell in love.[19]

We all have a place, or perhaps many, which bring back intense, unforgettable feelings. Some associate such happy memories with the countryside, the forest or the mountains, while for others it's the sea, a lake or a river. In general, it has to be said that beautiful landscapes provoke feelings of relaxation, of spiritual tranquility in us. Contemplating nature and landscapes has been the lifework of innumerable artists and writers throughout history, as Sir Kenneth Clark, the British art historian, once observed: "*the appreciation of natural beauty and the painting of landscape is a normal and enduring part of our spiritual activity.*"[20]

Furthermore, scientific research shows that the contemplation and appreciation of beauty can help reduce stress, improve mood, foster imagination and creativity, and all in all, help recharge our batteries: "*Considered from the perspective of the cognitive approach, landscape perception becomes a process of interpretation, mediated by emotional responses to sites, perceived meanings, and physiological reactions (e.g. stress reduction).*"[21] According to research: "*Generally, the natural landscapes gave a stronger positive health effect compared to urban landscapes,*" and the greener, the better.[22]

These feelings of peace and tranquility are what Jean-Jacques Rousseau experienced during his stay on the island of Saint-Pierre, in the middle of Lake Bienne in Switzerland, where he wrote *Reveries of a Solitary Walker*, a memoir in which he explores some of his most intimate feelings, beliefs and ideas about life and happiness.[23] The Geneva-born philosopher wrote that he had experienced these reveries since the age of five, but that alone, during his boat expeditions on Bienne or walks around the island of Saint-Pierre, he underwent moments in which reality and fiction, reasoning and emotion coalesced in a natural environment evocative and conducive to inspiration.

Such solitude leads to a state of contemplation, which for Rousseau is the closest thing to happiness: "*The happiness that my heart yearns for is not composed of fleeting moments (…) But if there is a state in which the soul finds a situation solid enough to comport with perfect repose, and with the expansion of its whole faculty, without need of calling back the past or pressing on towards the future; where time is nothing for it, and the present has no ending; with no mark for its own duration, and without a trace of succession; without a single other sense of privation or delight, of pleasure or pain, of desire or apprehension, than this single sense of existence,—so long as such a state endures, he who finds himself in it may talk of bliss, not with a poor, relative, and imperfect happiness such as people find in the pleasures of life, but with a happiness full, perfect, and sufficing, that leaves in the soul no conscious unfilled void. Such a state was many a day mine in my solitary musings in the isle of Saint Pierre…)*"[24]

Is Rousseau referring to something akin to meditation, or simply to the pleasurable observation experienced by bucolic and landscape painters?

We've all surely experienced similar moments over the course of our travels. There are particularly lyrical moments, which some might call tacky: sunsets at the sea, snow-capped mountains on a sunny day, the lushness of a forest, or the drama of a waterfall. Perhaps you associate those images with the company of family or friends, or perhaps, like Rousseau, they bring on reverie. What would be your lake of reveries, the place where you would reach that state of bliss?

At this point, let me pause for a moment and ask a question: Do you think you would be happy spending the rest of your life watching sunsets? Surely it would be like eating nothing but chocolate cake, day after day. There would come a time when it would be so cloying that you would get sick of it and desperately look for something else. As the saying goes, variety is the spice of life. You may have wondered why many people who live in coastal cities buy homes on inland streets without ocean views. In addition to the lower price, they're probably less windy, require less maintenance, and their occupants wouldn't feel the need to permanently contemplate the sea; after all, that ocean view is just a few streets away whenever they want it.

In reality, as their name suggests, dream homes are a chimera, more a refuge from the hubbub and routine of the world than true paradises. We enjoy them precisely because the rest of our time, of our life, is dedicated to work or study, family and friends, or to our hobbies and leisure. We withdraw to reverie, to those idyllic places, to rest, recharge our batteries and then return to our tasks. Rousseau himself acknowledges that part of his happiness in Bienne had to do with *dolce far niente* (doing nothing) and instead refers to the "most luxurious idleness."[25]

Let me explain. I believe we should seek out the places that make us happy; perhaps those favorite spots to spend weekends or vacations, and of course, if you find a corner of the world where you feel particularly good, why not spend time there? But my point is that we don't attain happiness through a state of contemplation in some favorite place. Remember the chocolate cake.

Instead, I would say happiness is best understood as a state of mind that takes into account all the moments of our lives, the good and the bad, those sources of learning, that make us more resilient, understanding and humble. One of the books that most helped me to understand that happiness cannot be conceived without including unhappiness or sadness, which are the obverse and reverse of our lives, was British writer C.S. Lewis's autobiographical *A Grief Observed*.[26] The author of *The Lion the Witch and the Wardrobe* recounts his brief marriage to a woman who was far more good-humored and full of life than he was, but who passes away after a lengthy bout of cancer. Lewis explains that it is in the moments of greatest happiness that we must anticipate that there will come a time when we will be unhappy, precisely when our loved ones die. And at such difficult moments we should remember how happy we were, and perhaps smile. Happiness and sadness are like ying and yang, they cannot be understood without each other.

Returning to our lake of reverie, one of their key characteristics is that these are places where we feel safe. For Holly Golightly in Truman Capote's *Breakfast at Tiffany's*, immortalized in Blake Edwards' film by Audrey Hepburn, this means the Fifth Avenue jewelry store, because nothing bad can happen to her there. Again, we've all felt something similar in certain places in the cities we've visited.[27]

Writing just two years before his death, Rousseau brings the last of his ten walks in the *Reveries* to a close with a reference to the words inscribed on the tomb of a prefect disgraced during the reign of the Roman emperor Vespasian: "*I have spent seventy years on earth and lived but seven of them,*" concluding: "*Happiness is a permanent condition, which does not seem designed for man, while here below.*"[28]

Rousseau actually died at the age of sixty-six, presumably unhappy for most of his life apart from his stays in Bienne. Persecuted for his ideas, unsuccessful in love, unsociable and condemned for offloading his children to an orphanage, at least he had the opportunity to live his reverie in his favorite place. Perhaps, in the end happiness, of one form or another, is always possible.

## 6.5   Will We Ever Really Understand Humor?

Did you know that the first traffic jam on New York's Broadway was caused by a philosopher? When the French philosopher and Nobel literature laureate Henri Bergson visited the city in 1913 to give a lecture on his 1907 book *Creative Evolution*, such was the public's interest that the queues brought traffic to a standstill.[29] Bergson had gained a reputation as a good speaker and attracted large audiences, a rare phenomenon to this day, given that while the intelligence of philosophers is usually beyond question, charisma is not their forte. But as Bergson showed, when entertaining, they can capture the public's imagination. Perhaps Socrates had that reputation, in the same way that Michael Sandel of Harvard University fills auditoriums today. This was also true of Ronald Dworkin, my tutor at Oxford, whose classes were always packed.

One of Bergson's most interesting works is *Laughter: An Essay on the Meaning of the Comic*,[30] but he was not the first philosopher to speak of humor. In his Politica, Aristotle writes that "*youths are not to be instructed with a view to their amusement, for learning is no amusement, but is accompanied with pain,*"[31] an assertion that seems to have been taken literally in the Middle Ages. For his part, Immanuel Kant explained that "*Laughter is an affectation that comes from a strained expectation being suddenly reduced to nothing,*"[32] a statement unlikely to prompt so much as a smirk.

Straddling philosophy and psychology, Sigmund Freud devoted an entire book to humor. In *Jokes and their Relation to the Subconscious*,[33] he analyzes the essence of humor, its forms and its relation to dreams. An observation: The examples he uses are not very funny. As he explains, a new joke is considered almost as an event of general interest and passes from mouth to mouth like the news of a very recent victory, not unlike the videos posted on social networks today.

On the other hand, his consideration that smutty jokes are verbal sexual aggressions, and that those who laugh at them behave as spectators of this aggression, gives food for thought.

In an attempt at synthesis, he defines the joke as "*playful judgement, the coupling of dissimilar things, contrasting ideas, sense in nonsense', the succession of bewilderment and enlightenment, the bringing forward of what is hidden, and the peculiar brevity of wit.*"[34]

More recently, Indiana University's Matthew M. Hurley, Daniel C. Dennett of Tufts, and Reginald B. Adams Jr. of Pennsylvania State University, have formulated a more canonical and scholarly definition, although I'm not sure whether many comedians would concur: "*Humor happens when an assumption is epistemically committed to in a mental space and then discovered to have been a mistake.*"[35]

It has to be said that most serious books about humor are anything but humorous, as New York Times magazine reporter Deborah Solomon found when she asked comedian Chris Rock what's funny, to which he replied, "*You want to know what's not funny? Thinking about it.*"[36] E.B. White would have agreed: "*Analyzing the meaning of humor is like dissecting a frog: few people are interested and meanwhile the frog is dying.*"[37]

Bergson's book, however, is more entertaining and useful than many in exploring why some jokes work, perhaps because he avoids a specific definition of humor. Instead, his philosophy prizes intuition over conceptualization and he provides myriad examples and offers categories of what is funny.

Nevertheless, he makes a couple of statements that in my opinion miss the mark: Firstly, he argues that "*comedy does not exist outside of the pale of what is strictly human,*"[38] even though zoology shows that primates certainly experience such feelings, and there is even evidence to suggest that other species may appreciate humor. Humans laugh with their pets, who seem to get the joke.

His second error is arguing that humor requires the presence of others. While laughter can be contagious and empathetic, and as babies we tend to reciprocate a smile or laughter, it is also possible, and I would say even advisable, to appreciate humor when we are alone. Laughing in private can give us insight into ourselves, providing us with inner resources to keep our spirits up. A good read with entertaining passages, or watching a comedy alone can provide moments of genuine fun. It's worth experimenting with different authors to see which click with you. For me, there are two movie classics that never fail to cheer me up: the Marx Brothers' *A Night at the Opera* and Howard Hawks' *Bringing Up Baby*.[39] All in all, as Scottish philosopher Adam Smith explains, " *Society and conversation, therefore, are the most powerful remedies for restoring the mind to its tranquility (…) as well as the best preservatives of that equal and happy temper, which is so necessary to self-satisfaction and enjoyment.*"[40]

For Bergson, there are two main types of comedy: verbal, through the use of language; and situational, through conflict between characters and circumstances.

Verbal comedy is the product of wit, the ability to use language to provoke laughter by saying what one does not mean, by playing with the meaning or pronunciation of words, for example, puns, or by Freudian slips. Wit is the ability to think or come up with ideas on the spur of the moment, to see the funny side of things. This ability is not innate, but acquired through social intelligence and working memory resources. The former relates to the ease we get along with other people and is a form of emotional intelligence requiring a proactive attitude, rather than depending merely on one's sociability, assuming that one is sociable in the first place. You may have met a comedian off duty, as it were, and been struck by their seeming humorlessness, but it makes sense for them to rest when they are not performing, either adopting a different persona, or perhaps simply being their true self. But this shows that, to some extent, joking requires preparation. If you want to be funny at any kind of public event, in addition to improvising with anecdotes, jokes and shenanigans, it's a good idea to put some work in beforehand.

In relation to situation comedy, Bergson identifies three main resources.

- *Repetition*, which relies on the comic potential of saying or doing the same thing again and again, to the point of absurdity. You will remember the famous scene in the cramped cabin in A Night at the Opera, which has since become a visual synonym for any tiny space. Outside, Groucho is making the breakfast order, with Chico adding to each request "and two hard-boiled eggs," which Harpo seconds with a honk and that Groucho then confirms, ad nauseam. I'm often tempted when somebody is reeling off a long list of demands to add a sly "and two hard-boiled eggs…"
- *Inversion*, when a situation is turned around or roles are reversed in an unexpected way. Impersonation is a very recurrent form of this, and again the Marx Brothers movie is benchmark stuff. Take the scene when Harpo, Chico and Ricardo, traveling as stowaways on an ocean liner to New York, impersonate three famous aviators, whose long beards and uniforms turn out to be the best disguise. This allows them to leave the ship until their ruse is discovered and they have to confess to the authorities.
- *Interference of series*, or what we might call comedic paradox, any situation which exists simultaneously within two independent series of events and is capable of being interpreted in two entirely different meanings at the same time. Again, we need look no further than A Night at the Opera: a doughty heiress, Mrs. Claypool, played by the ineffable Margaret Dumont waits impatiently at her table in a luxurious restaurant for Groucho, who is already beyond late. When she asks for a waiter to search for him, shouting his name as he walks round the tables, it turns out that he has been dining animatedly for an hour with an attractive young woman, right behind Mrs. Claypool.

Beyond the categories of resources Bergson formulates for understanding jokes, and given that humor has many and varied sources, ranging from the innocuous to the cruel, I would add three more pieces of advice.

- The first, from Freud: " *innocent jokes are bound to be of more value to us than tendentious ones, and trivial jokes of more value than profound ones.*"[41]
- The second, from Polonius in Shakespeare's *Hamlet*" *Since brevity is the soul of wit, and tediousness the limbs and outward flourishes, I will be brief. Your noble son is mad,*"[42] or as the popular proverb says, "Good things, when short, are twice as good."
- The third, taken from personal experience: in order to be funny, be kind. Treat your friends and colleagues with tact and consideration and they're more likely to laugh at your jokes. If you have leadership responsibilities, be prepared for people to laugh at your jokes out of respect for your position rather than your comedic talents; that said, others won't.

Let's return to humor as a sign of positive feelings, and how this works from a physiological perspective. Studies on this phenomenon are relatively recent, partly because, as we've seen, there has been no general agreement on what constitutes humor, although there is growing interest in its analysis. In a 2003 article by Wild, Rodden, Grodd and Ruch, in which the authors state that this is the first attempt to clarify it, they explain that " *the expression of laughter seems to depend on two partially independent neuronal pathways. The first of these, an 'involuntary' or 'emotionally driven' system, involves the amygdala, thalamic/hypo- and subthalamic areas and the dorsal/tegmental brainstem. The second, 'voluntary' system originates in the remotor/frontal opercular areas and the ventral brainstem. These systems and the laughter response appear to be coordinated by a laughter-coordinating centre in the dorsal upper pons.*"[43]

Laughter—doing it or observing it—activates multiple regions of the brain: the motor cortex, which controls muscles; the frontal lobe, which helps you understand context; and the limbic system, which modulates positive emotions. Turning all these circuits on strengthens neural connections and helps a healthy brain coordinate its activity.

These observations have led psychologists, coaches and educators to recommend laughter as a regular, daily exercise, highlighting its physical and mental benefits.[44] Don't let situations where you can have fun or joke with others escape you: it's as healthy as playing sports.

## 6.6   Why We Need to Learn to Laugh in the Workplace

Work and the office are a serious business. No laughing matter. You can make jokes about your boss or colleagues, but it's usually best if they don't find out: Work puts food on the table, and as we've been told from infancy, don't play with food.

This association between work and seriousness leads many of us to keep a straight face as we go about our business: At meetings or interviews, we should avoid mirth, be practical, get to the point, avoid preambles, anecdotes and other unproductive circumlocutions. After all, we're being paid for the hours we put in, so not focusing exclusively on executive tasks is surely a waste of time?

For many years, I thought that seriousness, the appearance of diligence and productivity, reflected specific cultures and work environments. For example, Anglo-Saxons are unsmiling, work-oriented and focused, while Latinos are lazy and talkative. This is a cliché shared by many, but misleading in reality: The personal experience of most of us will bear this out. That said, anybody who has worked with colleagues from other countries or abroad, will have noticed different approaches to going about things, and also of course, humor's place at work.

I will always remember the rigidity of institutional protocols in Japan, after a meeting with the president and senior management of a large corporation in their meeting room in Tokyo. We were instructed beforehand on greetings, order of speeches and topics to be discussed. The facial expressions of our interlocutors were flat, and there was hardly any nonverbal communication other than nodding. Needless to say, I stuck to the letter of our script.

In contrast, I have always appreciated the protocol and guidelines governing meetings in North American organizations, where a sense of humor is not only tolerated, but welcomed. When I was fortunate enough to be the first non-Anglo-American chairman of the board of AACSB Global, the association of business schools, I specifically prepared myself so as fit in. In addition to studying *Robert's Rules of Order*, the reference manual for managing board meetings,[45] I practiced the four duties that seem to me to be basic for the chairman: sticking to the agenda, trying to involve all members, formulating the actions or decisions taken and, not least, finishing on time.

In addition, I have seen the beneficial effect that a sense of humor can have on board meetings, despite their formality, especially in smoothing over differences, ironing out mistakes or errors, and even apologizing. If, for example,

I skipped an agenda item, I would joke about my confusion. If I spilled my glass of water, I would highlight the clumsiness that has prevented me from ever playing a musical instrument; jokes at my own expense, or pointing to external circumstances, and always avoiding allusions to other people, which inevitably cause offense.

You have probably also noticed that Americans frequently use humor in their presentations and speeches, often from the very beginning. It is a way to break the ice, to attract attention, to empathize and connect with the audience. It is an effective resource, but not an easy one to use properly, because it requires less work to be serious than to be funny. Moreover, it is not easy to come up with original jokes that make diverse audiences laugh. My advice, based on experience: If you find a joke that works, use it and perfect it. Comedians also hone their jokes at every show, and their success lies in having scaled steep learning curves over the years, as well as, of course, having good gags in the first place.

Writing in the Harvard Business Review in 2014, Alison Beard noted: "*working adults are 'in the midst of a laughter drought.' Babies laugh, on average, 400 times a day; people over 35, only 15. A recent study of Gallup data for the U.S. found that we laugh significantly less on weekdays than we do on weekends. Work is a sober endeavor.*"[46]

Recent research shows that leaders with a sense of humor are 27% better able to motivate others and inspire admiration than their unsmiling counterparts, and that their employees identify with the company by 15% more, as well as being twice as likely to solve problems and creative challenges, all of which translates into better performance and results. This is consistent with Gallup data showing that one of the factors that significantly improves job performance is having a friend in the workplace, someone to laugh and share jokes with.[47]

Taking a humorous approach to meetings and professional gatherings is a practice that will strengthen your leadership and make your work more entertaining. However, there a few guidelines worth following.

- The first is not to turn a meeting into an open-mic session. You must know when and how much humor to apply. As Beard explains, "*you're certainly not going to walk around the office lobbing one-liners like Bob Hope, cursing like Richard Pryor, or slinging insults like Ricky Gervais.*"[48]

A good belly laugh can bring people together, but not every encounter requires such catharsis. Sometimes, a smile-inducing comment is enough; we've already seen the salutary effects of wit.

- Secondly, we must avoid offending other people or groups with our jokes. The advice of Dale Carnegie, the master of public communication, whose first lesson was "don't criticize," remains pertinent, as illustrated by anecdotes about Abraham Lincoln, Clark Gable and Guglielmo Marconi.[49]

Furthermore, never tell the same joke to the same people twice: In addition to appearing dull, you will fail to meet one of the requirements of jokes, which is the surprise factor.

- Thirdly, do not let jokes and fun get in the way of the meeting's agenda. Humor should be a tool that serves good management, not detract from it.

The question of whether to use humor in circumstances of extreme gravity or adversity is a delicate one, and I believe there is no one-size-fits-all maxim. I remember after my mother's funeral, one of my best friends made a hilarious comment at which I could not help but laugh. In that moment of deep sadness, that joke had a relieving, relaxing effect, which also made me smile and adopt a positive attitude, thinking of my mother.

In short, given that we spend two-thirds of our time working, why not occasionally use that space as an opportunity for enjoyment, entertainment and learning?

## 6.7    Finding the Strength to Go On: Resilience Explained

How long can a prisoner of war subjected to repeated physical and mental torture be expected to survive? One of the best-know POWs of the Vietnam War was James Stockdale, who was held in the Hoa Lo camp—later dubbed the Hanoi Hilton—after his plane was shot down in 1965, and was not released until eight long years later, in 1973.

His Vietcong captors would occasionally separate one of Stockdale's fellow prisoners to subject them to intense interrogation or film them making forced confessions in which they rejected their role in the US intervention in Vietnam.

But Stockdale understood from the outset of his confinement that he would have to prepare himself mentally and physically if he were to survive the ordeal and return home to his family. Years later, he explained the process in an interview with celebrated management writer Jim Collins:

*I never lost faith in the end of the story, I never doubted not only that I would get out, but also that I would prevail in the end and turn the experience into the defining event of my life, which, in retrospect, I would not trade.*[50]

Stockdale also taught his fellow captives to learn to resist torture and to feel a sense of control in not giving away anything during interrogations. On one occasion when his guards gave him a razor so that he could shave himself ahead of a recording, he instead partially shaved his head with a reverse mohawk.

In his interview with Collins, Stockdale explained that his companions who failed to overcome the harsh captivity were, paradoxically, the optimists, those who lived in the hope that they would soon be released: first Christmas, then Easter, then by summer, until all hope was gone.

Collins described the experience as "Stockdale's Paradox," which consisted of a duality that combined unwavering faith in a good outcome, along with the permanent drive to overcome immediate difficulties and recurring obstacles. In short, the essence of resilience is an unalterable confidence in the future, combined with the daily struggle over adversity.

Resilience comes through character building, the repetition of behaviors and mental exercises. In many educational institutions, especially in military academies, this is drilled into students over a period of years. It is a quality that is useful for leaders in all fields, especially in business, and at times of extreme uncertainty such as today's. Entrepreneurs understand this all too well, after all they are serial losers: Triumph only comes after repeated failure. Success is simply the other face of defeat.

Literature provides us with any number of examples of resilience. One of the earliest is the biblical story of Job told, on whom Yahweh and Satan placed a bet to measure his loyalty and fortitude. After losing family, property and his health, he continued to accept God's designs. Eventually, he was rewarded and given a new family.

In *The Odyssey*, Homer entertains us with the exploits of Ulysses, subject to the whims of the gods as he and his crew try to make his way home. How many lives since then have been described as an odyssey? In essence, our lives are simply are series of experiences and conflicts, a journey that over the course of which, if we are fortunate, we learn the power of resilience.

We have recently emerged from a period when most of the planet was in lockdown: an appropriate stage on which to test and practice our resilience. That said, the "ordeal" paled when compared to what Stockdale and his fellow POWs went through.

In any event, resilience is not the same as patience. It is not passive. Neither is it merely resistance and endurance, and much less apathy. It requires being pro-active, taking the initiative and using our inner strength to achieve our goals. That is why seeking solace in alcohol or drugs is of little use at such times as we currently face, however tempting.

With this in mind, I'd like make a few recommendations that might help in maintaining and strengthening our resilience along the lines of *mens sana in corpore sano* for the many difficult weeks ahead of us.

- David Hume, the Enlightenment Scottish philosopher, wrote: "*Nothing is so improving to the temper as the study of the beauties, either of poetry, elo-quence, music, or painting*," he wrote in his brief essay *Of the Delicacy of Taste and Passion*, published in 1777.[51] The work is easy to read and of particular use for managers and action-oriented professionals. Its main the-sis is that cultivating the liberal arts and humanities generates happiness and helps to develop the resilience necessary to face the adversities of life.
- Physical exercise and sport, as well as eating moderately, play a vital role in strengthening the personal discipline that lies at the core of resilience. That said, as the vaudeville song recommends, "*a little of what you fancy does you good*" and can certainly help us see the light at the end of the tunnel.[52]
- At times like this, we should also take advantage to cultivate our friend-ships and camaraderie with colleagues, and of course seeking expert advice if needed. Over the last few weeks, I've taken the opportunity to rekindle old acquaintances and talk to people I haven't connected with in a while. Building consistent and lasting personal bonds strengthens our collective sense of trust, and also expands the circle of individuals who can be used for counsel and encouragement.

In harsh times that challenge our resilience, Barack Obama's message of hope resonates: "Yes We Can." We can get through the disaster unfolding around us, just as previous generations persevered and overcame the unprec-edented challenges they faced. And by showing resilience, we will have given greater depth and meaning to our own existence.

# Notes

1. Aristotle, *Eudemian Ethics* (trans. B. Inwood and R. Wood) (Cambridge: Cambridge University Press, 2013), beginning.
2. J. Sellars, *Epicurus and the Art of Happiness* (New York: Penguin, 2022) p.15.
3. Marcus Aurelius, *Meditations* (London: Penguin, 2006); p. 35.
4. https://archive.schillerinstitute.com/transl/schiller_poem/ode_to_joy.pdf.

5. A. Smith, *The Theory of Moral Sentiments* (ed. K. Haakonssen) (Cambridge, Mass.: Cambridge University Press, 2002), p. 59.

6. *Deconstructing Harry* (Hollywood Pictures, 2007).

7. J. Huizinga, *The Autumn of the Middle Ages* (Chicago: University of Chicago Press, 1997).

8. U. Eco, *The Name of the Rose* (New York: Vintage, 1992).

9. Aristotle, *The Nicomachean Ethics* (London: Penguin, 2004).

10. Aristotle, *Eudemian Ethics* (trans. B. Inwood and R. Wood) (Cambridge: Cambridge University Press, 2013).

11. J. Pfeffer, "The Narcissistic World of the MBA Student," *Financial Times*, November 7, 2010.

12. S. Iñiguez, *In an Ideal Business* (London: Palgrave Macmillan, 2020), Chapter 6.

13. C. Wilson, "Leibnizian Optimism", 80 Journal of Philosophy 11 (November 1983), pp. 765–83.

14. Voltaire, *Candide: Or Optimism* (London: Penguin, 2009).

15. Ibid., p. 149.

16. D. Kahneman, *Thinking, Fast and Slow* (New York: Farrar, Straus and Giroux, 2011), p. 255.

17. J.H. Carter, *Never Met a Man I Didn't Like: The Life and Writings of Will Rogers* (New York: William Morrow, 1991).

18. Plato, *Apology*, 21d, in *The Last Days of Socrates: Euthyphro; Apology; Crito; Phaedo* (ed. H. Tarrant) (London: Penguin, 2003).

19. https://www.poetryfoundation.org/poems/43281/the-lake-isle-of-innisfree.

20. K. Clark: *Landscape into Art* (London: Penguin, 1961), pp. 15–16.

21. B. Kara: "Landscape Design and Cognitive Psychology Procedia: World Conference on Psychology and Sociology 2012," Social and Behavioral Sciences, Vol. 82 (2013), pp. 288–291.

22. M.D. Velarde, G. Fry, G. and M. Tveit, "Health Effects of Viewing Landscapes: Landscape Types in Environmental Psychology." 6 Urban Forestry and Urban Greening (2007) 199–212.

23. J.J. Rousseau, *Reveries of a Solitary Walker* (London: Penguin, 1980).

24. Ibid., p. 91.

25. Ibidem.

26. C.S. Lewis, *A Grief Observed* (New York: Harper Collins, 2015).

27. Breakfast at Tiffany's (Paramount Pictures, 1991), based on T. Capote, Breakfast at Tiffany's (New York: Vintage, 2012).

28. J.J. Rousseau, op. cit., p. 109.

29. https://qz.com/1468694/broadways-first-traffic-jam-was-due-to-a-henri-bergson-philosophy-lecture/.

30. I refer to the Spanish version: H. Bergson, *La Risa* (trans. R. Blanco) (Buenos Aires: EGodot, 2015).Kindle.

31. Aristotle, *Politics*; Book VIII, Part V.

32. Quoted in H. Bergson, op. cit., loc. 769.
33. S. Freud, *Jokes and Their Relation to The Unconscious* (ed. J. Strachey) (New York: WW Norton, 1990).
34. S. Freud, *El chiste y su relación con el subconsciente* (Buenos Aires: Greenbooks Editore, 2020), Kindle ed., loc 98.
35. M.M. Hurley, D.C. Dennet, R.B. Adams, Inside Jokes: Using Humor to Reverse-Engineer the Mind (Boston: MIT Press, 2013), p. 13.
36. D. Solomon, "The Funny Formula", *The New York Times*, November 12, 2006.
37. https://www.ncbi.nlm.nih.gov/pmc/articles/PMC2269245/.
38. H. Bergson, op. cit., loc. 146.
39. *A Night at the Opera* (Metro Goldwyn Mayer, 1935); and *Bringing Up Baby* (RKO, 1938).
40. A. Smith, op. cit., Kindle loc. 522.
41. S. Freud., op. cit., loc. 352.
42. W. Shakespeare, *Four Tragedies* (ed. T.J.B. Spencer) (London: Penguin 1995); Hamlet, Act II, Scene 2.
43. https://pubmed.ncbi.nlm.nih.gov/12902310/.
44. Janet M. Gibson, *An Introduction of the Psychology of Humor* (New York: Routledge, 2019).
45. H.M. Robert, D. Honeman, T.J. Balch, D.E. Seabold and S. Gerber, *Robert's Rules of Order*, 12th ed. (New York: Public affairs, 2020).
46. A. Beard, "Leading with Humor", Harvard Business Review, May 2014. https://hbr.org/2014/05/leading-with-humor.
47. Ibidem.
48. Ibidem.
49. https://dalecarnegieboston.tumblr.com/post/20350676146/dont-criticize-condemn-or-complain.
50. Collins, J., "The Stockdale Paradox". JimCollins.com. Retrieved on 2008-07-02 from http://www.jimcollins.com/lab/brutalFacts/.
51. www.davidhume.org/texts/etv1.html.
52. https://monologues.co.uk/musichall/Songs-L/Little-Of-What-You-Fancy.htm.

# Index[1]

---

[1] Note: Page numbers followed by 'n' refer to notes.

© The Author(s), under exclusive license to Springer Nature Switzerland AG 2023
S. Iñiguez, *Philosophy Inc.*, https://doi.org/10.1007/978-3-031-20483-8

Printed by Printforce, the Netherlands